STUDYING BRITISH CINEMA
THE 1960s
BY
DANNY POWELL

auteur

First published in 2009 by
Auteur
The Old Surgery, 9 Pulford Road, Leighton Buzzard LU7 1AB
www.auteur.co.uk

Designed and set by Nikki Hamlett at AMP Ltd, Dunstable, Bedfordshire

Printed and bound in India by Imprint Digital

Cover: *Blow Up* © BFI Stills, Posters & Designs

British Library Cataloguing-in-Publication Data
A catalogue record for this book is available from the British Library

ISBN 978-1-903663-88-2 (paperback)
ISBN 978-1-903663-89-9 (hardback)

CONTENTS

ACKNOWLEDGEMENTS

I'd like to thank my wife who continues to put up with me.

DEDICATIONS

For my son, Jake.

AUTHOR'S NOTE

The Sixties is well known as a vibrant and revolutionary time in Britain. This book aims to show how British film was instrumental in the creation and reflection of the period known as the 'swinging Sixties'. By tracing films from the beginning to the end of the decade and focusing on classic movies it also aims to follow the changes that took place in Britain, examining the myth and trying to establish the reality.

INTRODUCTION

Much has been made of the social and cultural shift that took place in the Sixties and how it irrevocably changed the country. Traditionalists have often described it as the beginning of a spiralling decline in British society's moral standards and a shedding of 'common sense' values, in favour of an immoral free-for-all that signalled the end of traditional notions of community. A more liberal view is that the Sixties witnessed an opening up of Britain's hypocritical and class bound culture resulting in a greater freedom for all, a greater equality of opportunity and a further movement toward a modern and peaceful post-war climate.

Whatever the opinion, there is no doubt that the Britain of the Sixties has as strong and coherent image as any other decade with so many iconic images providing a sense of familiarity with this exciting time. And to this day film and TV continue to reproduce and recreate this golden age. Ironically, however, this seemingly cohesive image emerged at a time that struggled with competing discourses and ideologies, which inevitably produced new experiences. Thus, although we may feel we have a picture of the Sixties in our minds, this may not be as accurate as we think, as the iconic images of the time may obscure a more complex reality. It is perhaps in recognising this, that we may better understand how the Sixties became a defining era for the country. We may also understand more about the resultant Britain and how the media, including the British film industry, played a key part in defining Britain's new identity.

> 'The films of the time reflected what life was like for young people in a rapidly changing moral climate.' (Richard Lester, *Hollywood UK* BBC4)

If an advertising agency had been given the task of rebranding a product with an identity crisis, it couldn't have created a better one than the image cultivated by the combined forces of the media in post-war Britain. It was in this new age of advertising that the country, and especially the capital, became a brand, a product marketed to the rest of the world through an image which combined lifestyle, fashion, music, sport and commerce. This product would come to be known as 'swinging Britain' (or swinging *London*, such is the centrality of the city to this image) and would shape both the resultant character of the country and perhaps more importantly in a new media age, the perception of Britain to its inhabitants and to the rest of the world. This very British image ironically is also in part the result of the influence of America and a new global culture, in a country that was itself trying to adapt and change in a new world order.

For a brief time, after post-war austerity, it might have seemed as though Britain was back on top of the world. The country that had built an empire was establishing a *cultural* colonisation through a radical new style and concurrent image that was a worldwide influence. The country was exporting pop music, fashion and invention to the rest of the world and it seemed as though Britain was once again a global force. However, fashion is transient and the long-term actuality was quite the reverse.

Studying British Cinema: The 1960s will through the films of the time, follow the fortunes of Britain and attempt to establish how a bereft nation became, for a brief moment, the epitome of a new modern world. It will, through the analysis of key films of the decade, explore how Britain's identity was re-established and reconstructed and how these films are key artefacts which tell us much of the story of the age. We will examine the change in social mores, values and attitudes through the lens of a movie camera, to establish how the world of film played a part in convincing the public that there was no more exciting time in which to live than the Sixties. It will examine how the films of the day reflected the inward battle of the nation, which eventually resulted in an outwardly unified image exported to the rest of the world, and how this period continues to define Britain today.

The films selected are absolutely not intended as a definitive guide. No survey of this kind can be that. There are great films missing from the list, which are either absent due to the limitations of the format or because they do not meet the purpose of the book, which is to introduce key issues and debates arising from the films of the period, to explore the dominant views and attitudes of the age through movies and to establish how the world of film has played a part in establishing a construct by which we continue to make sense of the era.

It is also at once necessary though somewhat spurious to delineate any age by decade and it is somewhat misleading. There are films released both before and after the Sixties that tell us much about the time; but, again, for the purpose of the book which forms part of a series, we have focused upon those whose release date fell within the specific time period (thus, one film memorably associated with the period, *Performance*, actually released in 1970, is absent, although it will be included in a forthcoming volume on British cinema of the 1970s). Though the Guide examines films that deviate from the dominant view of the period and can be read as contrary to the goal of constructing a coherent picture of the age the movies are ultimately selected because they contributed to the construction of the zeitgeist, or seem in direct reaction to it, with each chapter focusing on a key text that illustrates important issues and themes.

THE SIXTIES CULTURE

The history of the much vaunted 'swinging Sixties' is often called into question as being one cultivated and nurtured by a privileged elite who enjoyed a dream lifestyle of self-indulgence and hedonism. The famous claim that if you can remember the Sixties, you weren't there, reinforces this notion. This view of the Sixties is in large part prevalent due to media influence:

> '…when asked about the Sixties, there seems to be a qualitative difference in people's response – they seem to be confused about what really happened and what the media had said was happening…Most people under forty, in describing the Sixties, at least defer to the media Sixties.' (York, 1980: 182)

Indeed it is difficult to identify exactly where and when the Sixties phenomenon took place such is the diversity of accounts that claim to have borne witness to its explosion. One of the key artefacts often pointed to is a 1966 article from the American magazine, *Time*:

> 'This spring, as never before in modern times, London is switched on. Ancient elegance and new opulence are all tangled up in a dazzling blur of op and pop. The city is alive with birds (girls) and beatles, buzzing with minicars and telly starts, pulsing with half a dozen separate veins of excitement. The guards now change at Buckingham Palace to a Lennon and McCartney tune and Prince Charles is firmly in the long hair set.' (Halasz, 1966: 32)

This view of London perfectly illustrates how the media combined myth, history and pop culture to suggest dramatic change. The language revels in new slang and hyperbole and in so doing all but tramples over reality. For this American magazine there is only the language of hype, which involves all the old archetypal images of tourist London, combined with the excitement of the new until the two become fused. Thus even as Britain was moving into the modern age, it was carrying with it all the old associations and, critically, it was being defined by the US.

The country *was* changing but it was not the wholesale change with which we are often presented, which somehow manages to combine iconic images of royalty, Routemaster double-decker buses, the Kray Twins, Twiggy, flower-power, Julie Christie, the Beatles, David Bailey, Carnaby Street, free-love, the mini and the mini-skirt. If this abiding impression is to be believed, these were exciting and hedonistic times where anyone could achieve anything, moving freely through society irrespective of background or class. But was this true or have these symbols in representing the period come to over-simplify its complexities?

> 'What happened…was the rise, or fabrication, of what became known as "Swinging London". In 1962 the American statesman Dean Acheson famously said: "Britain has lost an empire and not yet found a role." Now we had a role as the style and fashion capital of the world.' (French, 2006: 3)

This is not to say that something culturally significant didn't happen in the Sixties. There were significant changes in legislation that would allow Britain to become more permissive, but the reality of everyday life for most people was still quite conservative:

> 'I didn't remember the Sixties being a great time of pleasure. I think there was a lot of energy about and I think an optimism. If there was a lot of pleasure going on I think it was in the next street.' (Ken Loach, *Hollywood UK* BBC4)

The truth was that for the majority of people, the 1960s, particularly, the early part of the decade, was not unlike the Fifties. Yet history records that Britain and, in particular, London became the focus of world attention and the Union Jack synonymous with mod style and fashion, inseparable from the idea of London as a cultural centre of exciting, innocent and naïve freedoms. The media was crucial in this process of amplification, representing ideas of a new mood of excitement and translating them into a reality which became imitated and accepted. Dick Lester's film of The Beatles, *A Hard Day's Night* (1964) was central to this:

> '…he caught and intensified the appetite for "Now" excitement that The Beatles amplified: the "classlessness", "youth", "revolt"… starting to feed into the media…which in turn would feed them back in magnified form into society, creating the illusion which in fact became a reality that Britain was the place where… "its all happening".' (Walker, 1974: 242)

On the back of this wave of excitement came the idea of a 'scene', which was inhabited by young 'swingers' and the *Time* article even printed a map of the places connected to this youth revolution:

> 'Of course "swinging London" was always a highly selective composite based predominantly on the fashionable western districts of Chelsea, Mayfair and South Kensington.' (Donnelly, 2005: 92)

In other words, despite the exciting idea of a socially mobile meritocracy, it was still those privileged communities in the well-to-do parts and who could afford a certain lifestyle, that were living a version of the swinging freedom which had been a media creation:

> 'But as with all mythical constructions, it corresponded to an important imaginative reality and the myth had a cultural resonance which transcended the tiny cliques who made up London's interconnected "scenes".' (*ibid.*)

And for those inside the circle, it may indeed have seemed that this was a new way of life:

> 'I wouldn't say a majority…. one only knows a certain group of people and maybe it's a minority but it seems to me that a good time is much easier to be had by all now than ever before.' (Julie Christie, *Hollywood UK* BBC4)

Thus it was that Britain's *self*-perception would change to accommodate its new role and, with the help of its American cousins, this role would be nurtured and distributed globally, combining old world charm with modern style, and the press, the music, television and film industries would reinforce this impression and market Britain successfully to the rest of the world. The consequence was that it became an outward truth, as fiction and reality collaborated to produce a genuine phenomenon which was allied to and driven by other shifts in behaviour and attitude, the most dominant of which was a new consumerism.

The growth in disposable income, particularly available to the younger generation was producing a culture in which individual identity was of increasing importance. The availability of consumer items to those who had endured the aftermath of World War II was encouraging people to define themselves by lifestyle. While the older generation could now purchase domestic items such as washing machines, fridges and cars, the younger generation were spending their money on disposable items such as fashion and the pop music which was being promoted in the magazines and on television.

The availability of such items reinforced the impression being disseminated by the media that these were truly classless times. Many of the new stars of swinging London were from lower-middle-class or working-class backgrounds and these were the people upon whom the media focused. Michael Caine, The Beatles, Twiggy and David Bailey all embodied the changing times where a talented person could shape their own destiny. This perception was crucial in developing a view of the age that belied the reality:

'Take all this thing now about the working-class actors and writers. It's simply a release of certain talents from that class…The real working-class has nothing to do with the theatre today. The railway porter, the chap on the fish dock in Hull, they're not interested… Why should they be?' (Tom Courtenay, quoted in Walker, 1974: 127)

It was, however, essential to society's change that the public accepted this view of a new Britain in which social mobility was not only possible but, to the working-classes, essential.

'And so it became 'cool' to be working-class and British… it was hardly surprising that a society based on mass domestic consumption became dominated by its biggest market, in other words, the industrial working-class.' (Sandbrook, 2005: 199)

SIXTIES FILM

The Fifties had seen a continued decline in cinema attendance that had begun in the previous decade. During the war many women had attended cinemas but now they had returned to domestic duties and with the development of television there was now even less of an incentive to go to out for entertainment. Such was the concern for the ailing British film industry that in 1957 in an effort to support British film-making, the government reduced Entertainment Duty, a tax on box office takings (it was abolished in 1960). This, however, wasn't enough to halt the decline and between 1955 and 1963 two thirds of the cinema audience and half the cinemas themselves disappeared.

It is against this background that Britain surprisingly became a force to be reckoned with producing films that would be enjoyed the world over, attracting film-makers from across the globe who would make cinema that would express the changing times and social upheaval.

Sixties film is most often associated with a raft of techniques that were experimented with by film-makers at the time who were prepared to play with narrative and to break the logical construction of film to create new meaning. The techniques would include the speeding up of footage, the jolting surprise of time lapse or quick cuts and obvious transitions. Actors would employ the Brechtian technique of addressing the camera and thus distancing the audience. This 'swinging style' would accompany the swinging times but would leave some critics cold, who would see this style as a reflection of American ideas:

'Fantasy sequences in which anything becomes possible, slapstick in which the world collapses into chaos, outrageous visual jokes, distancing devices such as the use of the narrator, inter-titles or direct address to the camera….' (Murphy, 1992: 3)

Our predominant and lasting impression of Sixties film may be more akin to Austin Powers than the films actually produced. But it is through the selection and prioritisation of certain representations that we are left with history and because the Sixties was the first real media age, it can tell us more than most about media influence in the development of a cultural identity that still exists today:

'Whatever the swinging Sixties are going to be remembered for it won't be films. The moment you saw a red London bus go through the shot you knew you were in for a rotten time.' (Alan Parker, Personal View: *A Turnip-Head's Guide to British Cinema*, ITV, 1986)

Of course there were Sixties exploitation films which tried to ride the wave of excitement but British film was far more diverse than the hackneyed impression given above by Parker. The iconography of red telephone boxes, pillar boxes and buses, combined with landmarks such as Big Ben and Buckingham Palace were employed but even those that deal with the swinging lifestyle associated with the times do it in a variety of ways and not all of them depended on tourist attractions for their appeal.

In fact the film-making of the period didn't begin with London at all. For the perceived revolution to take place there had to be a catalyst and this began with the rise of social realism, a movement that was concerned with a greater awareness of the working-classes through authentic representation of this social group, previously all-but ignored by domestic cinema. This could not have been further from the swinging style of film mentioned above and reflected a very different Britain to that which we may associate with the period. However, the social realist movement marked a clear turning point in British cinema history.

The Fifties had begun to see the end of the measures put in place to help restore the country after the war. The period of reconstruction and the associated deprivations such as rationing were superseded by a period of wealth and development. The post-war rebuilding process had necessitated a huge growth in industry and this meant nearly full employment. The consequence of such burgeoning industry was a work force who were benefiting directly.

Not everyone, however, was impressed with this new affluence and some pointed to a deeper malaise that was affecting the nation. In the wake of the Suéz debacle[1] and the Profumo affair[2], there were strong criticisms of Britain's economic performance when compared with other countries. It was observed that much of what was being consumed was imported and that Britain was falling behind other countries. The nation was ripe for change and it needed new ideas and new values:

'At the heart of the problem…was a systematic failure of leadership, caused principally by the dominance of self-reinforcing elites in the country's public, cultural and commercial life… "the Establishment" was alive and well, centred around a few aristocratic families, the top public schools and the domination of Oxbridge. Its continued power had a stultifying effect, preventing Britain from mobilising the dynamism of its brightest and best among the wider population.' (Donnelly, 2005: 49)

The nation was, however, beginning to change and sociological writers such as Richard Hoggart (*The Uses of Literacy*, 1957) and Raymond Williams (*Culture and Society*, 1958) recognised that working-class life in particular was changing. Despite growing affluence it concerned some that something culturally important would be lost in these changes. Hoggart spoke of the 'shiny barbarism' of the growing influence of glamorous pop culture that was being imported from America. At the root of this culture was the development of consumerism, commercialisation and the mass media:

'His central argument was… mass culture gives the working-classes cheap sensationalist entertainment, enervating, dulling and eventually destroying their sense of taste; meanwhile the working-class environment itself is being torn up and replaced by the cheap glitter of affluence…' (Sandbrook, 2005: 172)

Although this argument raises issues of cultural tourism and a rather over romanticised view of working-class culture, it also raises the notion of a changing Britain which was waking up to the existence of the working-classes who were adapting to new values.

'Social realism', often referred to as 'kitchen sink' drama, reflected the importance of traditional working-class life but ironically had its roots in the middle-class drama of the theatre. The English Stage Company was a young theatre group established at The Royal Court theatre in Sloane Square. The group was producing young talent such as Joan Plowright and Alan Bates, who would go on to star in *A Kind of Loving* (1958). The deputy to the artistic director George Devine was Tony Richardson who would go on to direct *The Loneliness of the Long Distance Runner* (1962).

On 8 May 1956, Richardson directed the opening of a play by John Osborne that would shock traditional theatre goers with its gritty content and would become a significant point in the development of the new wave, beginning a link between theatre and film that would be a feature of the movement. His play, *Look Back in Anger*, about the frustrations of a young man called Jimmy Porter took place in an attic flat and did not change scene throughout. The dissatisfaction of the central character was to become emblematic of the times, a figure that would be repeated in a variety of guises and texts throughout the period.

Although it didn't please everyone, the play seemed to echo a feeling of the times and portrayed a new type of young person, whose development was at once seen as a threat and the future. The figure of Porter reflected an age in which education reforms had produced young people who despite their background were now gaining access to a standard of education previously unattainable. This, however, had in turn led to an inevitable bitterness as they felt disenfranchised from a society that had been constructed to benefit the privileged elite.

The Royal Court publicity described Osborne as a 'very angry young man', a term which became synonymous with a group of writers whose only real link was that they recognised the imbalance of power in the nation. The 'braying upper-class voices on newsreels, the odour of unearned privilege in parliament and the courts, the tired nostalgia for war' (MacDonald, 1995: 7) had been identified by these writers as being symptomatic of Britain's decline.

The term became part of the new movement and the angry young man would come to embody the spirit of the age, a frustrated working-class male who would often have contempt for those around him and be compelled to rail against a system designed to keep him in his place.

The original Angry Young Men, who were mostly the products of grammar schools, were soon superseded by working-class writers who really *did* represent the younger generation. The new wave writers that followed in Osborne's wake identified with Hoggart's view of northern industrial Britain. Novels and plays quickly appeared from writers who wrote about the features of a Britain that had been ignored and was now undergoing rapid change: *A Taste of Honey* by Shelagh Delaney, *Billy Liar* by Keith Waterhouse, *Saturday Night and Sunday Morning* by Alan Sillitoe and *A Kind of Loving* by Stan Barstow were all made into films in the early 1960s:

> 'Above all, there is a pervasive sense of frustration, insecurity, loneliness: the central characters often feel stifled by their environment, threatened by change or the expectations of others, dissatisfied with the drudgery of their lives but resigned to their inevitable lot.' (Sandbrook, 2005: 186)

This was a cultural breakthrough. By using working-class lives as the subject matter for the stage it raised issues about the construction of society and for some this was fascinating. Lindsay Anderson, one of the new wave film-makers, praised *A Taste of Honey* for being 'a real escape from the middlebrow, middle-class vacuum of the West End' (Anderson in Laing, 1986: 89):

> 'New wave writers were interested, like Hoggart, in the old world of Northern terraces, poverty and violence. What brought the new wave together was a series of common themes and interests: a focus on the working-class; aggressive attitudes to sex and women; a deep suspicion of modernity and mass culture; intense cultural nativism; a persistent strain of nostalgia…and a curious combination of indeterminate anger and political apathy.' (Sandbrook, 2005: 174)

The plays, however symptomatic of the changes afoot in society were also illustrative of the dichotomy between the media representation of the new 'revolution' and the actuality. Despite all the talk of a new society where social groups mixed freely, here were dramas of the working-classes being acted out to predominantly middle-class audiences for their amusement. If the new ideas were to impact on society, it would have to do so via a different medium:

'While kitchen sink plays inevitably reached only a limited audience, the fiction of the New Wave, especially when adapted for the cinema, appealed to the wider public.' (Sandbrook, 2005: 185)

FREE CINEMA

'British cinema (is) still obstinately class bound; still rejecting the stimulus of contemporary life, as well as the responsibility to criticise; still reflecting a metropolitan, Southern English culture which excludes the rich diversity of tradition and personality which is the whole of Britain.' ('Free Cinema Manifesto 3')

It was the film movement of Free Cinema that developed into the new wave. A group of young film-makers, who had all worked with the Royal Court Theatre, who would all go on to make social realist feature films, produced early film work that was determined to show the real lives of the working-classes, a group who had been noticeably ignored by the media and whose representation in film had been limited to crude stereotypes.

The film-makers, who included Karel Reisz, Lindsey Anderson and Tony Richardson, made short films that were screened between 1956 and 1959. As with the idea of swinging Britain, the term Free Cinema was a way of grouping disparate forces. The film-makers, who were having difficulty getting their films seen, grouped their work under this heading in order to attract attention. Anderson labelled their work to encourage the idea of a group principle. Free Cinema declared a manifesto at whose root was the intent to show working-class lives as they really were by making a series of documentary films which rebelled against the stagnant middle-class culture that pervaded British film:

'The number of British films that have ever made a genuine try at a story in a popular milieu, with working-class characters all through, can be counted on the fingers of one hand. This virtual rejection of three-quarters of the population of this country represents more than a ridiculous impoverishment of the cinema, it is characteristic of a flight from contemporary reality.' (Anderson in Sandbrook, 2005: 191)

These films would revitalise the film industry with a new outlook on contemporary living by simply showing a side of life which had previously been overlooked:

'…the views of the world which emerge from Free Cinema films are recognisable, the result of preoccupations common among intellectuals in the second half of the 1950s. Broadly, these preoccupations were: a sympathetic interest in communities, whether they were the traditional industrial one of *Wakefield Express* or the new, improvised one of the jazz club in *Momma Don't Allow*, fascination with the newly emerging youth

culture (*Momma Don't Allow, We Are The Lambeth Boys, Nice Time*); unease about
the quality of leisure in urban society (*Nice Time, O Dreamland*); and respect for the
traditional working-class (*Enginemen, Every Day Except Christmas*).' (Lovell and Hillier,
1972: 142)

Funded by car manufacturer Ford and the British Film Institute (BFI), these low-budget
films showed microcosmic moments of working-class living which were set to music or
had post synched sound. They caught the public's imagination and when screened at the
recently opened National Film Theatre (NFT) had the public queuing around the building.
It was a triumph of marketing with even the words Free Cinema written in capitals to
ensure that the movement, such as it was would gain attention. Although only intended as
a one off, the theatrical screening was repeated and the new wave can thus be attributed
to 'a fruitful conjunction between the polemics of Free Cinema and the actualities of the
Royal Court Theatre' (Eaton, 'Not a Piccadily Actor in Sight': 32).

Richardson and Osbourne went on to form Woodfall Films which was responsible for
some of the major successes of the British new wave cinema.

THE NEW WAVE

The preoccupations of the Free Cinema movement were developed in the new wave
and at the centre of this movement was the issue of class. There were the 'haves' and
the 'have nots' as there had always been – but the Sixties had given rise to a generation
that had higher expectations than those previously. The youth were beginning to
question their elders and in so doing undermine the very authorities and institutions that
dominated the culture. The Establishment was now under threat and it would have to
change to accommodate.

The new wave questioned the established order, bringing its ideas to a far wider audience
than Free Cinema had been able to. Like its embryonic predecessor, it kept the same
values, showing the divisions inherent in society by focusing attention on previously
ignored factions of society, the working-classes, particularly those in the north. These films,
however, would be fully developed stories that reflected more accurately the characters'
lives and thoughts. Their language would be that of everyday life, not of middle-class,
Southern England, the exact antithesis of those privileged classes who were emblematic
of a Britain that had had its day. The social realist movement portrayed the lives of those
who had, for too long been ignored. The films would feature the 'angry young man' of the
stage, and reflect him back to those he represented.

The films were beginning to question, like many theorists of the time, the way that society
functioned and instead of just demonising the youth as hooligans or deviants, there was a
clear shift in trying to understand the motivations of the protagonists. If they were rebels,
why were they rebelling? Who were they rebelling against? After years of unquestioning

obedience to authority, this generation were the first to try to understand reactionary behaviour, as just that, a reaction *to* something. In this way they were attacks on the Establishment and the dominant cultural order as they showed characters who refused to view themselves as inferior:

> 'We [British New Wave] produced works which showed these people who had never known their place and had no intention of it and were determined to get somewhere or at least they were interested in knowing what made themselves, and in some way society, work.' (Lindsay Anderson, *Hollywood UK* BBC4)

And it wasn't just the attitude of the characters that was shocking; it was the manner of their depiction on the screen which pushed the limits of acceptability. The language and the depictions of sex and violence were signs that a new morality was emerging, something that would cause the censor to re-evaluate its standards.

Class divided society and shaped life expectations. The working-classes had for generations lived in small communities, often built around industrial manufacturing, and weren't expected to leave those communities during their life. But this was changing in the face of new transport links, new technologies, affluence and educational opportunities. Thus the hero – or the anti-hero – of the new wave was someone who could question their designated role, who would be dissatisfied with the status quo.

The angry young man became a figure to represent the new generation, someone who typified the frustrations of the average working-class youth in films such as *Saturday Night, Sunday Morning*, *The Loneliness of the Long Distance Runner* and *Billy Liar*, three examples of the kitchen sink dramas which broke taboos and were clarion calls to the working-class youth of the day. These films showed a very different perception of Britain than that of 'swinging London', but which, at the same time, established a very definite British identity and style which were to be reproduced in both television and film over the next decades, accepting class differences to be part of the nation's identity and making the British new wave a vital part of sixties British culture.

Many of the films revolved around a central character that had some sense of identity apart from their peers, their family and their community. The kitchen sink dramas, as they became known, focused attention on specific members of communities who stood out, for their refusal to conform. They were people who wished to achieve fulfilment though individualism. The rise of youth culture had been accompanied by the rise in importance of self-expression and forged a new belief that society should be a meritocracy, that everyone should have the chance to achieve their own fulfilment, irrespective of their background or class.

The consumer boom of the Fifties, despite the 'never had it so good' rhetoric had led to different expectations of lifestyle and some would say to a greater discontent revolving around ideas of class:

'A class that had previously defined itself as producers now had to define itself as consumers.' (Welsh in Barrow and White, 2008: 100)

The new wave provided a commentary on Britain and in so doing was an indicator of changing times. The Labour Party would soon be elected, breaking a long period of Conservative rule. Harold Wilson would replace the rather staid figure of Harold MacMillan who seemed to personify bygone times.

To portray these lives accurately a new breed of actors was needed. Working-class people were no longer to be represented as simple comic stereotypes of the George Formby vintage, so new wave actors would be selected from different backgrounds. Tom Courtenay and Rita Tushingham typified the age, with broad accents from the north of England.

The film equipment was also new, employing lightweight 16mm cameras using faster film stock than previously available, which allowed filming to take place without the necessity of the studio. This reacted better in conditions of low light, which meant that filming could take place on location, which allowed not only more creative freedom but became a statement in itself. The ability to more easily shoot outdoors lent itself to the new wave themes and thus a new gritty realism was borne which perfectly engendered the themes explored in the films.

Shooting outside became a radical statement of intent to escape the artificiality of the studio films that had gone before and goes some way to convey the realities of life through real locations. The fact that the films were in black and white may have been an economic necessity but also added to the sense of verisimilitude. Now the films which developed Free Cinema's intent to portray ordinary lives could shoot in the industrial locations that would bring the aesthetic of realism to a wider audience than previously.

The films would become known for the use of *mise-en-scène* which would often depict the industrial landscape. Mines, canals, factories and large conurbations of terraced housing put on screen a culture that was built around the industrial revolution but was now on the verge of decline. These brooding settings with smokestacks alongside embryonic suburbs visually demonstrated the changes taking place as the characters are torn between the old way of life and embracing the new. There is also a clear conflict represented between the older and the younger generations and a clash of cultures and values.

'Throughout the New Wave, modern commercial entertainments are brash, gaudy and superficial, in contrast to the rugged, authentic masculine values of the old working-class culture.' (Sandbrook, 2005: 200)

This disparity is usually shown in the central character who often wishes to change their own circumstances but are unable to do so, thus positing them on the edge of a new age, but not quite ready to embrace it. The characters don't share the outlook of the older generation but mistrust the new and a feature of the films is the arrival of new entertainment such as TV. It is clear, however, that one type of lifestyle is ending. It is the end of an era:

> '...the New Wave reflected not poverty and inequality, but affluence and apathy; it sought not to build a new Britain, but simply to lament the disappearance of an old one.' (Sandbrook, 2005: 204)

Despite the arguably romanticised view of the working-class it is not to say that the films are overly moralising. One of the key features of the new wave was the movement away from traditional narrative function which works toward closure. The films are explorations of character in relation to circumstances and surroundings. That these factors are often oppressive and repressive means that the individual's characteristics are often a reaction to their circumstances and cannot be judged in simplistic fashion. At the core of many of the characters is an inner conflict, which reflects that of society and the films often follow the character's personal journey.

However, their journeys are often fruitless and the stories finish without closure, leaving the audience to conjecture as to what will become of the character. This uncertainty can be seen to reject a male anxiety in the face of change.

The young men of most of the stories embody a traditional masculinity and indulge themselves in actions which are often very aggressive toward women. This masculinity is often demonstrated by the central character's unwillingness to 'settle down'. In becoming domesticated the men are viewed as having lost their masculinity:

> 'The explanation for all this lies in the identification of supposedly feminine values with modernity and mass culture. Women were closely identified with the new affluent society because its products – washing machines, cookers, televisions to entertain the housebound mother – seemed to benefit working-class women more than their husbands....' (Sandbrook, 2005: 201)

The ability to be able to sleep around or have more than one partner is something by which the new wave characters demonstrate their independence and a new found freedom. This freedom is something that develops as the age continues and later it can be seen as a development that particularly affects women; but in the new wave films, it is the men who show their dominance in an aggressive sexuality, something by which they can reinforce their masculinity, which seems to be under threat.

Despite focusing on the working-man, the films do not attempt to address the problems of social inequality. For these characters there is no redemption. They are rejecting the communities that surround them and are reacting to changing times but seemingly only by developing a new individualism, not by wholeheartedly embracing the new. This view of themselves as separate from the community could free them if it were accompanied by mobility, but they are in most cases reluctant to change their circumstances. Inherent here is that the conditions for self-advancement don't yet exist or that these characters in particular can only recognise the changes but feel unable to yet take advantage of them:

'... Britain's post-war Education Act ... had opened up places for them in high schools and universities and allowed them like Jimmy Porter, to convert the energies that had been blocked so long in the limited aspirations and menial jobs available to working-class children into intellectual self-assurance. They had been educated, like Jimmy, into articulated contempt for its outworn institutions and class-bound attitudes, but saw no means of changing and replacing them.' (Walker, 1974: 42)

In this way, the films clearly demonstrate the changing times. The pull of the new world is occurring at the same time as collapse of the old communities but while the old communities still exist there is an inertia, which cannot be eradicated until society changes to accommodate the disenfranchised:

'Indeed, in many instances the anger of the New Wave really meant a combination of personal ambition and a vague resentment at a changing society...There is very little working-class solidarity in the literature and films of the New Wave: instead the working-classes are splintered by sexual tensions, individualism, selfish personal quarrels and the breach between skilled and unskilled workers.' (Sandbrook, 2005: 202–3)

Perhaps mirroring the personal cul-de-sacs which many of the new wave characters find themselves in at the film's end, 1963 was referred to by *The Evening Standard's* John Davis as 'The Year the Kitchen Sink Went Down the Drain'. The story of working-class Britain was becoming ridiculed as depressing and the sight of 'that town from the top of that hill' was a simplification of movies that had marked a real turning point in British film. The movement not have had the artistic impact of the French Nouvelle Vague but it was exceptionally influential as a reaction against an oppresive, class-based society and boasts many fine films.

'I think that this new English cinema was much more professional, much more sincere, not trying to impress by some peculiar style, in fact it had more depth to it.' (Roman Polanski, *Hollywood UK* BBC4)

However, the cultural change may not have been quite the revolution that some desired and the British new wave has arguably been marginalised by film history in favour of those London - centric 'swinging' films:

'Now to even to talk about those writers, those subjects, those films in terms of kitchen sink was an extremely middle-class thing to do but I think that that feeling, that tradition is very strong in this country and has remained so.' (Lindsey Anderson, *Hollywood UK* BBC4)

SWINGING BRITAIN

If the country was to be seen as a changed place, no longer could the culture be represented by the polarised and simplistic representation that set rich against poor or old against young that had typified the new wave. It was now important to describe a new way, a new culture that would emerge in its wake. The nation had to be seen to react to the dissatisfaction and find a positive way forward which would embrace, not eschew the new pop culture, while simultaneously trying to hang on to a British cultural identity in the face of Americanisation. The films that followed were predictably a mixture, as Britain searched for a new voice. They could not be categorised as a movement in the same way that the new wave films had, and their ideological message was as confused as the times. They would feature stylistic experimentation as well as new liberal values which weren't easy to define. Instead of rebelling against the old, it was time to embrace the new, but it would be the iconography of both that would define them. Set in the throbbing commercially orientated excitement of the metropolis, the new popular culture would be seen as offering a myriad of experience and perhaps for this reason, the film of 'swinging' Britain would be harder to delineate:

> 'Swinging London became the dominant motif of mid-Sixties British cinema, displacing the northern industrial towns and black-and-white social realism of the early Sixties 'New Wave'. In line with the more optimistic sensibility that they depicted, almost all films were now shot in colour, often with a *mise-en-scène* that emphasised bright primary colours.' (Donnelly, 2005: 95)

The films that followed in the wake of a new wave set largely in the industrial North of England were in part reactions to them as the zeitgeist of the Sixties relocated to the capital. Where the new wave films showed a brooding discontent based on an awareness of class differences, the post-new wave films emphasised a new positivity that explored the excitement of potential. There was now dramatic cultural change afoot, but it would be constructed in the London where the idea of a 'new' Britain could be reflected in the home of glamour and commerce, alongside the iconic and ironically traditional sights of the capital. In order to construct this new beginning the media would be central in defining the era.

Thus these so-called 'swinging' films depicted a new modern world in a familiar landscape. Instead of focusing on the drab claustrophobic world of angry young men and their industrial workplaces, an alternative reality was constructed around a spirit of new freedoms and liberation which would convey a feeling of a changed Britain, a modern Britain in which the class differences that fuelled the new wave were no longer relevant. The country's youth no longer needed to feel discontent:

> '…by 1964 the "New Wave" had spent itself. "Swinging London" had been born, an increasingly frenzied saturnalia whose cult was the new and the now, a world of colour supplements, pirate radio, glamorous television commercials, dolly birds, discos

and boutiques. With the backing of the Hollywood giants, British film-makers set out to capture the glitter and the glamour. Sober realism and earnest social comment gave way to fantasy, extravaganza and escapism; black and white photography and Northern locations to colour and the lure of the metropolis; Puritanical self-discipline to hedonistic self-indulgence; plain truthful settings to flamboyant, unrealistic decorativeness. Films became locked in a heady spiral of mounting extravagance, febrile excitement and faddish innovation.' (Aldgate and Richards, 1999: 216–17)

The ethos of free expression would alter conventional attitudes but also traditional means of expression and as the notion of this new, freer Britain was rather difficult to identify, so the films would often not convey any cohesive message or outlook with image triumphing over ideology – for some, style over substance. As the decade continued the more experimental and deconstructive the films became with an ever greater exploration of fantasy to express ideas that were not easily articulated.

How then can we view the rise and fall of the new wave and what does it tell us about the changing face of Britain? One feature we should acknowledge is that the films, despite their depiction of working-class lives, re-established the dominance of middle-class culture by relocationg and redefining the rebellion. This is no great surprise, as from a Marxist view it is the dominant order which controls the media. By allowing a new representation of the working-classes it could be seen to have elevated them to a new status or cultivated a certain view of the working-classes by bestowing on them a certain 'cool'. This can be seen as a response to the growing Americanisation of the culture, in which the ideas of a meritocracy are established in Britain. It can also be seen as a way of integrating the working-classes into believing a perception of a new classless Britain, which would continue into the swinging London films and would further incorporate the idea of a literal movement from south to north, to a new centre of excitement and cultural change.

The idea of social movement was central to the American Dream and Britain in this period was adopting American values. The idea of a meritocracy was given credence by a society which had to reinvent itself as a consumerist society. As explored by Hebdige in his book *Subculture*, far from turning the Establishment over in some sort of revolution, the media plays an active part in adapting the danger posed by the youth to the existing culture and despite being seen by many as a threat it is merely a part of the process of change to allow the integration of the counter culture into the mainstream. The raised profile of working-class stars would bring no great change to the systems in society; it would merely give the outward appearance of change. Hoggart's observation that the new culture was an empty smokescreen gets to the root of the problem, that the new mass culture would distract the masses from actual societal change (Hoggart, 1957).

As a part of the media, of course, film contributes to this representation but perhaps it is the cultivation of celebrity and stardom around British cinema that indicate the real changes that took place in the era and how the media constructed the idea of a 'swinging

Britain' that actually didn't exist beyond a small group of people in London and the pages of newspapers and magazines. Instead what we may see from the films made after 1963 is that the changes were stylistic rather than substantive, that is to say they were based around a change of presentation rather than a dramatic change in lifestyle.

Therefore the films of the mid-Sixties reflect a breaking of taboos that is far less dramatic than one might suspect. These films often demonstrate much of the confusion and the struggles that lie beyond the media manufactured façade of swinging Britain and show how the depiction of the excesses associated with the period is limited. They embody an attitude rather than a coherent theme and approach the changes in the decade through different perspectives almost as if trying to make sense of the era.

There is, however, a clear and identifiable link between the swinging London films and the new wave – their focus on the young. There is a colourful enthusiasm which embodies a more positive approach than the new wave and a developing relationship between pop music and British film, which would continue in the following decades.

And there is a new adventurer in this age of media, consumerism and commercialism. The independent female became an iconic sign of change, rejecting the values of domesticity and marriage and threatening the masculine-dominated ideals of the previous age. The mini-skirt and the contraceptive pill became weapons against women's subjugation, and the films explored the potential for women to change their role in society.

This new found freedom inevitably has its limitations and many of the films, which deal with ideas of pleasure, recognise new restrictions. The commercialisation of culture has led to confusion between what is a media perpetuated fantasy of pleasure and what is actually pleasurable. *The Knack* (1965), *Darling* (1965) and *Blow Up* (1966) in particular show the confusion in terms of a media constructed dream of freedom and reality.

There is an awareness in these films of the growing role of the mass media as it becomes more aware of youth culture as a commercial proposition. And ironically, the films show the ideological influence of the media, while at the same time constructing much of the phenomena of Sixties Britain. This is the development of the age of mass communication, as outlined by McLuhan, who claimed that 'the media is the message'. The media was generating much of the reaction of the age and was in large part responsible for shaping perceptions (McLuhan, 1964).

The films of 'swinging Britain' show an increasing interest in the manufacture of image and identity. Pop stars, advertisers, models and photographers are shown in films which reflect a society adopting new commercial values and many of the films communicate a sense of loss in the face of a growing superficiality as well as the promise of exciting change. There is a noticeable discomfort with a society based on less concrete ideals and there is an uncertainty which underlies the celebration of the new freedoms portrayed.

Accompanying this uncertainty there is a growth in the importance of psychology as the country struggles to make sense of the changes it is undergoing. This re-evaluation of the way in which people think reflects a dispensing with taken-for-granted certainties of the previous generation and allows for the views of those previously seen as marginal or condemned as outsiders to be accommodated. This 'individual' view of the world is endorsed by the production of films that demonstrate individual perceptions. The growth in popularity of *auteur* film-makers such as Antonioni, Anderson, Roeg and Kubrick, whose views of the world were both strange and wonderful, endorsed the importance of personal perception which would continue into the Seventies.

However, as the idea of 'swinging London' recedes, the liberal ideas that underlie its creation lead to experimentation (and, some would argue, excess) and film-makers show a willingness to push not only film language and narrative limitations to the extreme but also controversial content. Britain's time as a symbol of inspiration at an end, the mood of positivity is replaced by a growing disillusionment and disenchantment with a society which is still unrepresentative and which has actually changed little, despite the ferment of the Sixties. It is still a country of tradition and heritage, rather than modernity, now suborned to a large degree by American perceptions.

This guide will provide a narrative from the beginning to the end of the decade, 'joining the dots', as it were, through the films of the time, examining differing representations of time and place in an effort to make sense of the complexities of a changing nation, highlighting cinematic changes in style and outlook that were crucial in communicating, evaluating and constructing British identity in this famous decade.

Footnotes

[1] Post-war Britain learned to its cost its dependency on America and was forced into a humiliating u-turn when it tried to wrest control of the Suez Canal, an important trade link between Europe and the colonies, from Egypt who had nationalised it, removing it from British authority. Britain launched an attack on Egypt without consulting America, assuming it could rely on its support. America, however, saw things differently and threatened to sell its holding of Sterling reserves and cause the collapse of the British currency if Britain did not withdraw. This was a realisation for many of Britain's reduced standing in the world and confirmed that it was no longer a world power.

[2] John Profumo, Secretary for War, in the Conservative government was discovered to have had an affair with showgirl Christine Keeler. His affair with Keeler, who reputedly also had a relationship with an attaché at the Soviet embassy, raised issues of national security. Profumo initially denied their relationship in the House of Commons, but then later had to admit he had misled the House. This scandal rocked the government and was seen by many at the time as exposing the hypocrisy of many of the standards of an out-dated Britain.

CHAPTER 1: A GLIMPSE OF THE FUTURE — *PEEPING TOM* (COLOUR, POWELL, 1960)

Films to watch: *Victim* (1961), *The Leather Boys* (1964)

SEX

The 1960s are perhaps best known for radically changing sexual attitudes and behaviour but until the latter part of the Sixties there was actually very little evidence of films with explicit sexual references or depictions. Any change in film representation necessarily reflects changes in attitudes and any film-maker in the early Sixties wishing to confront themes of sexuality in a time still dominated by conservative values would run the risk of the censor's veto. Film's portrayal of such matters was necessarily tentative.

Homosexuality for instance was closely associated with perversion and was still a criminal offence in 1960 but with new legislation, perceptions of sexuality and normative behaviour were changing so fast there was confusion from the public about how to react to themes of this nature which had barely been touched upon in the previous decade.

The early Sixties saw the Wolfenden Committee's report which led to the decriminalisation of homosexual acts conducted in private between two adult men, then defined as being 21 years of age and over. Although this new legislation didn't endorse homosexuality, decriminalising it would inevitably lead to a re-evaluation of attitudes redefining a 'perversion' as a sexual orientation.

INTOLERANCE

The struggle for openness in such matters shows the conflict of the early Sixties: that in a time which was beginning to accept and legitimise certain types of behaviour or lifestyle, there would be a transitional period where certain practices, though acknowledged, had to remain somewhat underground. Moral indignation at marginal lifestyles was still high and one film and its maker would pay a particularly high price for this very British intolerance:

> 'In 1960 it was vilified as being exploitative, perverse and downright nasty in spite of the fact that there is very little explicit violence or sex.' (McNeill in Barrow and White, 2008: 104)

Michael Powell's *Peeping Tom* is a film that focuses on a form of fetish, voyeurism, and argued its relevance to the audience, highlighting attitudes toward sex and morality which expose the myth of the Sixties as a decade of instant sexual liberation. In a country that produced the 'Carry On...' and 'Confessions Of...' films, discussion of the repression of sexuality can never be far away and it is important to reflect upon how quickly the country had to adapt to a new morality to understand the context of the audience reaction to this film.

Tolerance for psychological problems as medical conditions was not far advanced and critics could not forgive director Michael Powell for presenting a character that was by mainstream society's standards deviant and expect him to engender sympathy. Powell, one half, together with Emric Pressburger, of the creative team who made some of Britain's best loved films, including *The Life and Death of Colonel Blimp* (1943), *The Red Shoes* (1948), *A Matter of Life and Death* (1946) and *Black Narcissus* (1947) would not work as a director in Britain again.

His colourful visual style was and still is best associated with the innocence of bygone times, filmed as it was in the bright cinematography of Technicolor. His films were synonymous with a Britain of stiff upper lips and a strong sense of moral duty. Even Powell himself was a reflection of a certain middle-class Britain, born to a well-to-do Kent family. Thus his unflinching exploration of a character who was a societal pariah seemed even more extreme to the audiences and critics of the day.

HATEFUL

> 'I thought it was the most hateful film I'd ever seen.' (Derek Hill, film critic, *A Very British Psycho*, Channel 4)

Today in the age of production-line teen-slashers, *Peeping Tom* seems a rather tame, if unusual, piece of cinema verging on the melodramatic but at the time it caused uproar. Its themes of perversion, prostitution and psychological damage were unnerving and what reinforced this unease was the presentation that made the viewer complicit in the murders, examining the voyeuristic pleasure of watching such content while refusing to condemn the central character whose motivations were located in the cruel behaviour of the parent.

This extreme reaction when considered in its context can be used to locate some of the conflicts which were to become major issues of the age. It is a film that has often been described as being 'ahead of its time' and perhaps this is because it embodied many of society's fears of a new age.

In his essay 'Under-The-Skin-Horrors' (in Ashby and Rigson, 2000: 222–32) Adam Lowenstein examines reactions from contemporary critics and points to their frustration at the film's 'direct emotional realism' which erodes barriers between an audience who would have enjoyed British horror, then derided as a crude mass entertainment, and one with 'taste'. Implicit in this criticism, Lowenstein argues, is the assumed division between the middle-class reviewers and the 'nuts' who pay to watch such fare, the working-classes.

Quoting Pierre Bourdieu, he explains that the very concept of taste is to 'fulfill a social function of legitimating social differences', and that the hostile reaction to *Peeping Tom* was a reaction to what Hoggart had noted about the nature of post-war Britain, namely that 'the great majority of us are being merged into one class.' He goes on to explain that Hoggart was of the opinion that the 'emergent mass culture is erasing traditional class-specific cultures and creating a "faceless" and "classless" mass society that he considers to be "less healthy" than the one it is replacing'. This view shared by one the characters in *Peeping Tom*, Maxine Audley, the only character who recognises the danger the protagonist presents and who comments, 'All this filming isn't healthy.'

MASS CULTURE

This view of the threat of mass culture reflects a Britain which is on the edge of a dramatic cultural change that will force it to examine itself. In film-making which shows awareness of audience motivations and the role of cinema, the *Peeping Tom* of the title, Mark forces his victims to do exactly that, reflecting back fears both in the micro level of the story, with the use of his camera, blade and mirror but also on a macro level, reflecting the terrors of a society plummeting headlong into an age of uncertainties. It is this fear of a society without clear class divisions, of 'us' and 'them', that marks the character of this new age.

Thus cinema actually takes on a wider significance, as a sign of the times, a product of mass entertainment, and of the subversion of an accepted morality:

'Its saying, not only is cinema not an escape, it can actually make life worse.' (Charlotte O' Sullivan, *A Very British Psycho* Channel 4)

In *Peeping Tom*, British society expected to see, and perhaps did see, a film that was 'itself an example of mass cultural entertainment' which was 'also saturated with images portraying the very manifestations of an "unhealthy" mass culture mentioned by Hoggart, including movies, pornographic pin-ups and the commodification of sensational violence' (Lowenstein in Ashby and Rigson, 2000: 224).

Irving Kristal, editor of Encounter commented in 1960:

'…we are on the defensive against "mass culture" which is what "popular culture" has become. Whereas "popular culture" was the culture of a class (the uneducated), "mass culture" is a culture shared to a greater or lesser degree by everyone. We all watch the same TV shows, read the same advertisements and see the same movies. As a result of the increase in popular wealth, popular taste now has a coercive power such as civilisation has never before witnessed. By its sheer massive presence, "mass culture" tends to crowd culture of every kind to the margins of society.' (Murphy, 1992: 117)

While for some, the prospect of a society without class barriers was hugely exciting, for others it meant an invasion of lower-class values. This perception of a mass culture spreading insidiously across the nation via low brow entertainments is reflective of a middle-class fear that will see the erosion of class divisions and with them the protection of standards and privilege which only those who had the necessary breeding and education could possess.

VOYEURISM

Peeping Tom seems to embody the fear of a Britain on the cusp of change. Mark's voyeurism speaks of a society about to enter an age where the visual is the main mode of communication. Mark (Carl Boehm), like Thomas, the photographer in *Blow Up* (1966), is an image-maker and there are many shared values between the two characters. Both are detached from the world around them and both aspire to a freedom which they are unable to attain. However, society's reaction to the two is markedly different and reflects the dramatic shift in Britain's outlook from post-war conservatism to the much vaunted liberalism of the swinging decade. Mark, like Thomas, may be someone who creates images but, unlike Thomas, he is not valued but rather is despised and loathed for his activities in a very different cultural climate. While Mark's cruelties are repressed and exist below the surface, Thomas can give vent to his, indulging in the freedoms available (albeit, not fully satisfied by them).

However, despite Mark's depraved activities, the film suggests he is not to blame for his actions. He is merely someone who reflects society, quite literally recording its fear and conversely its own fascinations. The girls he takes photographs of are objects of both threat and illicit pleasure for the so-called respectable members of society, but noticeably Mark takes little personal interest in this. He is a documentary-maker and even when he is pursued to his death he maintains the need to record events, the reactions of society to his actions.

Mark is inseparable from his camera and carries it everywhere. He is not so much a character as a lens through which society is filtered. He is lost without it and only knows life as an experiment which he has to record. His psychological state is the result of his father's actions whose experiment has made Mark a deviant, someone on the outside of society who knows its dark underbelly and predilections. Mark, however, is exonerated from any blame because his condition has been inflicted upon him:

> 'We sought not merely understanding but sympathy and the critics did not seem prepared for this.' (Leo Marks, *A Very British Psycho,* Channel 4)

Many Sixties viewers, however, could not but see darkness in this figure. Mark warns of the attractive and hypnotic pleasures of the new technologies and new attitudes that will be embraced during this period. He is also a servant of this society's need for such pleasures, producing the images which it craves and simultaneously punishing those who help produce them. It is in this exposure of double standards, of simultaneously watching and disapproving, that *Peeping Tom* reveals its message. It:

> '…mirrors from the start our own gaze as we watch the film, letting us know in no uncertain terms that the film will, in a sense, be watching us watching. We are the peeping Toms of the title and the film knows it too.' (McNeill in Barrow and White, 2008: 104)

The era is not yet ready to embrace the permissiveness associated with the age; in *Peeping Tom,* it remains hidden and suppressed. However, it signals a change in accepting its presence and not merely dismissing it as deviance. Mark's depiction as the most normal of psychopaths is unnerving and the implication that the mass pleasures he helps to produce are satiating repressed by society puts the 'blame' desires squarely on society's shoulders. Such pleasures are enjoyed by a cross section of society, who indulge to varying degrees, yet cannot confront or accept them and instead choose to ignore or condemn them. Mass culture was forcing the dominant middle-class values to admit this repression as unhealthy.

The effectiveness of *Peeping Tom* is that when the punishments are meted out it is our punishment that is inflicted and in making it a film about film, the lens is squarely pointed back at ourselves and it is a so-called deviant (Mark) who does this for us. This of course was intolerable to a society that prided itself on its own civilisation and held itself up to the rest of the world as the example of moral rectitude. In short, it was an attack on the British character.

DANGER

The film opens with a shot of an eye, immediately introducing the theme of watching to the audience. We are then confronted by a darkened street scene with a woman looking in a shop window. A figure enters the scene whistling but we don't get to see their face, only their point of view. What we do see is a camera concealed in their coat which is switched on before moving toward us and fading out. The sound of the whirring film is dominant as the camera, through which we are now looking, moves toward the dispirited woman who is turning away from the shop. Through the view finder we see the cross hair which targets the woman as if through the viewfinder of a gun.

In such a presentation, the camera becomes a weapon in which the woman is framed. She becomes a target and without knowing it she is condemned to death. As she will inevitably reveal her immorality so she will just as inevitably be punished. Thus we the audience are posited as both viewer and murderer.

The sound of a piano heightens the tension as the camera moves to look at the lower half of the woman, objectifying her. She turns toward the camera before dispassionately stating, 'It'll be two quid.' Thus the connection between sex and money is established immediately and we are consenting to payment. This implication of the audience in the act of soliciting is indicative of the film's intent, involving them in the sordid activities of sexual thrill seeking. Although there is no audible reply the camera follows the woman into an alleyway and a hand is seen throwing Kodak cine film into a full waste bucket (like a packet of condoms?).

The camera follows the woman into her flat where she gets undressed with boredom, paying no heed to her visitor, until there is a sound of metal and a flashing reflective light lands upon her face. She is now paying full attention, looking shocked and stunned, hypnotised with fear. As dramatic music builds the camera closes in on the woman who begins screaming in terror.

AUDIENCE

And so the first murder takes place, with no view of the killer. Instead the viewer is positioned as the killer as the prostitute is murdered and forced to watch her own death, and we as an audience are complicit in the murder. This can be seen as motivated by a fear of women, and the female sexuality which was to dramatically change during this period:

> 'It is not difficult to see to detect problematic male sexuality and fear of independent women as the major reactionary dynamic at work in *Peeping Tom*. In that sense it is very much a film of its period.' (Street, 1997: 78)

The text undoubtedly punishes women and reflects the tendency of the horror genre to both objectify and condemn the 'immoral' woman, but there is more than just a fear of the changing role of women at play in *Peeping Tom*; there is the attendant audience fear of a loss of morality. The viewer is forced to inhabit a scene of squalor and, though clearly an artificial cinematic squalor (making the point that this is a cinematic pleasure), the audience is forced to confront its involvement in a side of life it would rather ignore:

> 'Sexuality is taken out of the closet and exposed to sight…Sex is portrayed as threatening, as aligned with institutional power.' (Landy in Street, 1997: 78)

During the 1960s Britain would inevitably have to confront this fear and the Profumo scandal was the real life embodiment of this combination of immorality and power. It was inevitable that Britain would have to accept that what was widely viewed as unnatural and immoral was not actually easily divisible from civilised society but rather was another part of that society and could be found in the most unexpected places. *Peeping Tom*, in refusing to condemn its central character for deviance, refused to separate the deviant from the normal and this underlying sexual power was revealed in the Profumo scandal.

The film, then, echoes the scandal of the age, lifting the lid off surface respectability and demonstrating for those who cared to listen, that Britain could no longer continue to close its eyes to its own identity. Crucial to this self-discovery is the role of the media which is an integral part of the new Britain.

UNHEALTHY

The implication in *Peeping Tom* that cinema is an unhealthy past time connected with the perception of a mass audience, seeking thrills without guilt, is at the centre of the text and the film's self-awareness constantly reminds the audience of their part in the 'entertainment'. If the entertainments of the mass age are salacious, it is only a reflection of those who crave it.

Peeping Tom's self-reflexive nature is a precursor to the Sixties style and this feature is recurrent, beckoning in an age of the self, where the films constantly ask questions relating to the individual as a product of society. The nature of film begins to be more introspective and examines the construction of reality rather than assuming what we are watching is 'real'. The idea of image production and psychoanalysis is central to the idea of questioning the self and both elements are present in *Peeping Tom*.

The film's title sequence repeats and emphasises this self-reflexive style and shows a projector playing back the scene we have just witnessed in black and white. The process of watching it again is a rather uncomfortable and disorienting process, especially as it infers that we are sharing some of the same pleasures as the solitary figure who we see watching the film. He rises from his seat as the murder reaches its climax and we see an extreme close-up of the woman's mouth screaming before he falls back into his seat. The shot of the projector is superimposed with the name of the director, Michael Powell, an acknowledgement of his own complicity.

This multi-layered beginning positions the audience firmly in the world of the cinema. Despite the down at heel setting of the first murder which could be connected to the real world, it is portrayed in the artificiality of the cinema set, before being replayed in black and white, the chosen medium of the new wave film-makers concerned with the 'real'. This blurs the distinction between real and fictional representations in the film. The self-reflexive quality of the beginning of the film makes it one in which the processes of film-making and film-watching are evident, which can truly be said to be ahead of its time.

The next image we see is of a sign on the back of a car which reads 'police'. The camera moves up to reveal a street scene. This is the murder scene we have witnessed, although it is more 'real' in its daytime appearance and this time we see who is behind the camera. One of the investigating officers spies the cameraman and asks him to which newspaper he is attached. The man looks shocked and frightened before calming himself and replying, *The Observer*, a blackly comic touch. The cameraman, Mark, is young and good looking, perhaps not the monster we had anticipated.

TITILLATION

Thus the inherent titillation of many horror films is denied as we, the audience find out who the murderer is and far from being the hideous faceless monster we might expect, is a very amenable and respectable looking young man. In so doing *Peeping Tom* defies expectation and immediately takes away some of the pleasures of the genre. If we are to engage with the killing, we are not being permitted to remove ourselves. The difference between 'them' and 'us' is thus erased as the film shows us that it is the ordinary and everyday who will be portrayed as responsible for the horrific in this film.

The press take photographs as the body is removed on a stretcher, depicting 'respectable' society's need for salacious horror, and the young cameraman backs away to the other side of the street, continuing to film intently as the body is taken away, showing little difference between his actions and the media reproduction of images for the waiting public. He films a woman who he passed on the stairs the previous evening and her sympathetic reaction to the crime before the shot dissolves to the exterior of the paper shop where the media disseminate their entertainments.

Mark dismounts from his scooter, pausing briefly to look at nude glamour photographs which decorate the shop door and are for sale in the form of postcards. The shopkeeper chastises him for being late before asking him which magazines sell the most copies, to which he replies in ritual fashion, 'Those with girls on the front covers but no front covers on the girls.' 'Exactly', he responds, 'it's just the same in the work you do for me.'

Thus Mark's line of work is revealed, but, far from being condemned as distasteful, it is the proprietor of the shop who is condemned in the text. He is someone who uses Mark's interest in photography and, unbeknown to us, pornography, and exploits it for material gain. His assessment of what sells shows his opportunism in cashing in on society's shifting attitudes toward pornography which is far from a minority interest as his comment indicates. The growth of the media is revealing the levels of interest in sex, and society will have to adapt its morality, challenging standards that in the previous decade would have been set in stone.

RESPECTABILITY

To emphasise this view of a barely repressed sexuality simmering beneath the surface of mainstream society, Powell introduces a figure of the Establishment, as an older gentleman enters the shop and asks for copies of broadsheet newspapers *The Times* and *The Telegraph*. He is immediately defined as a 'respectable' member of society and is played by the much loved comic actor, Miles Malleson, who appeared in many British films. Mark meanwhile looks at the front cover of the morning's *Daily Mirror* which shows the face of the murdered girl. The contrast between the cheap sensationalism of the tabloid press and the better papers is made only to be ridiculed as the gentleman of the Establishment then shows he has other interests than the news.

He cautiously asks the shopkeeper for euphemistic 'views'. Behind him shelves are littered with glamour magazines, indicating a high demand. The newsagent finds some pictures under the counter and the man keenly looks through a portfolio before being disturbed by a young girl in school uniform entering the shop. This juxtaposition of the elderly gentleman with the naïve schoolgirl is particularly poignant and suggestive, and the audience at the time may have found it particularly uncomfortable, implicating the supposedly respectable in society's moral decline.

The gentleman, returning to the counter asks for a copy of all the photographs contained but declines the shopkeeper's offer to be included on the shop's mailing list: 'Oh, no. I'll look in again', he answers and the shopkeeper gives him a bag marked 'educational books'. 'Well, he won't be doing the crossword tonight,' the shopkeeper cheerfully remarks.

This comical undermining of middle-class respectability reflects the double standards of a society in which someone who seems to embody conservative values can, beneath the surface be as morally bereft as the next person. Mark, a murderer, is made to appear normal in comparison with this ridiculous figure who cannot maintain his façade of respectability and it is Mark's very normality that makes him an uncomfortable figure throughout the tale. This was particularly disturbing to a contemporary audience for whom immorality was something that existed 'elsewhere'.

REPRESSION

Milly (Pamela Green), a glamour model, poses in front of a faux Parisian backdrop, reflective of Joseph Yanni's view that, at this time, 'sex was regarded, if it was regarded at all, as an exclusively Continental pursuit' (*Hollywood UK* BBC 4). Britain's refusal to acknowledge sex was seen in its use of foreign actresses such as Bridget Bardot or Simone Signoret in sexualised roles. 'Come on sonny', she says pointedly, 'make us famous.' This, however, isn't an industry that will provide any fame, its underground nature, more likely bringing shame or infamy to its participants who are presented as working through necessity.

She talks of the murders and how it nearly happened to her when she was caught with another man by her fiancé. Mark meanwhile is busily positioning her. 'Can you fix it so the bruises don't show?' she asks. Mark looks intently at her inverted image under the black sheet. The use of the black sheet enhances his position as a hidden viewer, a secretive watcher.

VIOLENCE

Milly's conversation establishes her as a strong female figure and exposes male fantasy but it also acknowledges the threat of male violence for women that break accepted gender behaviour. Her accent and attitude expose the myth of her sexually provocative image, constructing a real person who is able to control and use her sexuality. The backdrop of Paris is another artificial setting and can be related to the fictitious one that opens the film. She ridicules Mark as an artist and the idea that through his photographs she can achieve fame. She recognises that she is confined in her role in society, one in which, despite her bravado, she is vulnerable to, and mistreated by, men.

Milly asks Mark about his full time job and he answers that he takes pictures. 'This sort?' she says, splaying her legs open on the bed. 'No Milly,' he says peeved by her crude behaviour. Milly represents the threat of a sexually independent female. She is aware of her role in selling sex but her open attitude is a threat to male power and society's superficial standards. When the shopkeeper enters with a tray of tea he offers it 'on the house.' 'Some house,' she replies and adds, 'I hope it falls around your ears.' Once again she triumphs in exposing the façade of respectability. Her candid attitude to sex gives her power and her criticism of the newsagent exposes the exploitative nature of this work.

Milly, like Mark, is a glimpse of the future and can be compared to *Darling's* Diana. Her use of sex as a currency in a new commercial culture shows her to be trying to exert control over her life and indicates she will be able to take advantage of the permissive age. She recognises that she lives in a male-dominated culture and that masculine created representations of women underlie aggressive attempts to control women. It is this view of Sixties woman as a figure of sexual power that will come to play such a key part in the age.

The other model, Lauren, tells Mark it's her first time being photographed and we realise why when she turns to reveal a disfiguring scar. Mark is mesmerised and seems fascinated by the girl. 'Don't be shy', says Mark as he moves slowly towards her. 'It's my first time too.' 'Yours?' Lauren asks baffled. 'In front of eyes,' he stammers to the girl who is bemused and transfixed.

The capturing of Lauren's image is referred to in terms of sexual experience and a loss of innocence. The act of capturing natural image is a private one which Mark has kept to himself and contrasts with the constructed images he makes for public consumption. His fascination with Lauren's disfigurement shows that rather than turn away from that which society finds uncomfortable he is prepared to confront it and furthermore he is fascinated by it. He exposes, through his lens, the darker desires of the culture.

This is disconcerting for an audience who is expecting to see the hideous made thrilling and seeking entertainment from it as the film continues the brutal confrontation of audience pleasures. The 'normal' way of looking at Lauren is to look at her body, objectifying her sexuality; but this is ruined if we are forced to look at her face. We are even prevented from enjoying her disfigurement as a horrific moment, as we might in a conventional horror film, which again blurs the distinction between 'normal' and 'abnormal' behaviour.

OUTSIDER

Mark, coming home passes by the ground floor window of the building in which he lives. His attention caught by a party, he stops and watches. The revellers are oblivious to his presence at first but then some guests notice him at the window. As they all turn to look Mark is transfixed but as he realises that he's been seen, he moves quickly away. One of the guests identifies him as 'that chap from upstairs'. The camera follows him through the hallway, where he pauses again to listen to the sounds of the party. He continues on his way toward the stairs when Helen (Anna Massey) throws open the door and introduces herself but Mark, clearly uncomfortable with social contact, retreats upstairs.

Mark's movement back and forth from one side of society to another is disquieting. He passes between social environments which becomes a theme for much of the cinema of the period but does not belong to any. He is not clearly defined by class but rather by his work. Mark's position is that of an outsider, someone removed from mainstream by his emotional detachment the alienation we see later in *Blow Up* which, for Antonioni, describes the modern condition. Nonetheless he serves to link separate worlds. The party is a depiction of 'normal society' and is typical of the middle-class depiction of Fifties films but Mark's appearance at the window is a visible threat to the social order and community.

The now familiar shot of the projector running begins a scene in which Mark is alone in his room. He again sits in darkness transfixed by events on the screen. The relentless, dramatic music plays as Mark watches the murdered prostitute's body being removed from her flat. Events are played back to us as though in a silent cinema, before there is a knock at the door. Mark hurriedly removes the reel of film before placing it in a metal cupboard, and emerges from the darkroom into his flat, answering the door to Helen who has brought him a slice of birthday cake.

The subsequent conversation establishes both of these young people's personalities. Helen is enthusiastic and impetuous, while Mark is rather shy and self effacing. Both seem young and innocent but Mark's inner turmoil is beginning to be explored as his need for peace and his attachment to his father is revealed. Mark's childlike willingness to please Helen shows him to be a vulnerable character, but one enslaved by his secret passion.

Mark reveals his role in films and his ambition to become a director, which indicates his desire to take control of his life. He takes Helen into this darkness of the back room where he works to show her one of his films but after taking a reel of film from a shelf he hesitates and selects a different film.

DARKNESS

The room is symbolic of a greater darkness. The space devoted to Mark's film-making equipment far outweighs that allocated to his living quarters which are cramped. It is as though his life takes second place to his work and something that dominates him but he has to hide. In this sense it is the very symbol of repression. Mark conceals this side of his character but it ultimately takes over his life.

Mark shows Helen a series of short home movies of when he was a young boy. The first sequence shows him sleeping in his bed before being awoken by torchlight in a state of upset. The second shows him voyeuristically watching a kissing couple from on top of the wall. He turns to laugh at the cameraman, his father. Helen disapproves. The camera returns to the couple as she comments on the strangeness of the subject matter. Mark offers to switch it off but she declines and sounds intrigued. Helen's reactions are indicative of the theme of the film, as she shows signs of behaviour that the audience are indulging in. She says she is appalled by the content, but persists in watching.

The next sequence shows a timid Mark coming into a room dressed smartly as it is revealed that it is footage of his seeing his mother's corpse. Helen is amazed that this was filmed and Mark shows her the funeral and the burial, then his mother's 'successor', a young woman at the beach, drying her hair. The next sequence shows him posing with his new mother, telling Helen that she married his father six weeks after his mother's death and his father is shown presenting him with a gift – a camera.

The subject of the family is portrayed in a particularly disturbing way. Mark's childhood, born to supposedly respectable middle-class parents has had a profound effect on his life and, unlike most portrayals of the family from the time it is not a reflection of happiness and security. Mark's life has been tainted by his own father and there is a significant questioning of assumptions of the family as being a haven from danger. This is in contrast to Helen who has had a secure upbringing, despite only having one parent.

As the camera closes in on the boy playing with the camera, he turns it toward his step-mother-in-law as she films. As one camera gazes into another, Mark is hypnotised, while Helen implores him to turn it off. Finally she flicks the projector's switch and says, 'Let's get out of here', before fleeing the room and Mark.

FILM

The self-reflexive nature of this sequence, examining the interaction between the viewer and the film, of the need to document life and the way in which the role of the camera is itself foregrounded is reminiscent of the explorations of the French New Wave, which examined the relationship between film and its audience. It is in its knowing construction that it resembles the work of Jean Luc Godard who would dissect the nature of narrative film; but while Godard's work would be held in esteem, Powell's experimentation was vilified and only appreciated in retrospect.

The extreme reaction Peeping Tom engendered tells us much about British attitudes of the early Sixties. While the film was deconstructive and adventurous in its style, it ventured too much into the area of morality and its observations of Britain were not appreciated. Mark and his camera were too questioning of an audience which didn't want to see itself or face the threat of change it represented. Mark's character portrayed moral uncertainty to an audience that was used to certainties:

'What could be more disturbing, however, than a film which probes the very mechanisms of cinema itself, revealing our own perversity....' (McNeill in Barrow and White, 2008: 104)

This examination of the relationship between cinema and its audience continues in the next scene. A voice on a telephone amplified by a speaker is talking about a proposed film: 'Is it commercial?' film producer Don Jarvis asks, looking at a model of the set. He tells his secretary to take a memo to all producers and directors, 'In light of the new economy drive, if you can see it and hear it, the first take's okay.'

We cut back to the studio where filming is taking place. The director is badgering the lead actress, played by Shirley-Anne Field. She attempts to faint a number of times before the director is finally satisfied.

The careful delineation of scenes is demonstrative of an industry driven by profit. Powell's ironic depiction of the studio executive considering a new project and the cost implications of the current film, while looking at a model of the set, exposes the 'reality' of what we are watching. At every stage of the film the layering of realities examines the way in which the audience engage with the text and what drives its production.

Mark, in his day job of focus puller is working on the set and reveals to a crew member that he is meeting someone for a drink, a young actress called Viv (Moira Shearer). That evening she gets herself ready in the dressing room, preparing herself for the secretive meeting with Mark as though preparing for her part in an illicit performance, which of course she is. She hides from a security guard, before making her way toward 'E-Stage'. The door closes behind her. She whistles a tune which is mimicked in the darkness of the set before a light flashes on to melodramatic and sinister music. As she calls out Mark's name more studio lights come on in an obviously stage-managed performance.

Mark reveals himself, descending dramatically on a hydraulic lift. Viv, fearing discovery, suggests they should cancel their plans but Mark tells her they won't be disturbed as he has put the red light on. He tells her that they have both waited a long time for this, to make what he describes as a 'perfect' film. The elusive nature of Mark's film is indicative of the difficulty of all film-makers: the impossibility of capturing 'reality' but his elevated position in the studio shows him to be in control for the first time. He is no longer the uncertain character seen earlier. As an image-maker, here in the studio, he is an authoritative figure as he attempts to construct his own reality.

Mark makes preparations while Viv dances to warm up before asking how her to act 'being frightened to death'. She jokes she would rather die laughing, before sitting in the box where her body will be hidden. A close up shows the red light and the title of the film, 'The Walls are Closing In'. The knowing title of the film indicates its self-aware presentation and the red light indicates both sex and danger. It is not just for Viv and Mark that the walls are closing in, it is for us as viewers as Powell employs some heavy-handed dramatic irony.

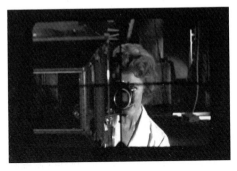

Mark checks his viewfinder again and tells Viv she can look through the studio camera if she wishes. As she does so he tells her he is 'photographing you, photographing me'. The self-reflexivity of the scene shows the pair duelling for dominance. Just who is constructing reality here? Viv is oblivious to Mark's motivations and she tries to frame him in camera, but Mark as the image-maker sits in front of the camera and tells Viv to take her position. As she stands with her back to him, he raises one leg of the tripod...

PSYCHOLOGY

Viv complains that she feels too relaxed and asks Mark to set the tone. He asks her to imagine a man who wants to kill her. 'A madman?' she asks. 'Yes, but he knows it and you don't,' he replies with dramatic irony before demonstrating the weapon, holding his tripod toward her and murdering her.

The indication that Mark is aware of his own problems shows a different approach to psychology that would gain in popularity as the decade moved on. Mark may have a disorder but that doesn't mean he is unable to function or unaware of it. His complex character questions assumed notions. The simplistic label of 'madness' was questioned throughout the Sixties as the popular interest in psychology grew and with the rise of another discipline, sociology, came the belief that people could be labelled rather unhelpfully by society if their views were significantly different. This is arguably another significant reason for the film's rejection, as the text does not simply present accepted ideas but asks the viewer to confront previously unquestioned beliefs.

Viv's murder follows that of the prostitute's and Mark's actions can be interpreted as exacting revenge on women who refuse to live in dread of society's conformist standards. She is another independent, confident and probably sexually active character who wants to indulge her desires. She is fun and free-spirited and lives without fear until Mark shows it to her. The characteristics that she exemplifies are very much those of the new age. She lives for the moment and enjoys dancing, music and male company; and the consequence is that she must be punished and this is what Mark does, for the audience's pleasure.

Yet Mark always feels that he has failed, perhaps due to the fact he can never wholly eradicate these women. In killing them and filming the murders, he does so for his father, the patriarchal figure in his life and this could be seen as Mark's attempt to serve the needs of a male-dominated society. The figure of the independent woman, however, will continue to thrive and will come to develop as an important aspect of this new media age. By filming them, he guarantees their survival.

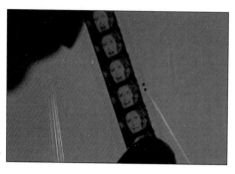

That evening Helen and her mother Maxine discuss Mark. Maxine is again drinking heavily. It is clear from the conversation that she doesn't trust him, claiming he 'walks stealthily'. Maxine Audley's character is someone who, despite her blindness, is able to see what those around her can't. Precisely because of her lost sight she is not tempted by the allures of the new visual age and warns her daughter against Mark.

Helen goes upstairs to talk to Mark who becomes disturbed as he thinks about the film he is developing. Helen, however, tells him about her writing short stories for children and that her first book is about to be published: a story about a magic camera. Mark is startled but then becomes excited.

The scene emphasises the innocence of their relationship, as both Mark and Helen are again portrayed as young children; but the duality of Mark's character, of the double life he leads, of the darkness that underlies his obsession with filming suggests he is 'tainted' by the allure of mass culture. Though Helen is attracted to Mark, she is not tempted by his obsession with his camera. Her writing shows a leaning toward literature, considered a more wholesome and intellectual pleasure.

The idea of the child or childishness was something that the Sixties embraced, as children are free from many of the burdens of adulthood. Mark and Helen are two sides of the same character. One is unspoilt and protected by her sightless mother, the other corrupted by his camera-fixated father. For Mark there is an inner struggle. Helen is opening his eyes to the prospect of a new life, one without the obsessive addiction to his filming but he his finding it almost impossible to free himself.

Once again the difference between reality and film is blurred as we see an extract from rushes of a film before we realise the director is now watching back the film in the viewing room with a few of the cast and crew. He expresses his disappointment and the need for comedy which is then supplied by Powell in a scene that combines the macabre and the comical. Back on the set the director instructs the lead actress how she should ask for a variety of trunks and indicates that the final one selected should be the blue one – in which Viv's body is contained. Mark looks nervous but continues to do his job while the actors run through. As the blue trunk is pulled out with considerable effort by the actor involved, Mark takes out his camera and begins to film as the terrified actress faints, much to the dismay of the director who thinks she has fainted in the wrong scene, once again confusing reality with fiction:

> '...the real horror intrudes on the artificiality of the film set...The film's persistent disturbance of the parameters of the fiction adds to feeling of disquiet it creates in the spectator.' (McNeill in Barrow and White, 2008: 107)

As the film draws to its denouement, rather archetypal investigating officers are introduced, discussing the Soho murder. Soho, of course, is not only home to sex but also the British film industry. The chief expresses his bafflement at the expression on the murdered girl's face. He cannot work out what it was that caused such terror. This, of course, is key to the film's meaning as we, the audience, explore the fear instilled by the camera.

Arriving at the film set, the officers take a look at Viv's body, which has the same expression as the prostitute's. They begin questioning the crew and Mark tries to film them. As he talks to one of his colleagues, who asks him why he is filming he tells him he is completing a documentary. In a conversation loaded with double meaning, Mark tells his friend that he doesn't mind being caught and admits to being 'crazy'. Mark's construction of the 'documentary' gives him control over events. His filming of the policemen, suggests that, far from being 'crazy', he is completely aware of his actions.

Later, Helen is reading aloud the story of the girl's murder from a newspaper. Once again the public's appetite for such stories is reinforced. Her mother asks about Mark's job in films, clearly suspicious of him and then senses his presence before he appears at the window. Mark's position as an outsider is noted by Maxine, who comments at his occupying the window. She is the one character who recognises the threat Mark poses. When Helen invites Mark in to meet her, Maxine asks Mark about the murdered girl but he denies knowing her. Helen persuades him to dispense with his camera for the evening and locks it away. Removing the object of his obsession, he becomes calm and relaxed. He tells her he feels something but can't express it, indicating his camera is his means of expression, but as they leave for the restaurant they are happy.

When they return home they express their delight at the wonderful evening and Helen acknowledges that it was particularly enjoyable without Mark's camera. She goes to fetch it and as she brings it out, she points it at herself. Mark, terrified, snatches it back and tells her he will never film her, as everything he films, he loses.

Helen tries to dissuade Mark from sitting up looking at films but he tells her that he has some work to do and then he'll try to find the faces she needs for her book. She kisses him and he closes his eyes. Once gone, however, he presses the camera to his lips indicating how it is the true object of his affection.

In his flat Mark looks at Viv's terrified face on the reel of film. She has been reduced from a person to an image, the very epitome of the modern age. She has been killed by the filming but lives on. Hearing a noise and shining a light into a corner of the room he discovers Maxine, who has let herself in. She questions Mark about the films he plays every night. There is a reversal of roles here as Mark has become the hunted and Maxine points her stick at him in the manner of the tripod he uses to kill his victims.

Mark leads her toward the screen which is showing Viv's murder. Her terrified face is projected against his back as she reaches a hand up and asks what he is seeing. As the film ends he throws himself against the screen, complaining that the lights fade too soon and that he has missed his opportunity. Distraught, he resolves to find another and, grabbing his tripod, he shines a light at Helen's mother and begs her to let him film her.

Instead he flees the room, pursued by Helen's mother. She tells him that 'all this filming isn't healthy' and that he needs help. Mrs Audley feels Mark's face and he comments that she is taking his picture. She asks him what is troubling him but he pulls her hands away and bids her goodnight.

Mark and Maxine's confrontation shows her as the guardian of moral values in *Peeping Tom*. She protects Helen from Mark's influence and when he tries to kill her he cannot do it as she has not been corrupted by the allure of mass culture. Her disillusionment, reflected in her drinking, seems to mourn something lost and though she pities Mark and recognises his need for help, her duty is to protecting Helen from his influence.

TRAPPED

The climax of the film shows Mark finally controlling his own fate. His final victim will be Milly, the model from earlier in the film using her to attract the attention of the police.

Above the newsagents, Milly complains at having to work as she is missing a date with her new boyfriend. Mark looks out of the window and sees the man tailing him. She complains that she needs to get on with the work but Mark films the man instead.

As he pulls the blinds down, Milly lies on the bed and wonders, 'Is it safe to be alone with you I wonder. It might be more fun if it wasn't.' Millie's wish for 'fun', however, is punished as Mark looms over her before the scene fades to black. He then leaves the newsagent and posts the key back through the letter box, being followed by the policeman.

Helen goes upstairs to Mark's room. She sits next to the projector and switching it on views Viv's murder. When Mark arrives, she asks him, 'That film, it is just a film isn't it?' He tells her it isn't and that he is a murderer. Helen's question is the question around which the significance of film functions. Can a film be just a film or does it capture reality? Mark's film is his life, not just a reflection of it. He cannot be separated from that which he films.

Mark picks up his tripod and asks Helen, 'Do you know what the most frightening thing in the world is? It's fear.' Mark shows how he placed a mirror above the camera and made the girls watch their own deaths, explaining in doing so the power of film. This self-awareness shows the danger of the camera and explains its earlier depiction as a weapon. Milly's body discovered, the police arrive, Mark breaking a window to film them. 'Look out', one calls. 'It's only a camera,' one of the policeman shouts, again associating it with a weapon.

Helen pleads for Mark to give himself up but he tells her how he has waited for this moment. He plays all the tapes and sets off cameras to take photos of his dying moments as he walks toward the tripod and its blade, before forcing himself onto it, thereby ending his documentary and his life. As the police burst in to find Mark's body and Helen still alive, the projector runs out of tape and we hear Mark's voice as a boy asking for his father to hold his hand indicating that Mark's behaviour is a result of emotional repression.

SUMMARY

Peeping Tom became a pariah in its time but viewed today it helps our understanding of a society which was on the verge of massive changes in its perception of the world. The real horror of the film comes not from the murders but our own thoughts of what lies waiting beneath the surface. For traditional mainstream society, it was as if its own repressions were like a dam about to burst.

The desire for permissiveness and what could go wrong if one represses tendencies that perhaps were more prevalent than we cared to admit showed a society in denial. The outlet of the mass entertainment of the cinema pointed the blame not at itself, which was acting as a mirror (like that at the end of Mark's camera), but instead just reflected society and its inability to accept what was all around.

John Costello argues that during World War II:

'the trend to permissiveness was firmly established with the commercialisation of eroticism in the films, television, and advertising industries which had followed the lead of the wartime pin-ups and girlie magazines.' (Costello, 1985: 370)

It is Mark's voyeuristic tendancy that would explode in the coming decade, and in this way the image-makers would capture the audience in the same way as Powell captures the predicament of a Britain on the verge of being hypnotised by it's own reflection.

The inference that the perversity was not to be found in the individual but in society was something that was just too much to take at the time. The unsettling thought that for a large percentage of the population there were passions which lurked under the surface and which were about to be let loose in an age which liberalised sexuality had to be deemed unacceptable but the fear was there and there is nothing more frightening than fear itself.

CHAPTER 2: KEEPING IT REAL
— *SATURDAY NIGHT AND SUNDAY*
MORNING (B/W, REISZ, 1960)

Films to watch: *Room at the Top* (1958), *Look Back in Anger* (1958), *A Taste of Honey* (1961), *A Kind of Loving* (1962), *The Loneliness of the Long Distance Runner* (1962), *This Sporting Life* (1963) and *Billy Liar* (1963)

LAMPTON PAVES THE WAY

'One feels that a whole new chapter is about to be written in motion picture history… I can say for myself that the only shock I felt was the shock of recognition, the shock of recognising ordinary, tawdry people on the screen in an extraordinarily bitter, adult drama, and the shock of realizing how rarely this had happened before.' (Arthur Knight, *The Daily Express*, 3 April 1959)

It is difficult to imagine, given the changes in censorship today, how the new wave films stunned Britain with content that now seems so innocuous. The above review of *Room at the Top* (1958), the first film recognisably from this movement, demonstrates what a shock it was to have the working-classes represented on the screen as leading characters. Something considered so natural today shows up the imbalance in class relations on screen until this time and how it was reinforced in the media. Indeed, to have a character so intent upon changing his social position reflected the climate of growing discontent among the lower-classes:

> 'In the Fifties British cinema was in a bad state… In a period of increasing affluence people were choosing to spend their money elsewhere. Movies had fallen behind the times but the thrusting northern hero of *Room at the Top*, provided a welcome challenge to the public school types who still seemed to dominate the screen.' (Richard Lester, *Hollywood UK* BBC4)

Of course, to many contemporary critics in Britain this was audacious and they found it difficult to accept that such characterisation as a fair reflection of the times. It is perhaps significant to note that America accepted the veracity of this particular version of reality far more readily:

> 'Not only do bourgeois morals take an awful drubbing here, but so does the general moral climate of our time.' (*The New Yorker*, 11 April 1959)

If Hoggart was worried that Britain was going to emulate America, then surely here was the evidence. Unlike most of the anti-heroes of the new wave, *Room at the Top*'s Joe Lampton reflected the acquisitive and ambitious characteristics of American values:

> 'The story has something of the nineteenth-century American rags-to-riches fable, but it also reflects the enthusiastic materialism and mobility associated with the late fifties. Instead of being about anger or even envy, it was really a tale of ambition.' (Murphy, 1992: 14)

It is, however, impossible for him to achieve social mobility through his industry and instead he decides to climb to the top through guile. Lampton became the forerunner to the anti-hero of the filmic angry young men who were to follow. But while he embraces the American Dream, the characters who typified the new wave were figures who couldn't adapt to the age of mass consumption and, although they rebel against the older generation, the films largely reject the attractions of consumerism.

REALISM

The film introduces another world to that shown in films of the previous age, concentrating as it does on the working-classes, beginning with a deep focus shot of a crowded factory floor. This is not the artificiality of the studio so apparent in *Peeping Tom* – this is 'real' life, shot in a real factory. The framing emphasises the uniformity of all the workers, stood as they are behind almost identical machines but then the camera then selects a single worker, whose thoughts we can hear above the din. The internal monologue tells us much about the character. Through his thoughts and feelings we have an insight into someone who seems the very embodiment of Hoggart's new youth. Based on Alan Sillitoe's novel it reflects Sillitoe's experience of working in a Nottingham bicycle factory:

'The filming in the factory, when it begins. Albert Finney is standing on the exact place where I stood on when I went into work at fourteen, so everything is so authentic that the film is like a kind of social document, apart from the story.' (Alan Sillitoe, *Hollywood UK* BBC4)

Arthur bemoans the monotony of his task at the lathe and every job he completes is merely a measure that brings him by increments closer to the weekend. As he works he looks around the factory floor and differentiates himself from his colleagues, with whom he seems to feel no common bond. Arthur's isolation is indicative of his individuality. When working on the film Albert Finney was conscious to communicate the sense of reality associated with the film movement:

'The reality of working at the lathe, I found that very exciting… when I was being photographed working at that lathe I could absolutely concentrate on what the character was supposed to do. There was no cheating involved.' (Finney, *Hollywood UK* BBC4)

His colleague, Jack he says 'wants to get on'; but this idea of self advancement in the workplace is anathema to Arthur who sees it as a waste of time. He sneers at Robbo, the foreman, having a 'load of worry and a fat gut' and he looks with pity at the older workers whose lives have been decimated by the war years. He talks of the way in which they have been ground down and makes it clear that he will not be used in the same way.

Arthur's character shows the rift that has taken place between the individual and authority since the immediate post-war years. He is, from the very start, placed in opposition to the character of Jack, whose attitude reflects the quiet obedience of the previous generation. The only worker with whom he associates his outlook is Fred, a young black man who 'knows how to spend his money'. This new perspective recognises the waste of young lives during the war and sets itself in opposition to those films which revelled in the celebration of victory that followed.

This opening sequence has already identified much of the difference between the Sixties and the Fifties. Arthur is of the new generation; he is an individual who puts himself first and feels no solidarity with others who work in the factory and share his experience. He sees work as futile and he prioritises fun ahead of any sense of duty, the downfall of the previous generation. The irony here, however, is that Arthur lacks any sense of fun. His attitude is one of resentment and bullish obstinacy, rather than carefree insouciance:

'Like the "angry young men" of the time, Arthur's anger is real but its focus remains unclear.' (Welsh in Barrow and White, 2008: 103)

Unlike many of his colleagues, Arthur doesn't accept his lot in life and shows no gratitude for what he has. He is aware that his purpose in the factory is to fulfil back breaking labour for those who own it and that he could work harder but he is also aware that if he does, his employers will not reward him. This knowledge, however, doesn't really help him, as he cannot change his situation. His awareness, in fact, has only made him more unhappy and discontent, which is his saving grace as a character. To convince himself that he isn't manipulated he refuses to buy into the core values, the 'propaganda' tying the rest of the workers down. Instead Arthur, like so many of the youth of the Sixties, devotes all his efforts to pursuing pleasure.

REBELLION

Saturday Night and Sunday Morning's depiction of an ordinary factory worker attracted large crowds upon its release, perhaps due in part to the sensational advertising but more likely it was because it went one step further than *Room at the Top* in establishing a raw anti-hero in the mould of American idols James Dean and Marlon Brando, with the same attitude and rebellious sex appeal. Britain's changing character was here made flesh in a very British hero whose roots lay in the American teenage rebel. He also served to highlight the class gulfs in Britain, his very appearance on the screen emasculating previous public school heroes of film. If Britain's previous generation of film heroes had embodied a traditionally British sense of fair play, here was a character that was highlighting the fact that these rules no longer applied and these sensibilities belonged to a different Britain, one rapidly becoming less relevant. Arthur's rebellion has at its root a growing awareness that it is this Britain that has kept his like in their place for long enough – and they will no longer be ignored.

The street scenes and those of the factory emphasise community but it is a community which is overbearing and claustrophobic. The thick smoke that blankets the town adds to the feeling of oppression as do the tight, uniform streets. Arthur's return home sees his journey juxtaposed with Jack's (Bryan Pringle) whose appearance on a heavy laden motorcycle and sidecar emphasise his lack of freedom. Arthur cycles past Mrs Bull, a local gossip who jealously guards the small row of terraced housing. Her resentment of Arthur is apparent; but while Jack's character is a faithful and obedient husband and worker, there is little to commend him to the audience.

Both of these characters are reflections of the community that Arthur finds infuriating and though one might expect to dislike Arthur for such a disrespectful attitude, the audience find themselves drawn to a character which refuses to become a victim and will not be consumed by notions of community which he sees as a means to make him conform. There is an insular and apathetic attitude that the communities breed that Arthur cannot tolerate and it is something that he sees even in his own father. He sneers at his dad as he watches the television, and tells of a man at work who has lost the sight of one of his eyes through watching too much television. Much is made of the media in new wave films. This new industry is responsible for the dissemination of the new 'barbarism' and, though glamorous, it is treated with disdain as it spreads its distractions over an increasingly soporific nation. It is associated with advertising, marketing and sales and has no integrity. Arthur's dad sits in front of the TV, a picture of apathy hypnotised by television, like one of *Peeping Tom*'s victims.

AFFLUENCE

Arthur readies himself for the evening ahead, his bedroom full of the latest fashions. He spends his money, like many of the new generation, on looking good, part of this generation enjoying new affluence. As he leaves his house he encounters Mrs Bull, still standing at the entrance to the alleyway and the gulf between the generations is shown as Arthur barges past her. As he does so she comments 'That Arthur Seaton's going to get a good bashing one of these days', indicating in the tradition of moralistic tales that Arthur will be punished for his lack of respect. This tale, however, does not conform to this tradition which we see later:

> 'It's a grown up film, where moral choices are complex and the issues are never entirely black and white.' (Robert Murphy, *Saturday Night and Sunday Morning* DVD, BFI)

In one of the early scenes Arthur is embroiled in a drinking contest at the local pub. This is the weekend he has been waiting for but despite one woman at the bar's assertion that he's 'having a good time', Arthur is spending the evening in an aggressive battle. Tellingly, he is pitted against a sailor. The use of a character in this context that in many post-war films would have been heroic shows how times have changed. With conscription abolished and the war over the sailor is no longer an automatic figure of respect or admiration, he is merely another anachronism to illustrate Arthur's plight. The victory in a drinking contest is a rather hollow one and Arthur has spent money that he has worked so hard for. Pointedly a rock and roll band in the background sing 'What do you want if you don't want money? What do you want if you don't want love?'

Arthur does not know what he wants and can only struggle to exert himself by being reactionary. Despite winning the drinking contest it does not achieve anything in itself and it is Arthur's infuriated inertia bred of dissatisfaction that many of the new wave characters demonstrate. For some, the new wave did not present rebellion but wallowed in the comfort of affluence:

> 'He is a well integrated person, a loudmouth, in a sense, who does nothing, not aware of being part of an oppressed class because he is too bloody comfortable as it is.' (Alan Sillitoe in Walker, 1974: 84)

As the evening draws to a close Arthur walks into another part of the bar, where the older generation are stood singing traditional songs. He spills drink over a woman who is disgusted by his behaviour, before falling headlong down a flight of stairs. Pride normally comes before a fall but at the bottom, Arthur smiles to himself. There is no shame for him and he lies on the floor laughing, revelling in his drunken state. This is as good as it gets, his thoughts numbed by drink and his urge to rebel satiated.

ADULTERY

Arthur cannot face up to his own problems and refuses to take responsibility for his actions. He persistently lies throughout the film and when he makes his way into Jack and Brenda's house (he is sleeping with Jack's wife) through the scullery window he shows little care for her reputation. 'You'll have all the neighbours talking you know,' she complains. 'You never think do you?' But what she means is that he never thinks of others, who form the community. He typically denies that he fell down the stairs, instead claiming that someone pushed him and that he won't return to the pub until the rail is fixed.

There is something of the child in Arthur, constantly pinning the blame to others and it is no surprise that he takes up with a married woman for whom he has no responsibility. He is so different to the upright heroes of the Fifties whose moral codes and values were so strict. Arthur would for many have been an example of moral decline. Arthur, however, refuses to adopt the morality of the middle-classes and he sees little point in telling the truth. To him there is little to be gained from honesty. The lies are part of a refusal to conform. And it is precisely the lack of responsibility that Brenda (Rachel Roberts) finds so attractive. Her misery is being married to a man with no passion and though she fears the repercussions, she is prepared to risk all for the pleasure that is missing from her life. At the pub she complains that Arthur's drinking is 'nothing to be proud of' but she clearly revels in Arthur's bad behaviour.

The biggest indication in the film that times are changing is the straightforward depiction of sex. While seeming tame by today's standards (the act of lovemaking is not shown), the forthright references to the sexual liaison between Arthur and Jack's wife, Brenda, is shown in a way that was considered shockingly frank at the time and the film was awarded an X certificate, a new certification which allowed new subject matter of a more adult nature:

> '…the frank presentation of Arthur's sexual attitudes, Brenda's adultery, and the unwanted pregnancy seemed adult and contemporary next to Hollywood films still labouring under a draconian Production Code.' (Welsh in Barrow and White, 2008: 99)

Brenda is keen for sex and wants to take advantage of her husband and son's visit to Skegness. She encourages Arthur not to stay downstairs too long and depicts a woman who is every bit as willing as her lover, a precursor to the independent women that will follow.

The next morning is more graphic as Arthur and Brenda are shown in bed together. Jack's picture is shown clearly, something at which Arthur smiles, as though he has achieved some sort of superiority. Brenda rolls over, exclaiming, 'That's nice', as Arthur strokes her. She openly refers to the previous night –'Hey, Arthur, what a time we had last night' – and they cuddle and kiss. Despite the restrictions of censorship, there is no avoidance of the issue of sex and despite criticisms of the new wave films that women were largely shown in stereotypical fashion, Brenda's attitude toward sex is bold. Robert Murphy notes that although women are not treated well in the new wave films, they:

> '…have a seriousness, an emotional weight, altogether lacking in the pathetically trivial
> roles women had to play in most 1950s films.' (Murphy, 1992: 33)

An additional consideration is the uncertain morality. Despite Jack's presence in the form of a photograph, there is no apparent guilt between Brenda and Arthur; rather, there is a genuine fondness and a feeling that both these characters are seeking happiness that eludes them in 'normal' life.

After a breakfast interrupted by Jack's return Arthur goes immediately to another pub where some friends are gossiping about the previous night at The Flying Fox. The woman is his aunt Ada, the other person his best friend, Bert and they take pleasure in a story about a man who paid for all the drinks the previous evening but showing little gratitude as he could afford a car, one of the consumer items becoming more widely available to the public. They emphasise the new: 'Can't beat a bit of fun can you Arthur?' his aunt asks, rhetorically.

THE GOOD OLD DAYS

Bert (Norman Rossington) tells another story of a man from the pit, who was remembering the 'good old days' but Bert was far from impressed. 'You tell me any more about the good old days and I'll split your head open,' he tells the man. The disparity between the older generational perspectives is highlighted. The idea that hardships of war brought out the best in the community does not make any sense to the younger generation who crave fun. This is the age of the individual and to them the community spirit is as relevant as the war. Arthur's auntie, Ada, played by comedienne, Hylda Baker, relates the struggle of raising the children in the wake of the war and how the country for some provided little opportunity with some opting to leave for Australia.

'Me and your mum had a struggle to bring you up,' she tells him. Arthur assures her that there will be no repeat. 'It won't happen again, I'll tell you that.' Arthur's view is reflective of his character. He believes that he is able to exert some influence over matters over which he has no control, in this case the economy, but this is not so.

In this scene Arthur meets Doreen (Shirley Anne Field) and persuades her to go on a date with him. Arthur's image as a carefree young lothario is enhanced as he flirts with Doreen who, unlike Brenda, does not dote on him but rather plays hard to get. Doreen gives as good as she gets but it is clear from her behaviour that she is not averse to his approaches. She tells her mother that she is talking to a 'bloke I know from the factory'

 and, despite initially refusing Arthur's offer of a cigarette, telling him she doesn't smoke, she then relents and accepts. 'Alright, I will have a fag.' She criticises Arthur for being a 'fast worker' and following a verbal jousting match agrees to go to the cinema with Arthur but emphasises her respectability (she will not sit on the back row).

MASCULINITY

Fishing on the canal, Arthur describes his philosophy of women – 'They all want a good time' – while accepting that 'this one looks different'. However, it is not Arthur's way to settle down as this would be an admission of defeat: 'I take a tip from the fishes. Never bite unless the bait's good. I won't get married until I'm good and ready.' Despite Bert's assertion that 'You've got to get married sometime haven't you?' Arthur angrily spits back 'Why don't you try it then'? and goes on to say that 'marriage costs too much', as it means he'll lose his wages for life. It is this outlook for which the British new wave is often criticised, representing young women as only interested in marriage, betraying a regressive male outlook. But although Doreen seems to fit into this category, largely through Brenda's representation, the film provides a:

> '…complex and empathetic look at the female experience of sexuality and marriage in the late 50's before the contraception pill and the abortion law started to have a real affect on women's lives.' (Welsh in Barrow and White, 2008: 102)

Therefore, although the new wave films can be criticised for their portraits of women, to be viewed within their context and can still be perceived as being adventurous in their examination of female attitudes.

Arthur's tirade does not stop there, however, and he begins an attack on society generally: 'I work for the factory, the income tax and the insurance already. They rob you left right and centre. After they've skint you dry you get called up to the army and get shot to death.' Arthur's attitude to women may well be sexist – he is clearly the product of a working class, male-dominated culture – but he is also (and this is what he finds far harder to articulate) the product of a culture that has used the working-classes for centuries to make money and make war. Arthur knows he is trapped and he recognises marriage as one of series of institutions that he's expected to conform to. If the middle-classes were puzzled about what the angry young men were angry about, it was because they were articulating a problem that had not been until this point visible. Society's reappraisal of class was forcing people to examine the hegemonic structure of society.

Bert's attitude is that of the majority. He echoes the thoughts of many working-class people, who accept the status quo and hope that luck will change his life. 'That's how things are, Arthur. There's no good going crackers over it. You've just got to keep working and hope that one day something good will crop up.' His acceptance is brought about not by having any faith in society but in recognising that there is no way out. To be dissatisfied is pointless. He does not want to recognise the inequality because he knows he cannot effect change.

Arthur still feels that he can control his own destiny but he knows, in his own words, that life is tough for those that don't weaken. His refusal to adapt doesn't mean that he exerts more control over his life; merely that life becomes more difficult. His view that his cunning will help him escape is contradicted as he inadvertently admits that he too will be caught, by the young and beautiful Doreen. Again, marriage is linked to other forms of society's constraints.

Arthur defends himself to Bert when they discuss his affair with Brenda. To his mind it is Jack's fault. Despite admitting that she shouldn't have chosen him, Arthur points out that Brenda has a choice and in refusing to accept the blame he insists that Jack has a part to play in his wife's adultery. Although this is not quite liberalism by today's standards (Arthur insisting that Jack can control his woman), Arthur does acknowledge Brenda's right as an individual to be more than just a housewife. It is perhaps in this way that Brenda is a forerunner of the less constrained female characters that follow in this decade.

COMMUNITY

As if to reinforce work's complete domination of the community, the next scene begins with the shot of the town in the shadow of the factory, the archetypal shot of the British new wave which speaks of the ill fated industrial communities whose lives were dominated by machinery of mass production. Arthur is inseparable from the town that has made him the person he is:

'Arthur is a son of the city, made for and by it, and these shots of the townscape emphasise this. Arthur, like the city, is to be at various moments observed and studied as part of, and contained by it. As the camera and the spectator scan the skyline, we are perhaps reminded that Arthur's is but one story in this compact working class community.' (Lay, 2002: 75)

The whistle calls the workers to their labour and there is no refusal. The overlapping sound from the exterior shot of the morning to the interior of the factory is that of industrial machinery. Arthur, of course, finds whatever distractions he can to alleviate the tedium and this time uses a dead rat to shock a female co-worker.

Arthur sits with Jack, whose character demonstrates his opposition to Arthur and in so doing lends understanding to much of Arthur's behaviour. Far from being a character with whom the audience sympathises, Jack is a cold and morose figure whose acceptance of his position as equal with his peers seems borne of complacency rather than any real solidarity. His claims that the tea that is good enough for others is good enough for him is the exact antipathy to Arthur's outlook. Whereas Arthur strives to separate himself from his peers, Jack is happy to conform. His assertion that married life is 'alright' is hardly enthusiastic and his deadpan manner reinforces the impression that he is lacking in emotion.

Arthur maintains that he looks after number one and when confronted by his foreman he deals with the accusations in typical fashion, denying everything. The phrase 'I'll believe you, thousands wouldn't', reinforces Jack's distrust of Arthur as he calls him a 'young rogue' and labels him a 'red'. This is far from accurate, however, as Arthur is someone who shuns community. Arthur claims that he did vote once but only to break laws, using his father's polling card, demonstrating his philosophy: 'That's what all these loony laws are for, to be broken by blokes like us.'

Later, Doreen and Arthur emerge from the cinema, and Doreen says, 'I knew the film would end like that,' a knowing reference to the fact that this film will not follow predictable conventions of cinema. It could also indicate Doreen's increasing influence over Arthur, as from this point in the story she begins to become a consideration in Arthur's life. Unlike Brenda, Doreen is a character who reinforces the view of the British new wave portrayal of women as misogynistic, with women either portrayed

as housewives or housewives in the making. Her conversations with Arthur are often demonstrative of her domestic intentions and she can be viewed as a somewhat manipulative character which succeeds in bringing Arthur into line where society fails. 'I'm not all that keen on boozing,' she tells him.

ABORTION

The revelation that Brenda is pregnant shows Arthur that his actions are not without consequence and at this point the audience could be forgiven for thinking that this will lead him to re-evaluate his life choices. However, this is no morality tale and Arthur, in typical fashion, tries to evade his responsibilities, first questioning whether the baby is his and then asking Brenda to have the child telling her, 'Another one won't make a difference.' Finally, Arthur decides to consult his Aunt Ada, who he thinks will know what to do.

The topic of abortion is raised and is one that is important in other new wave films such as *The L-Shaped Room* and *A Taste of Honey* as illegitimacy becomes more of an open subject. Arthur's hope is that Aunt Ada knows someone, or perhaps is someone, who can carry out the sort of backstreet abortion that was forced upon young girls who wished to protect their reputation. When she agrees to help he clearly thinks he has divested himself of the problem. Introduced to Brenda, Aunt Ada points out how women are the one's who have to bear the burden of illegitimacy. ('It ain't right, men get away with murder.')

That evening Arthur's conflict with his neighbour, Mrs Bull resurfaces as he encourages a man who has broken the funeral parlour's window to run away. When a policeman arrives on the scene Mr Bull tries to report him but he has fled. Arthur's perverse outlook on morality is shown when he condemns the man for being 'spineless' for not fleeing the scene. The next day Arthur exacts his own brand of childish revenge, shooting Mrs Bull with a pellet gun. In a comical scene Mrs Bull bursts into Arthur's house with her husband before returning with a policeman. Arthur denies shooting Mrs Bull but is reprimanded by the policeman and the reactions of the two parties exemplify the gulf in attitudes. Mrs Bull leaves with her husband proclaiming 'That put him in his place' while the younger generation celebrate by dancing because 'It's not every day you beat the coppers.'

The celebration fades into a shot of Brenda looking out over the town. 'I was just enjoying the lovely view,' she comments ironically as she views the industrial town.

Ada's supposed abortion has amounted to little more than 'old wives tricks' and Brenda now realises that Arthur is beginning to lose interest in her. Arthur has been seen at the cinema and despite his denouncing the 'bloody lies' she knows the truth: 'The trouble with you is you don't know the difference between right and wrong.' 'I don't want anyone to teach me either.' Arthur counters. Despite the chain of events caused by Arthur's actions he is unwilling to revise his behaviour. 'You'll learn one day,' Brenda says. 'We'll see,' he replies stubbornly.

Despite all that has happened and Arthur's refusal to change his ways he has a clear attachment for Brenda. Arthur recognises that she is trapped in the same way as he is and, though he feels no duty towards her, as they stand against the industrial background it is in the recognition of their shared circumstances that he agrees to get the 40 pounds necessary for her abortion. 'You're getting off lightly aren't you?' Brenda says, and though she is criticising Arthur, her statement has more than a touch of indulgence.

In contrast, the next scene shows that Doreen and Arthur are now planning for the future. Doreen is talking of marriage and, though they are still playing cat and mouse, their new roles are being established. Doreen chastises Arthur for his drinking but when he accuses her of taking too much interest in how he spends his money she denies that she has any. Arthur, however, tells Doreen that he likes her telling him off and in so doing acknowledges they have a future together. Doreen's criticism that Arthur doesn't take her anywhere lately leads Arthur to agree to take her to the funfair.

RETRIBUTION

The fairground is another typical new wave scene, developed from the Free Cinema shorts, showing the youth of the time at play. Through the use of lightweight camera it captures, in much the same way as Truffaut's *400 Blows*, the energy of the location with fast camera work and fast film stock that can capture the night time scene. It is such entertainments that indicate a spread of the type of mass leisure culture that *Peeping Tom* warned of, particularly those enjoyed by the young.

Arthur and Doreen's enjoyment is intercut with shots of a subdued Brenda trudging around the fairground with Jack and his brother who is accompanied by an army colleague. Brenda sees Arthur and he encourages her to meet him, where she reveals that she is keeping the baby. On becoming aware that Brenda is missing the men begin to search for her. Arthur and Brenda are chased through the fairground but Arthur escapes.

Later that evening Arthur leaves a pub, only to be found by the soldiers who beat him up on some waste ground. The scene is brutal and unaccompanied by music. The sound is natural and depicts violence in the most unglamorous way. Arthur takes his beating as though he wants it, as though it settles matters. His face is covered in blood and he collapses before the screen fades to black.

This climactic episode could be the prelude to a change in Arthur's character as a valuable moral lesson is learned; but here, in the new wave, there is no such resolution. The next scene shows the familiar view of the town and Arthur's terrace of houses as a statement of little having changed. The same signature track of the film is used, though now a little slower.

Arthur is in bed, and the voice-over communicates his thoughts: 'I'd had my bit of fun; it wasn't the first time I'd been on the losing side in a fight. I daresay it won't be the last. I'm a fighting pit prop who wants a pint of beer. That's me. If any knowing bastard says that's me, I'll tell them I'm a dynamite dealer waiting to blow the factory to kingdom come. I'm me and nobody else. Whatever people say I am that's what I'm not, cos they don't know a bloody thing about me. God knows what I am.'

Arthur's narration indicates confusion and anxiety at his position in a changing world and despite his obstinacy communicates a crisis of identity reflective of the changing place of the working-class;

> 'From the perspective of 1960, it seemed conceivable that the working class as it had been was an endangered species and *Saturday Night and Sunday Morning* reflects these feelings of uncertainty, confusion and social paranoia.' (Welsh in Barrow and White, 2008: 100)

As he looks out over the terrace the music takes on a more upbeat tone. There is optimism as normality is re-established and a feeling that life is back to normal. He looks out at Mrs Bull and his neighbourhood. Seeing Doreen approaching he smiles.

As she enters his bedroom she looks in his wardrobe. 'Are all these clothes your'n?' she asks, again alluding to how Arthur spends his money. Explaining his bruises, Arthur claims that he was knocked down by a horse and cart but when Doreen calls him a liar he confesses the truth and admits to the affair. Doreen questions Arthur's feelings toward her: 'You talk to me like I was a bit of muck. What do you take me for?' 'Trouble with me is that I keep bumping into things.' 'You'll have to look where you're going then,' Doreen replies, encouraging him to be more careful and to look to the future. Her growing influence over Arthur signals his gradual conformity and this is conformed as Arthur agrees to buy Doreen a ring.

The film fades to Doreen's house where the young couple make a show of Arthur's leaving for her mother's benefit before kissing passionately on the carpet, indicating the consummation of their relationship.

At the canal Bert hums the wedding march. Arthur admits that he's given Jack a lot to put up with and Bert defends him. Arthur's antipathy to marriage is revealed as motivated by a fear of losing out and turning into his parents. When Arthur perversely defends his need to enjoy himself and keep fighting, Bert asks him where all the fighting gets him:

> 'You ever seen where not fighting gets you. Like my mum and dad. They've got a television set and a packet of fags and they're dead from the neck up. I'm not saying it's their fault. It's so the gaffers can push them about like sheep. There's a lot more in life than what my mum and dad have got.'

Arthur and Bert's conversation highlights the pointlessness of his struggle. Despite not wishing to end up like his mother and father and recognising the need for change, he is not able to change his fate and is now committed to settling down. He catches a fish, a metaphor for his own capture.

The final scene takes place on a hillside. It's peaceful. Arthur and Doreen are living together at Doreen's mum's house. Arthur says he doesn't mind living in an old house but Doreen wants to live in a new one, with a bathroom. Arthur reminisces about blackberrying with Bert and claims there won't be a blade of grass remaining soon because of the new housing developments. He throws a stone at the sign advertising the new houses: 'And it won't be the last one I throw.' The modern housing is representative of a new era and, more significantly, the end of the old way. Arthur's pointless gesture shows his own inability to change with the times:

> '…the film ends with a dim perception of how a way of life has claimed him, as its claimed generations before him and will eventually tame him into social conformity….' (Walker, 1974: 84 –5)

SUMMARY

For some critics, the new wave films such as *Saturday Night and Sunday Morning* were not effective in communicating issues of class because they portrayed a romanticised or poeticised view of the working-classes that was actually a product of a middle-class perspective:

> '… by focusing on relationships the possibilities of the film changing the working-class and working-class culture are undermined because the social problems explored are framed in terms of personal, not economic or industrial, relations.' (Lay, 2002: 76)

But it was this very identification of working-class citizenry 'as people rather than members of a distinct class' (Lay, 2002: 75) that had been absent from British culture before the Sixties. There was now a need to acknowledge a group so marginalised on screen as to be almost invisible; and although the films do not actively explore working-class exploitation, it is questionable whether they need to make this explicit in order to make the point.

Films such as *Saturday Night and Sunday Morning* might be accused of romanticising the working-class experience, but they could also be seen to be undermining hegemonic ways of thinking about a social group and the place they inhabited, acknowledging the existence of other forms of beauty, other ways of seeing the world, a re-evaluation connected to wider issues or morality, taste and behaviour.

'The tension between the unpleasant reality and the beauty of images is also matched by the ambivalent effect of characters who are both attractive and morally disturbing' (Leach, 2004: 53)

The directionless anger exhibited by Arthur does not threaten political structures directly – as he himself admits, he as no political affiliation – but it does threaten the stability of his immediate social fabric. His lack of duty, obedience, respect and gratitude exposes a lack of faith in a society that gives him little in return. The frustrations that Arthur experiences are hegemonic and imposed by a culture in which there is innate and inherent inequality. Arthur has little or no opportunity to make a real difference to his own life. But what this and other new wave films do is redress the balance of a condescending culture that ignores or belittles the working-classes:

'Arthur Seaton, "terribly limited in his sensibilities" and "narrow in his ambitions" though he is, is still able to take advantage of full employment and a fat wage packet to assume a devil-may-care attitude to the world.' (Murphy, 1992: 30)

Saturday Night and Sunday Morning does not elevate its characters to heroic status but instead – more effectively, and in common with other new wave films – it raises the working-classes to a position where they become important enough to have their everyday tales recognised, their struggles acknowledged and their discontent heard. Arthur is not an admirable character but the film is far too subtle to trade in simplistic ideas of right and wrong. He is a character of uncertain morals, few scruples and a self-preservation that is borne out of a hard life. He doesn't aspire to the middle-class success of Joe Lampton, far from it. Here is the depiction of a rough working-class anti-hero, brooding and resentful at the life which he was given by society but doesn't seek to change it. Instead he entrenches himself in an attitude of brutal bravado which reflects his determination never to change and never to compromise for the sake of others. Arthur's rage, however, is impotent as he can neither recognise the source of his subjugation nor is he willing or able to confront it. His refusal to associate his plight with those in the same situation and his lack of solidarity with others in the community leave him isolated:

'I felt very strongly about the reality of it. I sympathised with Arthur's situation. I did sympathise with his feeling of being trapped in there or seeing himself at that machine for the next forty years of his life.' (Albert Finney, *Hollywood UK* BBC4)

Arthur's appeal was a warning to cosy middle-class society, which was awakened to the fact that the working-classes were no longer content with manual labour in the 1960s and that the pent up rage that Arthur felt was echoed across the nation. Though Arthur's childishness is often shown in spiteful games, his yearning for fun and a better life was being repressed and this youthful desire was about to change the nation.

CHAPTER 3: NEITHER HERE NOR THERE
— *BILLY LIAR* (B/W, SCHLESINGER, 1963)

MODERN BRITAIN

'The film is about a very specific moment when Britain changed from post-war Britain into modern Britain.' (Julie Christie, *Billy Liar* Criterion Collection DVD)

The radio announcer's voice which begins *Billy Liar* is typical of the Received Pronunciation that was representative of the middle-class media still emanating from London and communicating to the rest of the country in the early 1960s. The control of the media by the middle-classes ensured that theirs was the dominant voice but this was about to change.

Billy Liar signals a shift in the outlook of Sixties film and the end of the new wave. It was the only film of the movement not to be given an X certificate and had a much lighter-hearted approach than its forebears. The country was tiring of the tales of small town hardship and waking up to a new age of mass media which was beginning to appeal more to the young.

'Philip Larkin, the British poet, wrote that sexual intercourse began in 1963, between the end of the Chatterley ban and The Beatles first LP. That's where *Billy* was.' (Julie

Christie, *Billy Liar* Criterion Collection DVD)

As the camera tracks past rows of houses and flats, virtually indistinguishable from one another, the genteel voice of the radio announcer filters through the airwaves, penetrating the walls of homes across the nation and permeating the culture of the country. The sedate comfort transmitted through the airwaves offers contentment to those who are locked in anonymous lives by occasionally being given a dedication on the radio.

The country, however, is changing and though the first shot is of a suburban street, subsequent shots show rows of tower blocks before the culmination of the sequence shows the demolition of old Victorian terraces that used to be inhabited by the working-classes. As the radio presenter refers his dedication to 'Mrs Betty Bullock and her neighbours', she is revealed as having none.

RECONSTRUCTION

It is a profound shot that indicates both the end of something familiar and the beginning of something unknown and is symbolised throughout the film by a background of rebuilding. The empty space has yet to be filled but change has begun:

'It was not the first time I had used the idea of construction and reconstruction which was very much a thing after the war…and so it was a running thread of atmosphere.' (John Schlesinger, *Billy Liar* Criterion Collection DVD)

Billy Liar in one regard is timeless as it charmingly portrays the indolence and aimlessness of youth, the constant prevarication of relying on the promise of tomorrow. However, in another respect, the film is very much an indicator of the age. It is on the cusp between the end of the new wave and the beginning of 'swinging Britain' and this is reflected in the film's approach to northern life, which is no longer removed from the rest of the country but aware of the allure of London:

'…in 1963 cinema audiences were clearly beginning to lose interest in working-class realism…*Billy Liar*… took care to market itself very differently, with the emphasis on fantasy and the zany optimism which signaled the arrival of the swinging Sixties.' (Richard Lester, *Hollywood UK* BBC4)

The film combines new wave sensibilities and themes with comedy and fantasy, indicating the direction of film to come, showing a central character in the traditions of the angry young man whose inability to escape his surroundings shows a marked difference both in presentational style and a softening in attitude to what had gone immediately before. In

Billy Liar, significantly, the rebel is a woman.

And Billy is not working-class in the traditional sense. He has received the benefits of a grammar school education and he is far more aware of the opportunities that are available in a Britain beginning to change. He does work in a job that he resents but it is not the manual labour of Arthur Seaton. Billy's work is white collar and although he is unable to grasp the nettle, the opportunities are there for those brave enough to take a risk:

> 'There was much that was to do with my life in the north of England, in Hull, the longing to go to London, to make something of myself, so I could identify with Billy, utterly, totally. Some of the play was so close to home that I could barely get the words out.' (Tom Courtenay, *Billy Liar* Criterion Collection DVD)

Courtenay, who took over from Albert Finney in the stage version of *Billy Liar*, was quick to empathise with Billy's situation, and was the natural choice for the film but he also embodied a shift away from the manual labourer who Finney personified as a figure of the times. Billy's rebellion was articulated in the mind and he was a figure of self-expression, someone whose imagination would make him characteristic of a new outlook.

Billy Liar is a film which does not possess the shock value of the first new wave films but shows the nature of a changing Britain much better than perhaps any other of the movement. The dichotomy of the central character embodies many of the conflicts that were happening at the time and Billy's quandary is whether to live the life of his parents or embrace the new age that is beginning to impact on young people all around Britain:

> 'This film is not a big story…it is about a description of time, a class, a place…it's all about the choice a young person has.' (Julie Christie, *Billy Liar* Criterion Collection DVD)

Once the credits end, we are introduced to Billy's home life. We see his father, Geoffrey, (Wilfred Pickles) emerging from a Radio Rentals van before going inside. Ironically his father is distributing the very devices by which his son's generation is now having their imaginations sparked. No longer is the television being portrayed as a sedative; instead it becomes the inspiration for a generation as mass culture spreads. Inside his wife, Alice, (Mona Washbourne) waits for her record to be played on the radio like the many other housewives seen in the opening sequence. This is one family like many others whose entertainment is filtered out from London which is a long way away.

The dull domesticity is soon established as Billy's grandmother (Ethel Griffies) bemoans the state of the curtains. She and his father immediately discuss Billy, referring sarcastically to him as 'his lordship' and inquiring where he is before discussing ways to get him out of bed. A 'damp dishcloth' and 'a bloody good hiding' are their joint suggestions, reinforcing the old fashioned nature of the home whose values are hard work and a harsh lesson for those who don't.

OPTIMISM

Similar to *Saturday Night and Sunday Morning* we hear the lead character's thoughts but here they are daydream rather than brooding resentment, optimism rather than pessimism. The humour is frivolous and there is a sense of a new outlook of possibility. 'It was a big day for us. Democracy was back in our beloved land of Ambrosia.' The voice-over is used throughout the film to relate Billy's inner emotions which are portrayed in a series of fantasies. These are a reflection of his need to escape the world in which he lives and give access to his desires and frustrations. Unlike Arthur Seaton, however, whose thoughts reveal his inner anger Billy's reveal the suppression of reality or rather a manipulation of reality into something that is more to his taste.

The war-time imagery of this first dream shows the bombed out ruins of terraces. Billy is atop a tank and receiving the accolades of the grateful people who are throwing garlands at the heroic soldier. The overlapping sound of his parents show the narrative connection between Billy's fantasy and his reality – that he wishes to escape as does the dream itself, creating a strange combination of first and second hand experience. The northern streets are daubed with the celebratory 'Viva Fisher', an amalgamation of revolutionary rebellion and Billy's surroundings which give vent to his rebellious attitude.

Billy's fantasies are thus a reflection of both the character's inner turmoil and society's social revolution. His awareness of upheaval in the wider world is a catalyst for personal change, but throughout the film he is held back by the sort of loyalties, ties and commitments which were common to most living in this time. Billy has had his eyes opened to the potential of the new age through his access to education but at the same time he is expected to meet the standards which his family abides by but which are firmly entrenched in the past:

'It's just to do with conforming to your parents' lives.' (Julie Christie, *Billy Liar* Criterion Collection DVD)

He then begins to relate the bizarre tale of the Republic's left armed salute which was originated as a result of injuries received in the 'Battle of Wakefield'. This variety of characters that Billy invents shows that he has the capacity to take on whichever role he wishes in his dreams and to control every part of the world he inhabits – tellingly a republic a metaphor for his own independence – while the crazy stories he invents are indicative of the growth in surreal comedy that was to be a feature of Sixties cinema.

Billy's mother calls out that his 'boiled egg is stone cold'. The return to the day-to-day drudgery of his home life is disconcerting, emphasised by the camera which quickly tracks out from a metal coal scoop, a symbol of a fading age, which his mother is hitting as it impacts on his consciousness. 'Alright, I'm coming,' he calls, deciding that, 'Today's a day for big decisions.' But we see early on how Billy's character prevaricates and lacks concentration, resolving to write his novel and get up in the morning but being distracted by a nail that needs cutting.

Billy enters the breakfast room reading the paper in the manner of a stereotypical gentleman of leisure, sporting a coin substituting as a monocle in one eye. 'Cabinet changes are imminent I see,' he says mimicking an upper-middle-class attitude. 'You'll be bloody imminent if you don't start getting up in the morning,' his father replies, absurdly and, obviously habitually. Continuing in character, Billy greets his mother as 'mater' while his grandmother criticises her for letting him 'do as he likes'.

The exchanges between Billy and his family show the underlying tensions between the younger generation and their parents. Billy's adoption of an upper-middle-class attitude shows his desire to move in society but it is met with his father's platitudes that are aimed at keeping him in his place. The privileges of a better education are double edged as they have given Billy a better understanding of society's disparities but he lives in an environment in which his family is accepting of their place and have different values:

> 'Of course I think Billy was an artist. I think he did have talent it's only that he was such a frightened person ....It had to all retreat into his dreams. But he was in a very belligerent atmosphere. That father would be seen as almost abusive nowadays.' (Julie Christie, *Billy Liar* Criterion Collection DVD)

His father expects complete obedience from his son and he is disappointed at Billy, calling him 'hopeless' and deriding him as 'like a lass'. He does not recognise that Billy is part of a generation with a new outlook on life and that his indolence is a result of not knowing how to respond to the changes in society. Geoffrey's derision of Billy as being like a girl signifies a shift in gender roles, which is enhanced later in the film, as well as later in the decade. To his father, femininity is associated with weakness but the age of The Beatles, with their long hair and non-macho masculinity, is close at hand.

FANTASY

Billy opts to avoid confrontation, instead sublimating his desires below humorous characterisation; but even in such light-hearted whimsy there is an undercurrent of tension. In Billy's mimicking of the leisured classes there is an awareness that, had his birth been different, so would his lifestyle. While characters such as Arthur and Colin have limited expectations, Billy's awareness of class differences provokes ambition.

Billy's fantasies draw on a variety of sources throughout the film. His characterisations come from both British and American film, TV and news, demonstrating the influence of popular culture on the way he understands the world. Hoggart's 'shiny barbarism' is certainly alluring to Billy.

His mother points out that he was spotted the previous evening with a girl other than his fiancée, Barbara (Helen Fraser). Billy's behaviour indicates a shift in moral values as he is having relations with more than one girl. Tied as he is by his parent's values he denies it but shows irritation at the way in which his business is common knowledge. The age of close-knit community is not quite over and Billy tells his mother that whoever saw them should mind their own business, but his mother points out that it is their business and not to be so cheeky. Billy wants to be independent and free but to his parents he is still not of an age where he is ready to make his own decisions.

Billy demonstrates that he has heard all of his father's critical comments before by numbering them as he says them. The family is unable to communicate with each other; each familiar criticism is just a ritual that has ceased to have, if it ever had, any impact.

When Billy says that perhaps he will leave home, his father and grandmother are surprised in a manner that indicates he rarely answers such regular criticisms and has to repress his desires. However, by the time he tells them that he has been offered a job in London, the family are incredulous. 'What bloody job?' his father asks.

Billy tells them that he has been offered a job script writing with a famous comedian, Danny Boon, in London. His dream of becoming a scriptwriter and moving to London show the impact that the new media industries are having on the age but Billy's location and upbringing are a limit to his opportunities. To his mother and father London and the media are another world and when Billy tries to explain it is as though he is speaking another language – which to an extent is true, as Billy's hopes to move and earn a living from his imagination are completely beyond their frame of reference.

The language of the media, however, is one in which Billy is fluent: 'Look, do you wanna know or don't ya?' he asks in the manner of an Italian-American gangster. Billy is a product of the modern age and the new media, aware that the changing world is affording new opportunities to some and if he can free himself, he will be able to take advantage of these. In these scenes Billy is still treated like a child and his father even criticises his mother for not ensuring that he gets washed and dressed before coming downstairs in the morning.

His mother advises him to change his ways: 'You'll have to stop all this making things up Billy. There's no sense in it at your age. We never know where we are with you. I mean you're too old for things like that now. I don't know what we're going to do with you.' The paradox of his mother considering him too old for his behaviour and yet still taking responsibility for his actions shows one reason why Billy behaves as he does. It also informs the viewer of the difference between a generation grounded in practical post-war responsibilities and reality against one of imagination and freedom, one constrained, the next shedding these limitations.

As Billy shaves, his mother is in the background, out of focus; but as she draws closer, it is he that becomes out of focus as he begins to daydream. The screen wipes away to a fantasy that begins with his mother who has been transformed into an aristocratic figure, draped in fur and jewellery. She smokes grandly from a cigarette holder. In the background a piano is playing. 'Oh my God,' she says, 'how dreary, Billy's pissed again.' She laughs carelessly as it cuts back to him smiling in the mirror. This film- inspired fantasy shows the sort of representation of Britain that was common in many films prior to the

Sixties and to be a humorous reference in a new wave film nicely illustrates the widening differences in the ages.

Returning to the dream Billy's father is congratulating him on his dissolute behaviour. 'So glad you're going to London, you old loafer,' he says, dressed in tails and a waistcoat and brandishing a brandy glass. 'Simone and I were thinking about kicking you out of the old nest any day now. Better come into the library, so we can talk about the money end.' In Billy's world it is merely circumstances of class that are preventing his taking the opportunities available. It would be so easy if he were privileged.

Once again we cut back to Billy with the sound of his fantasy continuing but as the camera swings from a profile view of Billy smiling again to an over the shoulder shot, his father interrupts: 'And keep your hands off my bloody razor in future. You can't call a thing your own in this house can you?' There is a sense of claustrophobia in *Billy Liar* which is reinforced in many of the shots, as the close physical proximity of these characters enhances Billy's feelings of being trapped.

As Billy exits the kitchen his mother asks him when he is going to unlock his wardrobe. Billy argues that he has his private things in there and that it's his wardrobe, which his father disputes as he paid for it. While his mother asks for him to keep it unlocked, his father threatens to break it open. Billy's lack of control over his personal possessions shows his lack of autonomy, he is robbed of any independence by his parents who deny him the personal freedoms which would help him develop independence:

'...because youth weren't meant to have money. They weren't autonomous.' (Julie Christie, *Billy Liar* Criterion Collection DVD)

We see why he is reluctant open the wardrobe in the next scene when Billy opens it and a stack of calendars fall on the floor. He carries a pile of them to the bed. They advertise a funeral directors 'Shadrack and Duxbury'. Looking up toward his bedroom light fitting, the music builds and the lamp is pulled down by a detective figure, flanked by police, who shines the light toward camera. 'What did you do laddie, spend the postage money? Was that about the size of it? You were given those calendars to post last Christmas.'

The voice continues as now Billy, looking straight at the camera, is a convict in a prison cell. He stares smugly and stands resolutely in a dark shadowed cell as another voice intones 'William Terence Fisher, I have a warrant for your arrest on the charge that you did knowingly and willfully misappropriate two hundred and seventy calendars.' Now, however, the shot shows Billy agonised and tormented, looking out of the window before walking away to the other side of his cell in daylight, throwing himself against the wall.

The way in which the fantasy sequences in *Billy Liar* are integrated is a distinct break with the realism that characterised the British new wave and yet it achieves the same aim of expressing the internal desires of the character. Billy's thoughts, however, show that his world is dominated by entertainment and the mass culture which is beginning to take hold of the nation is providing a different reality for young people than that of Arthur Seaton; yet it is just as palpable, which is reflected in the directorial presentation.

Director Schlesinger shot in Cinemascope, allowing him a wider screen, which presented problems in framing but allowed him to include fantasies like speech bubbles appearing above Billy's head. By using such techniques he eschewed the stricter realism of his predecessors and indicated the future of British film in the period:

'I felt that cutting from reality to fantasy, immediately without any apology or explanation was the way to do it, it's just what jumped into his mind.' (John Schlesinger, *Billy Liar* Criterion Collection DVD)

It is in its developed use of fantasy sequences that the film heralds the revolution to come. The film shows a real rupture between the drab reality that Billy inhabits and the way in which for him and thousands like him, there is an escape provided by the breakdown of the post-war consensus. The spread of pop culture is eroding the grey inevitability of adult responsibility and demonstrating that fun is a real alternative, even a career.

This second dream, based on a crime drama, reinforces Billy's feelings of being trapped as well as introducing the sub-plot of the missing calendars. His interrogation is similar to that which he faces from his parents on a regular basis as he has to justify his actions, while the confinement of his cell merely reflects his incarceration in the house. As he takes the role of a prisoner, he is impersonating another prominent culture in Sixties drama, that of a glamorous outsider whose value is misunderstood by society, something Billy feels keenly.

While the first stage of this fantasy is reflective of how trapped Billy feels and manifests itself in his being a convict, it becomes a success story with Billy, once again becoming a heroic figure. It also demonstrates Billy's ambition in his becoming a success against all odds, discovered and applauded by society despite being disadvantaged, and even having a reforming affect on society itself. While melodramatic and humorous, the dream points to Sixties reforms and the dreams of a meritocratic society in which anyone can rise to the top regardless of background.

The fanfare, however, is interrupted by Billy's mother knocking violently on his bedroom door and calling for him. As he conceals the calendars under his sweater and tidies himself, he cannot resist striking a Napoleonic pose. Coming downstairs he tentatively comments to his mother, 'I might as well give in my notice today, if I'm going to go to London.' Feigning lack of interest, she answers that he needs to make up his mind what he wants to do. 'Work for Danny Boon.' he says decisively. His mother looks up, from her dusting, concerned at the strength of Billy's resolution.

'How do you know, Billy? You've never done that sort of thing before. You can't switch and change and swap about just when you feel like it. You've got your living to earn now.'

Billy's conversation with his mother reveals her fears for him but is representative of the conservative approach associated with the previous age. For his mother security and stability are core values reflected in family life, while for Billy the family is something claustrophobic and cloying which prevents him achieving his goals. Both his mother and father try to encourage him to follow a safe route as if there is nothing to be gained by trying to break away from their existing way of life.

Billy leaves his house and greets a neighbour before making his way down the hill. This depiction of suburban Britain shows the ties Billy is keen to escape. This safe and familiar life where people know each others' business is breeding sterility and Billy must escape it if he is to achieve his goals; however, if he does he knows he will lose this security, and perhaps disappoint his parents.

He marches as though in an army but is made to leap aside as a bicycle rings its bell, now back in the real world where he is ineffectual and his dreams of heroism are irrelevant. Later, on the main street he plays a childish game, closing his eyes and trying to make his way to the end of the street, promising himself that if he does, 'Everything will be alright.' There is a sadness which underlies Billy's comic presentation. Billy is a boyish character whose endless dreaming makes him loveable but the dreams are fostered by a frustration at being trapped and the saddest aspect is that Billy is trapped by those that he holds most dear:

'The thing that interests me about Billy is the way it was seen at that particular time. I know that now he would be seen as a victim but I don't think that then, with that particular outlook, he was seen as a victim. That's what interests me about this particular portrayal... you couldn't be in a more hopeless home.' (Julie Christie, *Billy Liar* Criterion Collection DVD)

Billy arrives late for work at the undertakers. 'Must be home time, Fisher's here,' his colleague Eric Stamp (George Innes) comments. Billy then engages in a comic routine with another workmate, his friend Arthur (Rodney Bewes) while Stamp sarcastically laughs, unimpressed. Developing the story of the calendars, Billy is warned that Shadrack (Leonard Rossiter) has been going through the books and is in a bad mood but Billy tells them he is handing in his notice today.

AMBITION

Eric finds a letter from Billy's mother to the radio presenter of 'Housewives Choice', Godfrey Winn, which Billy has failed to post. While Billy makes a phone call to the Midland hotel where Danny Boon is staying, Stamp laughs, reading out the letter, in which his mother gives him little chance of success in his ambition of writing songs as he has 'not had the training. We are just ordinary folk.' Billy's mother has the perception of herself as ordinary while those who are in the public eye are somehow different and to achieve this status one has to be formally trained. The new age will shatter these preconceptions and Billy reflects this different outlook, 'Well I'm not ordinary folk even if she is.'

Having flushed the calendars down the lavatory, Billy and Arthur leave the undertakers, greeting Shadrack's partner, Councilor Duxbury (Finlay Currie) but greeting him as Mister Duxbury. The music that accompanies the councilor's appearance is dour and, while Shadrack is to some extent representative of new times, certainly in his use of new technology, the councilor is from a bygone age. He corrects them, 'It's Councillor Duxbury, Fisher, that's my title, Councillor Duxbury. You wouldn't call Lord Harwood mister would you? Councillor Duxbury. Think on.' The youths mimic him and put on thick northern accents. The figure of the self-important councilor is a northern stereotype, his language and demeanour embedded in the values of the past, of an unquestioning respect for status, title and position in society which are all being threatened.

Billy runs into Barbara, his fiancée, who greets him enthusiastically, but he lies to try and get away from her, claiming that he has an important appointment. They greet each other as 'Darling' and 'Pet' and kiss each other on the cheek. Tellingly Billy puts on a different voice as though playing a role. Despite agreeing to get engaged to Barbara, he only seems to have done so to try and conform to convention and his reluctance to spend time with her reflects his wish to be free.

Puzzilingly Billy checks that Barbara's engagement ring doesn't need altering before hurrying away, but we quickly find out why he was enquiring about the ring as, in the café, another girl, Rita (Gwendolyn Watts) asks, 'Well, where's that ring?' Billy claims to have left it in the jewellers but Rita is angry, fed up with Billy's excuses. As she moves away, Arthur expresses his amazement. ('I can't keep up with your sex life.') The café is a reflection of an increasingly Americanised Britain and is the closest Billy gets in this parochial setting to the sort of lifestyle he craves. He runs away from Rita who is clearly not as easily dissuaded as Barbara but not before she becomes another of his machine gunned victims.

The contrast in the female characters once again shows the shortcomings in the representation of many of the women in the new wave. There is little exploration of their characters which amount to very simplified versions of womanhood:

> 'I can't say this film is great on women. At this point it's still a man's world. You've got the bitch, the virgin and the real woman, who's a fantasy. But I think that's fairly representative of the time. Of course, in his next film, *Darling* John (Schlesinger) went

on to deal with women's role in this changing world.' (Julie Christie, *Billy Liar* Criterion Collection DVD)

NEW WOMAN

And yet in the same way the film uses fantasy techniques innovatively, it also introduces a new sort of woman and the model for a generation. The introduction of what Julie Christie describes as 'the real woman' takes place as Arthur recognises a girl who has hitched a lift with a coal lorry. Reinforcing his early impression of her free-spirited nature, he recalls her having asked Billy to go with her to France. Billy's face lights up as he realises that it's his friend, Liz. This character, played by Christie, seems to capture an attitude which had not been evident in British film before. When Arthur asks what she does, Billy's answer spells out Liz's approach to life:

'Oh all sorts, waitress, typist, she worked at Butlins last year. She works until she gets fed up and then she goes somewhere else. She's been all over.' While Billy describes her we see Liz singing to herself in the van before music starts up.

Billy's comments show his admiration for Liz, whose carefree attitude he aspires to. Her ability to go wherever she likes and do whatever she wants shows her sense of adventure and becomes a prototype of the women who became main characters in the swinging London films. While Billy is confined and limited, Liz is free. It is noticeable that she has taken a job in Butlins, a holiday resort, reflecting the growth in post-rationing leisure activity, but it also associates her with fun and social movement:

'During the 1960s the commodification of travel opened up unprecedented opportunities for young single women to journey on their own. Promises of unprecedented freedom positioned travel as central to the period's single girl mythology.' (Luckett, 2000: 234)

The representation of Liz is truly groundbreaking and it shifts the attention away from Billy's plight. Suddenly, his fantasy has become a reality and she is the embodiment of the liberation which plays such a part in his dreams. Off screen, Julie Christie was to become the template for a whole generation of young women:

'That's the way a lot of young women were…it was just a question that we were allowed to be as we were on film…there wasn't anything remotely smart about anything that I had on or how I was made up or anything and that was the change. That how we were was how we were allowed to be presented.' (Julie Christie, *Hollywood UK* BBC4)

Liz swings her handbag in carefree fashion while Sixties style pop music plays. The music that accompanies her is absolutely crucial to her identity in the film, immediately lightening the tone and bringing with it a modernity that cuts a swathe through the streets of this northern town. There is a contrast between the older buildings and the new tower blocks being built and Liz is part of this change, her fresh young attitude symbolic of the age. In just this one sequence, she has captured the zeitgeist, the mood of the time, for the first time:

'The swinging bag entrance was a very good entrance for her into this movie and into movies in general…Julie has a kind of fresh, spontaneous quality which was right for *Billy Liar* because she had a free and easy style and that's what caught the audience, I'm sure.' (John Schlesinger, *Billy Liar* Criterion Collection DVD)

The characters of Mark and Helen in *Peeping Tom* had previously displayed a naïve and childlike quality and are early prototypes of a 1960s character type. The model, Twiggy's girlish appearance and poses would often try to capture her innocent appeal and as we shall see later, The Beatles are portrayed in a similar way. Such youthful behaviour is manifested in a sense of freedom and a rejection of responsibility. This is in contrast to Billy who has the role of child forced upon him by his parents. His father derides him for his lack of responsibility but Liz is free of this and captures a new 'joie de vivre':

'It didn't feel, oh look I'm being a new kind of girl or anything like that. I was just grateful that I didn't have to go through this ridiculous charade.' (Julie Christie, *Hollywood UK* BBC4)

Approaching another shop window Liz is recognised by the owner. In the window are a range of electrical products on special offer and a Top Ten of the music charts. The availability of pop music and such consumer items again shows a changing world but, even more, it is Liz's attitude as she talks to the man in the shop window that demonstrates this. She tells him she's been to Doncaster and when he asks the reason she just shrugs her shoulders, once more indicating her carefree mobility and they arrange to meet up later, though the nature of their relationship is not entirely clear:

'Now, she could be quite loose. I mean, she did what she wanted to do but… it was presented as strength. It was a wonderful part, actually, because on the whole women got quite a raw deal in the Sixties and Liz was quite unique.' (Julie Christie, *Hollywood UK* BBC4)

Liz's entrance signifies change and it is this change which the film captures so well:

'A sense of the flux and change going on in Britain, as well as its cinema, is present in *Billy Liar*. The Times's critic remarked, "Mr Schlesinger gives us perhaps the sharpest and most persuasive picture yet of that northern town in the throes of reconstruction."' (Walker, 1974: 167)

And Schlesinger, perhaps as an American, is acutely aware of the significance of the reconstruction and how it will affect Britain in introducing mass culture. One sign of this is the appearance of a supermarket, something repeated in *The Ipcress File* (1965).

CONSUMERISM

Danny Boon, the comedian for whom Billy wants to write, is introduced by a poster in the supermarket window. A crowd is clamouring to meet this celebrity and we see Liz through the glass. Thus the connection between a new celebrity culture and a new consumer culture is seen with both causing similar effects on the public. This is Hoggart's new mass culture coming true as the allure of 'shiny barbarism' is apparent. Boon is cutting the tape in an official opening ceremony for City Food Ltd. The manager takes great pride in welcoming 'Danny' by name and the crowd cheers at this personal address:

> 'The film is full of evidence of all those changing things. The supermarket which was ordinary was fantastic like opening a cathedral. The beginning of that kind of consumerism, all the working-class ladies shouting and screaming because they were so excited by this idea there was going to be this emporium of goods where they could consume.' (Julie Christie, *Billy Liar* Criterion Collection DVD)

The shot of the crowd reveals that it is mostly made up of older housewives who are all delighted at Boon's presence as he introduces himself with a clearly familiar catchphrase, 'It's all happening!' His showmanship is apparent and marks him out as someone who represents the older generation of music hall light entertainment that will soon give way to the pop music of the young. This experienced showman asks for a pretty girl from the crowd for a picture and selects Liz.

Here are more indications of changing times and yet there is a feeling that progress is limited certainly in this part of the world. The older women queue outside the supermarket, waiting to catch a glimpse of this clearly odious and superficial television star who is just like the other commodities they are purchasing, a package with an image. These women, unlike Liz, are associated with a growing commercialism, consuming the products of the entertainment industry. Their excitement demonstrates the distance they are from the manufacture of the media and, just like Billy's mum, they feel there is a gulf between someone like Danny Boon and themselves.

Meanwhile Arthur is watching as Mr Duxbury appears to be falling asleep in his office. Billy is busy typing his letter of resignation while Arthur tells him that he has managed to get him some 'passion pills' and promises that with 'two tickets to The Regal and a bag of chips', Billy will be 'well away'. The desperate excitement at the prospect of sex suggests that the permissiveness, for which the 1960s would become famous, certainly hasn't reached Billy's town, despite his best efforts to introduce it.

Billy enters Shadracks' office and, placing his resignation on the desk, speaks to his employer's empty chair, explaining in a formal voice his reasons for leaving, turning down the fictitious offer of a partnership in the business. He starts to talk of London, explaining how it is a big place and how he could lose himself in London. He repeats the words 'lose himself' into a nearby vase before playing with his own voice and gravitating into Churchill's famous wartime speech. He then picks up the CB radio and imitates a famous TV show, 'Emanuel Shadrack, this is your life.' This he repeats until he notices Shadrack at the door and pretends to be suffering a coughing fit.

Once again Billy's behaviour is a by-product of the media that he finds so seductive. Although he would like to achieve fame through this writing, it is the fame rather than the work in which he is interested. His actions in Shadrack's office show him mimicking media sound bites until they lose all meaning and demonstrate his susceptibility to the entertainments of the new age.

Shadrack, meanwhile is greeting some recently bereaved customers. He takes them to an ante-chamber, where music is being blasted into the room by a tape player that Shadrack is controlling from his office, demonstrating once again that new technology isn't always life enhancing. He returns to tell Billy that he will not accept his resignation until the matter of the missing monies is sorted out.

LIVING

Billy is sitting with Barbara in some old fashioned tea rooms, where she is discussing her plans for home furnishings. The sedate location reinforces Billy's relationship with Barbara, showing the difference between her outlook and his. Billy, agitated, looks keenly at her ring and asks to take it to the jewellers to have it altered and though she doesn't want to, he insists to the point of force, before apologising for his behaviour. 'I'm really not myself today.' Billy's identity, of course, is at the root of the film and exactly who he is when he is being himself, is not clear.

'It's a good job I've got these to keep me going.' He takes out some tablets and tells Barbara that the 'passion pills' Arthur has given him are energy tablets. He gives them to her, placing them in her tea before suggesting that they'll go for a walk somewhere quiet.

Taking her to the graveyard, Barbara is more concerned with the epitaphs to the dead than she is in sex. Quizzing her on how she feels, she replies that she is content but he tries to guide the conversation toward the subject of sex and attempts to passionately kiss her but she turns away, more interested in talking about their dream cottage in Devon. Billy tells the obviously much repeated story of their cottage, while he thinks of

Barbara dressed in seductive lingerie and kissing him passionately. Barbara, interrupting his fantasies, asks him if he is feeling alright as his hand has wandered to her knee.

It is no coincidence that this scene is set in a graveyard. Both Billy's workplace and where he takes Barbara are concerned with loss of life. He is trapped in his job and trapped in this relationship and Barbara's willingness to look forward to retirement and death makes Billy, who wishes to live now, react with a passion.

Returning home he is reprimanded again by his parents who criticise his manners. 'What are manners?' he asks, once again mimicking an upper-class voice. 'Talk sense,' his father answers. 'If that's what they learned you when you went to grammar school, I'm glad I'm bloody ignorant.' 'Ah, confessions,' says Billy before being told off for bring cheeky.

Behind the comic dialogue there is more social criticism as Billy, who has been able to access a grammar school education is using it to question the assumptions of his parents, not to mention the social order, its hierarchy and taken-for-granted ideas. The opportunities offered by such schooling are inevitably to lead those from other classes to criticise and alter the social structure.

Billy opens the door to Rita who is angered by not having found any record of the ring at the jewellers. He tries to convince her that she saw the wrong person but she is dismayed by his treatment of her and though he makes excuses, she does not believe them. When Billy tries to claim his father is his 'Uncle Ernest', Rita becomes angry again and tells him that she wants the ring tonight and commands him to take her dancing to the Roxy that night.

When his father quizzes him about Rita Billy claims that she's just a friend on her way to visit *her* Uncle Ernest on the new estate in Cragside. His grandmother comments about the new houses and about having upstairs and downstairs lavatories, while his father talks to him about marriage. He cannot understand his indecision over engagement or why he is seeing so many girls but when Billy tells him that he can't decide what to do he shares with him a rare moment of communication about how he and Billy's mother had little money when they first married.

The difference in outlook between Billy and his father is, of course, shown throughout the film but it is in this moment that we see it is the result of changing attitudes in terms of relationships which is causing the gulf between the two. Billy's relationships reflect that there is more freedom for the younger generation and that expectations such as choice of who to marry are now considerations. His father has not had the same opportunities.

However as they talk, Billy's grandmother is also still talking, this time joining in to comment on his parents' marriage. As Billy tries to explain the complication of the possibility of moving to London, she continues and the camera focuses on her to show how she is now dominating the conversation. Billy can't make his point and loses his temper, telling her, 'For God's sake, belt up!'

His father grabs him and pushes him into the kitchen angered by Billy's lack of respect. His mother tries to defend him but his father continues to criticise him for his 'phantom friends and blue suede shoes. If he wants to go to London, he can bloody well go', he shouts. His mother, however, states that he's not leaving and they begin rowing. Billy leaves the room to find his grandmother suffering a seizure. While his mother and father tend to her he resolves to rid himself of the calendars.

MODERNISATION

A shot of more demolition and more rebuilding work is seen. A crane is constructing a tall tower block and the sound of drilling is heard as Billy walks through the town. He begins to march proudly. As he walks past a rugby ground, we hear the sound of the crowd; Billy imagines himself as a leader, talking to the crowd: 'I offer you nothing but liberty, fraternity and equality.' Billy's voice is heard over the ground's tannoy as he continues his speech and now he has become leader of the Republic of Ambrosia, dressed in uniform with Liz his wife by his side. He makes a speech to the enthusiastic crowd, 'We will rebuild; cannon and mortar have devastated our drab and shoddy streets but this I pledge, the talents of craftsman will change the face of our cities. We will build towers, towers…no less.'

Billy's dream is about the modernisation of Britain, commenting on the post-war rebuilding of the country embodied by the new blocks being built. He promises the crowd a new future which is greeted enthusiastically by the mass of people but the tone is heavily ironic as implied by the use of direct gaze. There seems to be emptiness in the reconstruction that pales in comparison to the change implied by Liz, an attitude change, rather than a change wrought by the new commercialism

Still fantasising Billy is limping up a hillside where he meets Councillor Duxbury. Adapting to yet another role, Billy immediately adopts Duxbury's way of speaking and feigns interest as he tells him about the sweeping changes the modern age has wrought, the changes in the buildings, the loss of trams and the development of the city centre.

Continuing to the top of the hill Billy throws away the calendars before running away across the mountainside. The accompanying music gives a sense of freedom enhanced by the open spaces, in contrast to the claustrophobic spaces of the rest of the film. As he casts them away, he is literally 'wasting time' but this is what Billy enjoys and in doing so he achieves escape.

His reverie is short lived, however, and after a disappointing meeting with Danny Boon, who hadn't read Billy's scripts, he has his rendezvous with Barbara and Rita to keep. A gang of bikers introduce this scene, showing the growth in youth culture as they ride down a darkened street. They pull up outside the new Locarno bingo hall, where dancing is held, reflecting the new leisure entertainments. Both Rita and Barbara are waiting outside for Billy who is watching from across the road. Eric accompanies Rita inside but Barbara is left waiting as Billy uses one of the bikers' helmets and goggles to disguise himself. Inside young people are doing the new dance, the 'twist' to the music.

Billy spots Liz who is upstairs and joins her. She asks him about the scriptwriting and his book and Billy answers that it will be published next Christmas. Used to his lies, Liz tells him to count to five and then tell the truth and he admits he hasn't even started but then can't resist telling her he's sold some scripts to Danny Boon and has been offered a job in London. She asks him when he intends to leave but he becomes vague, he says it's difficult. To Liz, however, it's as simple as getting on a train but Billy makes excuses and tells her that she's had the practice.

The difference between Liz's attitude and Billy's is highlighted here. She is prepared to travel and sees life as an adventure, Billy is held back by his personality. He feels unable to do what Liz does and despite having both the capability and ambition, he is unable to change.

Billy's song 'Twisterella', written with Arthur, is played by the band on the stage but as he begins to enjoy it, his problems close in. He spies Shadrack and hides, then downstairs he bumps into Barbara who he convinces had the meeting arrangements wrong. On the dance floor, Barbara confirms her old fashioned status and complains she can't twist. She encourages Billy to go and get an orange juice but before they can they are spotted by Rita. As the women begin to fight Billy makes his escape but he is caught in a spotlight as the bandleader congratulates him on his new job with Danny Boon. Liz rolls her eyes and Stan shouts 'Billy Liar!' from the crowd.

INDEPENDENCE

His problems having come to a head, Billy escapes with Liz and they walk in the open space of the park and Billy asks her whether she finds life difficult. She asks him who he loves and he says he loves her. When, however, she states that she wants to marry him, he becomes evasive and she asserts that she wants to get married, not engaged, Billy says that one day they will. 'One day,' she echoes. Liz tells Billy that she is willing to have sex with him and informs Billy that she has had other lovers. But when she offers to tell him about them he declines and she seems disappointed.

Liz's openness and sexual experience are an early example of the liberated female figure which is to become so dominant in the period's films. Her independence is shown not only in her willingness to travel but also in her ability to have sexual relations outside of marriage and for this she feels no guilt. She is in contrast to the other female characters as she refuses to adopt established attitudes and deny her true feelings:

> 'It was unusual for any girl to admit that she was a sexy person. They pretended otherwise.' (Keith Waterhouse, *Hollywood UK* BBC4)

She accuses him of thinking that her sexual adventures are the reason she goes away but she says that she just has to get away sometimes. 'It's not you, it's this town, and it's the people we know. I don't like knowing everybody; I don't like becoming a part of things. Do you know what I mean? What I'd like be is invisible.' Billy explains that to be invisible, he has invented his own imaginary country. Liz, it seems, has done the same and says she knew Billy would do it too. 'Oh Billy, why are we so alike?' she asks.

But Liz's escape is not in her imagination alone; it is an actual escape and she defies social convention. Her free-spirited approach to life provides not only Billy with a figure of fantasy but also provided Britain with a new icon. Christie's bag-swinging Liz would become the embodiment of Sixties cool.

> 'Liz in *Billy Liar!* is attractive not only because she is played by Julie Christie and (unlike Babs) does not dress like her mother, but because she is cultured (unlike Rita) and has travelled not only to London but to Europe.' (Sargeant, 2005: 239)

A point-of-view shot shows they are being watched. Billy talks of how if they were married they could imagine themselves away together and, excited by this prospect, he proposes marriage. She accepts and they are about to make love when Stamp and some friends start shouting. They ridicule the lovers and run away to the playground, shouting and laughing. Liz encourages Billy to ignore them. 'They're not worth it, the whole place isn't worth it,' she argues. She tries to persuade Billy to come with her to London and he finally agrees.

Liz's character shows Billy what it is that is holding him back and she illustrates what the Sixties 'revolution' offered. To her there is the potential for real change which extends further than the dancing or the transient fashions of youth culture. For her sex is just a natural outcome of a genuine new freedom and she tries to explain this to Billy but the attitudes of this parochial town, typical of its time, are those which have shaped Billy's outlook and although he wants to change to do so he has to give up his pretences.

When Billy returns home it is to an angry father who tells him that his grandmother has been taken to the infirmary. He tells him to book a taxi as his mother is requesting his presence. When Billy tells him to go upstairs we find out the reason behind his father's anger who not only has discovered that he didn't post his mother's radio request but also now knows about the missing calendars and postage money. This leads to a row as his father criticises Billy's behaviour which has made him into a laughing stock in the neighbourhood. But this time Billy loses his temper:

'Grateful, grateful. Grateful for this, grateful for that. That's all I've ever heard. Grateful you're going to go to the grammar school…'

'Well it's a chance we never had.'

'And don't we bloody well know it.'

'I even had to be grateful for winning me own scholarship and what did you say when I came running home to tell you I'd won it. That you'd have to pay for the uniform and that I was to be grateful.'

Billy tells him that he's not grateful for his job and refuses to pay the money back that he owes. He tells his father he's leaving to go to London but his father derides his dream of becoming a scriptwriter, telling him that he needs to do a 'proper day's work' and reveals that he expects him to take over the family business so he can look after his mother when she's older.

ESCAPE

Billy angrily grabs his suitcase and goes to the infirmary. This is where he has the chance to break free from his situation. His mother offers to help rectify his problems the next morning but he tells her he won't be around. His mother looks hurt and tells him that he can't run away from his problems, but he tells her he is resolved to leave.

Billy's mother is called away by a nurse and he picks up a newspaper and makes up a story. When his mother emerges again she tells him that his grandmother died that evening. He gives her the cup of tea he has just bought but in a scene which characterises the traditional British stiff upper lip, she can't drink it.

This scene seems from another era. There is nothing at the infirmary that indicates the modern age and in the death of Billy's grandmother there is the passing of an era. The age of the welfare state has gone, as have the attitudes of community that produced it. The scene, and the performances, characterise an attitude that the Sixties would reject:

'I just love Mona Washborne's performance now. I find it quite wonderful there, dealing with that dreadful British uptightness and repression of emotion.' (Julie Christie, *Billy Liar* Criterion Collection DVD)

She asks what train he intends to catch and he tells her that he must leave or he'll miss it. 'We don't say much but we need you at home, lad,' she says to Billy. He tries to comfort her that he'll be back next weekend to visit and as he leaves his mother holds back tears.

Billy exits the hospital dreaming about a state funeral in Ambrosia where he is making a speech for the departed ('Great lady'). As the bugle plays Billy makes his way through a deserted shopping precinct. Arriving at the train station he asks for a single ticket to London. In the cafeteria, there is a soldier leaving. Stamp is drunk and Rita is holding him upright. She sees Billy and she berates him. 'You think you're somebody don't you. I'll tell you something, you're not, and you're nobody.' Billy apologies and offers the ring but Rita dismisses him as muck, and leads Stamp away. Rita illustrates exactly what Billy is trying to escape and her life with the similarly unambitious Eric seems to be mapping itself out.

Billy walks outside and meets Liz who had to walk as she missed the last bus. They move through the ticket barriers followed by some musicians. Billy, distracted and depressed, is preoccupied and asks whether she needs cigarettes or something to eat or drink. Liz doesn't want it but Billy says he saw a milk machine on the station and insists on going to get some. She warns him not to take too long. One of the musician calls out whether she would be willing to share her 'gaff' with him.

Billy runs to the milk machine and is warned by the ticket inspector that the train is about to leave. Billy pays his money but once he collects the milk, he stops with his eyes closed, listening to the guard's whistle and the sound of the train leaving. Liz looks sadly resigned at the window, accepting Billy will never change, while Billy himself runs onto the platform in an effort to convince himself that he meant to catch the train only to find that Liz knows his decision, as she has left his suitcase for him. Billy casts the cups of milk onto the track, relieved that he does not have to leave.

The final scene shows Billy returning home along a darkened and deserted street. At first he seems downcast but then he begins to march proudly and the military tune that accompanies his march builds as the camera rises to reveal that Billy is leading his army up the street. The music fades and Billy returns home to his parents' house, closing the door behind him. As the camera tracks backward the Ambrosian national anthem starts up in celebratory fashion.

The ending of Billy Liar, like the ending of Brief Encounter in the 1940s, speaks volumes for the attitude of Britain in the respective periods. Just like its predecessor, the division at the railway station is reflective of the values of the age. Billy in making the choice to remain on the platform, a vision of a previous age, makes the choice to stay in the past:

> 'Tom's (Billy's) choice was to go into this new thing which nobody knew about but which was presenting itself; of course, he chose not to because it's frightening…the aspect of freedom…free love, openness in gender roles, whether women were proactive and not passive which was all very frightening.' (Julie Christie, Billy Liar Criterion Collection DVD)

SUMMARY

Thus Billy's world of fantasy would become a reality as the Sixties progressed and though Billy Fisher was unable to take advantage of society's change, it would move on regardless. The angry young man was becoming a figure of the past and it was Liz's positive young woman who became the new defining character for British cinema of the period. The combination of Julie Christie's roles that would make her the standard bearer for the Sixties freedoms as her star persona would become inextricably linked with the new attitude:

'I think that in terms of fashion that Liz in more sophisticated surroundings would have been a beat. I think that's probably what she became when she went to up to London, sitting in coffee houses with black stockings and men's sweaters, playing chess, listening to jazz, discussing the meaning of life with artists and musicians and smoking dope, that's what I think Liz started to get into when she went to London. I mean she would have led the life I led probably.'

Billy Liar is a film that has a similar identity crisis to its central character; although it is in the new wave canon, it is often overlooked as it relies heavily on fantasy and is therefore somewhat anomalous in the kitchen sink oeuvre. It is a transitional film but this makes it no less powerful:

'..what films like *Billy Liar* remind us of is the extraordinary power the cinema possesses, against all the odds, of anticipating as well as reflecting social change, so that the films seem to be at one and the same time prophecies of and metaphors for what is happening or going to happen.' (Walker, 1974: 167)

And what was about to happen to Britain was to change it irrevocably.

CHAPTER 4: LIVING THE DREAM
— *A HARD DAY'S NIGHT* (B/W, LESTER, 1964)

Films to watch: *Help!* (1965) *Yellow Submarine* (1968)

SYMBOLS OF CHANGE

'I suppose…it all goes back to The Beatles. We were lucky enough that they were quite cool and hip and there weren't a lot of cool and hip people around…they became idols and like any idols they were copied. So that's why London is now cool and hip.'
(Julie Christie, *Hollywood UK* BBC4)

Christie's convoluted explanation of how London became cool seems, on first sight, an inaccurate if not entirely senseless comment as The Beatles famously came from Liverpool. However, in order to become famous they had to move south and it is this migration towards London as the cultural capital which was the trigger for their subsequent worldwide success.

Like *Billy Liar*'s Liz who leaves a northern town on the train, *A Hard Day's Night* articulates the same movement south in another train journey, one which many young people would emulate.

Thus the angry young men in their northern towns like Billy Fisher would be left behind, while The Beatles would show what could be achieved by boarding that metaphorical train. These four lads from Liverpool embraced the age of opportunity, and the result was a British-led phenomenon that put the country and its capital at the forefront of the sixties revolution.

'I was aware when we were filming it that they were producing an effect on the entire population of Britain for better or worse, which badly needed to be documented. I think they were the first to give a confidence to the youth of the country which led to the disappearance of the Angry Young Men with a defensive mien.' (Lester in Walker, 1974: 236)

The Beatles provided the perfect transition from the new wave to the swinging Sixties in their film *A Hard Day's Night*. For a start, instead of actors playing real people, we now had famous real people, from the north, playing themselves and all in the style of a documentary. Paul, John, George and Ringo are 'themselves', what could be more reflective of the reality? Here, arguably, are the seeds of both the reality TV boom of the noughties and the beginning of the infatuation with 'celebrity' that would dominate the entertainment agenda decades later.

Like the new wave films there is a strong sense of a class divided nation in *A Hard Day's Night* but the emphasis of the film is far more positive, emphasising that in this changing climate there is more opportunity than ever before.

In presenting The Beatles in such a way, they become messengers of changing times who show what can be achieved in this new meritocratic society. They bend the Establishment to their will and in so doing highlight the new freedoms of the age while those characters who refuse to change are shown as obstinate, stubborn and old-fashioned, belonging to a bygone age.

For Charlie Gillett the social realist authors and film-makers had social messages to get across, and the characters inevitably came second, functioning as conduits for the writers' ideologies. The Beatles though, exploded this image of working-class youth. For Gillett:

'their social message was rarely expressed, but hung around their heads like an aura of impatience with convention and evident satisfaction with wealth and fame.' (Glynn, 2005: 36)

In so doing The Beatles in *A Hard Day's Night* were an attractive alternative from what many saw as the self-imposed gloom of the new wave. No longer did working-class attitudes and backgrounds condemn one to a suffocating life in a factory. They were an example of what could be achieved in a new age of consumerism and pop music, if it were embraced. While Hoggart may have been worried by the threat to traditional working-class community by the new entertainments, The Beatles certainly weren't.

However, it must be remembered that this is an industry constructed view of a new band and, as such, it is a hegemonic construct designed not to overthrow the system but instead encourages a belief in a system that is accommodating new values and beliefs. If we can believe that The Beatles are representative of a new beginning in a formerly class divided nation there is no need for radical change. Their inspiring example would help divert the gaze away from a society that was still very much divided by class.

This contradictory position that The Beatles hold is at the heart of *A Hard Day's Night*, which is, of course, not a documentary but a stylised piece that never really allows the viewer to access reality. The presentation of events clearly plays with received notions of The Beatles' characters but also uses them to reinforce their position as honest, unpretentious, working-class lads in this way they can be seen as extending the process of making the working-class knowable, allaying the fears expressed in *Peeping Tom* about mass culture and softening the 'angry young man' into an actually rather approachable young man. In his conclusion to his book 'Culture and Society' (1958) Raymond Williams comments, 'The masses are always the others, whom we don't know, and can't know. Yet now, in our kind of society, we see these others regularly, in their myriad variations; stand, physically, beside them. They are here, and we are here with them' (Lowenstein, 2000: 224) and this is exactly what we are seemingly allowed to do in *A Hard Day's Night*. However we should be wary of believing that this is the case.

A Hard Day's Night was made to cash in on the band's early success and United Artists agreed to fund it with little notion of how popular the band would become or their lasting effect on the world. For UA this was a low budget, low risk venture the purpose of which was to introduce the band as people to their buying public:

> 'Get each boy on his own for a stretch of film and show him as an individual. Get away from any notion of The Beatles as a four-headed monster.' (Lester in Barrow and White, 2008: 124)

The film is quite aware of its positioning of the band and it at once reinforces and undermines the band's image, playing with our notions of them as individuals while reinforcing their role as a packaged commodity to be relentlessly sold. If this is the age of freedom, The Beatles, ironically lose theirs in promoting it as an ideal, a commodity in an increasingly commercial age:

> 'However duplicitous the reality, class, at least for British audiences, was a key ingredient in the attraction of The Beatles. Here as Richard Buskin notes, were "four ordinary boys next door…living out a fantasy on behalf of everyone else." To this can be added nationality, as the group's success made them patriotic symbols of a new social mobility and the classlessness that was advocate as the way ahead for 1960's Britain.' (Glynn, 2005: 36)

FAME

A Hard Day's Night begins with the band being chased by hysterical fans to the train station. The framing of the opening shot is immediately one redolent of imprisonment, the band members positioned to the left of the frame inside vertical lines formed by street lamps. The soundtrack covers the girls' screams and the quick movements of the camera immediately create the energy and dynamism of the film. There is a sense of reality, of being able to look in at The Beatles' lives and one of the earliest shots is of a camera peering in through a window at John Lennon as he looks outside at the frantic chasing fans. They rush by in a blur as The Beatles run to avoid them, the shallow depth of field often enhancing the background blur as the band runs away while the fans are pictured in a series of close ups. Despite their fleeing, there is never a feeling of real physical threat as the band is often pictured laughing and their attempts to hide are ridiculous and comical. The fan's role is instrumental in creating the phenomenon and the chase part of a game in which the band participate.

Thus the movie begins with a clear delineation of its representational techniques. On the one hand it is 'a day in the life of The Beatles', an insight into their way of life. However, director Richard Lester is also aware enough of the mechanics of the new media to make it multi-layered. There is self-awareness in its construction that shows the mechanics of an industry designed to publicise and promote products such as pop bands just the same as any other product. This is not an attempt to be completely authentic but rather to expose the creation of a sense of reality – and then make a mockery of it:

> 'The film has reiterated how the reality of The Beatles escapes the medium: our consumption is only of a symbol, mass produced at so many removes that only the belief can confer authentication.' (Glynn, 2005: 49)

In this way, despite the sense of fun there is an alternative reading on the nature of fame. By filming on a train there is an obvious sense of claustrophobia to capture The Beatles' sense of isolation imposed by their new found stardom:

> 'So that feeling of claustrophobia was how we tried to think of the whole first sequence, the whole first third of the film. In closed spaces: prisoners of fans, prisoners by car, train, small hotel rooms-do this, do that, sign this.' (Richard Lester in Glynn, 2005: 41)

Once on the train the tenuous plot devices are not concealed. Rather, the transparency of the situation is there for all to see. The boys search for a compartment and find Paul sitting with his grandfather whom he introduces to the rest of the band. John points out that this person is not Paul's grandfather but he insists he is. This use of a well known actor, in Wilfred Brambell, playing John McCartney, immediately undermines the tenuous reality and instead embraces artifice; they refer to him as being 'a clean man', a knowing inversion of the dirty old man Brambell was known for playing in *Steptoe and Son*.

Similarly, Norm, the band's manager is played by Norman Rossington, familiar to us from *Saturday Night and Sunday Morning*, while Shake, his assistant, is played by another recognisable actor in John Junkin. From the outset the film deals with the band as a commercial product and there is a conflict between their personal needs and the commercial requirements imposed by their manager. It is clear the band is dismissive of the care that their management have for them. 'You got back alright then?' Shake asks. 'No,' replies Lennon:

'Ever noticed how much celebrities are pushed around in public? Manager's guiding them, fans pulling at them, comperes patting them. You get to feel so much moveable property. What it feels like to be a Beatle: that's the first priority.' (Alun Owen, interviewed in Walker, 1974: 237)

Despite their innocent presentation, there is actually an undercurrent of The Beatles' worldliness. While Norm lectures them, Lennon is contemptuously sniffing up some 'coke' from his bottle. This antagonism is acted out in the manner of parents and small children. The separation of the generations is made clear as The Beatles are shown to have a different set of values to those of their manager, more in tune with their audience. Paul tells his manager not to lose his grandfather and he is told not to be so cheeky.

Their representation as young boys is consistent throughout and they even flirt with schoolgirls on the train, which reinforces their appeal to their fan base. When a stereotypical middle-class commuter, complete with bowler hat, enters the first-class compartment he is predictably at odds with their youthful carefree attitude. He looks at them with disapproval over his newspaper and makes a unilateral decision to close the window. The boys' request that the window be reopened provokes a discussion of rights and it is clear that the band is being promoted as a voice of the younger generation.

However, they never force the point and always keep the criticism good humoured. John flutters his eyelids and the extent of the younger generation's rebellion seems to be the eating in public and playing a radio. It could be argued that the use of pop music to rile the commuter merely shows him as a fuddy duddy and as he refers to the railway act, it is clear his only purpose here is to make the older generation appear redundant. Paul's flippant 'Up the workers and all that', merely reinforces the Beatles' lack of political edge and light-heartedness, while their pleading for rights because they too paid for their tickets is half-hearted.

IDOLS

The balance between The Beatles' presentation as rebels and cheeky teen idols had to be maintained and a scene of the band attacking another member of the Establishment was cut, as it seems the band had to be careful not to bite the hand that feeds. Another scene which was deemed too rebellious was cut from the film:

'Stuck in a traffic jam, the group is overtaken by a company director's Rolls. Lennon lowers his window and lets fly an imaginary hail of bullets at the executive in the back seat.' (Catterrall and Wells, 2001: 11)

This type of hard edged attack on authority will be seen later in the decade in *If…* (1968) but this film is careful not to make any political statements.

The commuter's complaint that he fought the war for the likes of them is met with derision – 'I bet you're sorry you won', and the boys reinforce their position as children, by poking their tongues out and asking for their ball back, after leaving the compartment. Here, however, we suddenly deviate from the faux realism established as the band members are seen running alongside the train. This employment of surrealism punctures any pretence the audience may harbour that the events on screen are 'real' and demonstrate, perhaps, that The Beatles live in their own world, where anything is possible. Thus, both the positive tone of the film and its style move it away from the anger and realism of the new wave and through The Beatles conveys a new mood:

'The general aim of the film was to present what was becoming a social phenomenon in this country. Anarchy is too strong a word, but the confidence that the boys exuded.' (Dick Lester in Glynn, 2005: 35)

Thus the crazy, surrealist humour, so much a feature of Lester's work who had filmed with the Goons, becomes a way of communicating The Beatles' attitudes to the world around them, where accepted modes of address and behaviour have been taken for granted by now can be broken and made to look ridiculous – by behaviour that is equally (but differently) ridiculous. Like Billy Fisher, in *Billy Liar* who invents his own world to cope with the one around him, so do The Beatles, who do not belong in the privileged surroundings they have access but neither do they accept that they should be contained by their class. Fantasy is now becoming not only an expression of dreams but a means by which to show an alternate reality which is occupied by choice.

'The film people I admired weren't making Presley movies. My interest was more on the Continent and therefore my heroes were Truffaut and *400 Blows*. Also *Shoot the Pianist*, where there are those little surrealist touches that come out of nowhere. It was that which led me to alter some of the early musical numbers, so that we got two realities bumping into each other.' (Lester in Caterall and Wells, 2001: 9)

PRISONERS

When Paul's grandfather goes missing, Paul and John enter a carriage full of girls to ask for help and John throws himself to the floor, claiming to be an escaped prisoner. Once again, the band is portrayed pleading with the only people who understand them and can grant their freedom, their own fans. Their crazy behaviour is a reflection of their wish to escape the dull reality of their lives on tour. Thus they invent their own and The Beatles often

escape their own situations by inventing new ones, which can be seen in the next scene.

Finding John McCartney in a private compartment with a woman, the boys put him in the cage of a luggage compartment, in which they begin to play cards. As 'I Should Have Known Better' begins the card game is exposed as a fiction as a wide shot suddenly reveals them to be playing the music, changing the non-diegetic to the diegetic. The schoolgirls meanwhile play out the roles of the Beatles' fans at one stage playfully grabbing at Ringo through the wire cage, at another being serenaded by John as he sings words of love. The filming of the song cuts a series of close ups together that enhance our familiarity with the fun-loving band and reinforce their personalities:

'The only freedom they ever get is when they are playing their music. That's when their faces light up. Had to get to know them pretty well to write the film, and that's what really made my mind up how to write it.' (Alun Owen in Catterall and Wells, 2001: 5)

As the train pulls into another station, the repetitive nature of The Beatles' life on tour is highlighted as the day repeats itself with yet another set of fans wildly screaming. The band is told to run straight into a waiting car, once again pursued by fans that they elude by comic escape. Inside the car we have another insight into The Beatles' existence as we see them pursued by very real looking, desperate, crazed fans. The film is now alternating between the actuality of The Beatles' life and the fictional construction of their situation.

The film is an industry product and it is difficult for it to be anything else. It is in its very acceptance of this and its willingness to highlight the process that it succeeds. It is a theatrical presentation of the idea of fame and as such presents the new phenomena for what it is, a complete media construction. The real fans are juxtaposed against the actors (who are sometimes playing fans), the staged chases alongside real chases. This leaves The Beatles in a sort of no man's land or, rather, a land where they can invent themselves in which sense they become representative of a new Britain. In this media determined age, however, they are scripted interpretations of themselves and we as the audience cannot be any closer to knowing them. This being the case we are presented with very two-dimensional scenes and conversations that don't ring true – and don't have to. In this new age, the image replaces the reality.

The hotel room, despite its luxury is a similarly oppressive environment to that of the train and though they are given whatever they want, it is clear that they need to escape their imprisonment. The bottles of HP sauce delivered on a tray remind us that despite their lives of new found privilege, they remain unaffected.

FUN

The next scene shows a fashionable club alive with dancing. Fashionable girls do the latest routines but this is not the tentative dancing seen in *Billy Liar*, this is the 'scene' that promises so much, perhaps the one that Billy imagined escaping to. The club is full of frenetic energy and the band is shown enjoying themselves with verité techniques that give the viewer a feeling that they are gaining an insight into the band's off-duty behaviour, where they are clearly at home.

The stuffiness of the older generation is being cast aside by the behaviour of the young. To demonstrate this, this scene is contrasted with the sterile environment of the exclusive casino where the older, privileged members sit around gambling, apparently without a hint of enjoyment. Signs of wealth and class abound although this status is punctured by Paul's grandfather who is also sitting at the table and does not take proceedings seriously.

The bare feet of one of the dancers in the club emphasises the informal and freer attitudes of the younger generation of which The Beatles are representative. The 'natural' camera work enhances the feeling of capturing the 'real' Beatles, shown dancing, smoking and socialising. This is at odds with much of the rest of the film, where the theatrical nature of the boys' scripted interactions gives the clear message of deliberate construction — yet this reality here is just as constructed as in earlier scenes.

The fly-on-the-wall view we are given as the camera often peers through the crowd to find members of the band creates ordinariness by reducing them to faces in the crowd. However, filmed at the same location, in Les Ambassadeurs club in Mayfair, both casino and the nightclub give the illusion of the division of the old world and new but reveal the actuality of a swinging London for the elite.

Paul's grandfather once again breaks the social rules of the club environment by taking on the role of a waiter in order to acquire gambling chips. His use of the formal dress undermines the distinction between those in waiting and those who are privileged by position. 'Bingo' he cries in a reference to the traditionally working-class game.

The Beatles return, like good boys, to complete their fan mail but discovering that Paul's grandfather has gone to the gambling club, they go to find him. The band members comment ironically on gambling and orgies taking place as if disgusted before excitedly leaving.

Two club members are discussing Paul's grandfather, whom they look on approvingly 'Lord John McCartney, millionaire, Irish peer'. 'Filthy rich, of course', one comments. 'He looks quite clean to me,' replies the other member. As the band arrive at the club, the manager tells them to behave. ('We know how to behave, we've had lessons,' counters John.)

Social comment is not really at the heart of the film but this sequence shows effectively how it is dealt with within the parameters of The Beatles' image. The club is an exclusive environment, supposedly only accessible by society's elite but The Beatles, despite their working-class origins, are able to gain entry through their 'fame'. While being lectured on how to behave by their manager, they are aware that it is not their behaviour that grants them their privilege. The band, throughout the film, are the exception that proves the rules. While they do not explicitly tackle society's boundaries they do so by implication.

MOBILITY

In *A Hard Day's Night* the Beatles are on a journey and they reflect the mobility that is available to this generation. The band begin at a train station and end the film by flying away in a helicopter but theirs is not just a physical journey, it is the mobility of being able to move through society. Throughout the film the energy conveyed is kinetic, from the movement of the camera, to the running, chasing and dancing that express this new vibrant way of life. The scenes in which there is stasis are reflective of the older generation.

The new Britain is moving forward, away from the past. John is in the bath mimicking a German voice, as though re-enacting the war but Britain's diminished stature in terms of world power status is pointedly remarked upon – 'Keep Britain tiny,' says Shake. 'Rule Britannia,' sings John before sinking the ships. The band are 'invading' foreign territory but it is through the new media and its global reach, which makes the war seem so outdated even quaint Britain's recent past has suddenly become history and the notions which it supported are openly ridiculed.

Entering a press conference at another hotel it is clear that such events rate very low in their priorities. They make a beeline for the drinks but are guided away, to the media circus. A crowd of photographers are waiting and though they grab for the sandwiches they elude the hungry band who appear superfluous at this media junket, which carries on regardless.

The press is shown indulging themselves on the free drinks while a series of non-contextualised answers are spoken over cross-dissolves of camera flashes and shots of the band:

'I've always liked that question.'

'I never noticed his nose until about six months ago.'

'And me mother asked before we left for America if we wanted any sandwiches.'

'And when I plugged her in she just blew up.'

The abstraction of answers to frequently asked questions takes away their meaning and makes the ritual of these press conferences redundant in their repetition. The edits emphasise the passing of time and the amount of questions the band have to answer, presumably until the questions begin to lose meaning.

George, meanwhile, has his photograph taken, altering his facial expression slightly for each one and we see the prints appearing on the screen, the mass manufacture of images. This technique is used at other points during the film and points to the commodification of the band as well as being an allusion, perhaps, to arch pop artist, Andy Warhol:

> 'Each image is stored, stacked mechanically to emphasise a repetitiousness mirroring of the industrial process…the boys are manufactured as a (Warholian) tin of soup – and, simultaneously, a celebration of variation within standardisation.' (Glynn, 2005: 60)

The press' questions are empty and trivial, demonstrating how out of touch they are with the public they represent. The Beatles in turn supply answers that though often ridiculous, are based in common sense and common parlance. While they mimic their questioners' accents and lambaste the pointlessness of the questions, it is all done in good humoured fashion. The fact that The Beatles are able to deal with questions framed to enhance their strangeness with such unerring ease, demonstrates their down to earth qualities and diffuses the threat of the youth culture which they represent (willingly or not). 'Are you a mod or a rocker?' asks one of the journalists of Ringo, 'No, I'm a mocker,' he says appositely, refusing to be categorised by the reporters:

> 'The "long Sixties" witnessed a recurring duality where the young were both celebrated as the harbingers of an exciting and prosperous future and condemned as exemplifying a new moral and cultural bankruptcy.' (Glynn, 2005: 5)

MEDIATION

The Beatles, in this way, help smooth the transition of Britain from old to new, presenting a cross over of the traditional and the modern. Thus the band embody the conflict within the age, but smooth over the edges and in doing so make acceptable the changing face of youth culture. They have the down-to-earth appeal of the angry young men but stripped of the anger and overt politics. For The Beatles there is no need for resentment toward the Establishment as social boundaries can quickly be traversed.

The band's distance from the world of traditional showbiz is established through their relationship with those who work in the media. Their role as outsiders is emphasised through the effete representation of those who work in the industry. Ringo's combination of childish petulance and resistance to the 'bourgeois' crew member interfering with his drums is rather like that of a child who only has one toy which he values above all else, reinforcing his working-class identity.

The shot of the band's performance enhances the role of the television production team. This repeats the emphasis on the industry mediating the band to its audience, showing how the images are produced and selected but the duality of the film can be seen as, once again, a series of close ups which show the band actually enjoying playing.

Throughout the film this is when the band are free, so although their image is being mediated and they are subject to the media industry, they remain true to their art and this is where their relationship is forged. The film gives the impression that there is no artifice to The Beatles and what you see is what you get, despite the best efforts of those around them. Of course, this is itself the artifice of the film.

The director, a tantrum-throwing queen played by Victor Spinetti, walks in and accuses them of going behind his back to arrange his removal. He explains that his direction of filming has been called into question by a 'musical arranger' who it transpires is Paul's granddad who has been stirring up trouble again.

The band again is shown as genuine as they ridicule the pompous figure of the director whose self-importance is shown by his attitude toward not only the band but his pride in his single award which only succeeds in highlighting his insecurities, again in contrast to the band's self-possession.

ENERGY

'Can't Buy Me Love' begins as they make their way down the staircase. The metal grille and iron bars are emphasised, consistent with the theme of the band's imprisonment. They run to a nearby field and an aerial view pictures them running back and forth in speeded up film footage. They have mock races and fights, falling down and lying down. A low angle shows them leaping upwards against the sky in slow motion.

The film language used in the scene communicates the band's energy. 'We're out!' Ringo shouts before the band are seen making their way down the metal mesh staircase. The frequent changes of camera angle as they go around and around convey a sense of giddy pleasure and viewed from beneath the staircase they are broken into a pop art pattern by the mesh and an eddying camera that shows their hurried steps.

Jumping over the discarded sets from the studio, they escape the artificial world and the iron bars of the staircase, making their way to the open space of a field, leaving the debris of the studio behind. Paul discards his jacket and John his hat as they shed their clothes and inhibitions. The aerial view shows them frolicking in a central square of a heli-pad.

The band are then seen, framed formalistically, from the end of a running track, with Paul holding an imaginary starting pistol. The 'race' descends into chaos as the band move in ridiculous ways before falling over.

Back in the square, with the song still playing, they stand at the corners before swapping places in the manner of a dance, the camera angle changing from above to a worm's eye view from one of the corners. The camera is distant and then becomes part of the games and Paul attacks it, moving toward and grabbing it. It then points downward as Ringo runs past and then reveals the pair of feet of the person filming, before showing George tap dancing.

Above and below, the boys are shown play fighting and as one gets up the others fall down. They run away over grass and are pursued by the aerial camera, and then they are shown jumping into the air in slow motion, the low angles making their leaps dramatic gestures, before Ringo is shown making his own leap which barely lifts him from the ground. The sequence ends with the aerial view of them once again running across the field and circling them.

This famous sequence with its varied techniques shows The Beatles at manic play and it has become iconic in its communication of Sixties attitudes. The band members are involved in activities that communicate freedom. They have escaped their manager, their commitments and their commodification as a media product and are free to do whatever they please. The location of a playing field is synonymous with childhood and in this vast open space movement is emphasised as they run, jump and chase.

There are, however, other interesting aspects to the sequence, which again draw our attention to the role of the camera. The idea of the representation of the band is toyed with by Lester, who while filming something free and apparently cathartic is actually underlining its artifice. The camera shapes our interpretation of the band, their freedom at times shown to be insignificant but at others to be majestic. The camera's involvement foregrounds its part in shaping events, and its place as a view of one of the band gives the illusion of our own involvement in what we are seeing. Lester is knowledgeable enough to reference other Beatle imagery:

> '…it again enacts the Beatles' existing photographic iconography, in particular Dezo Hoffman's shot from Liverpool's Sefton Park of the group leaping into the air….' (Glynn, 2005: 72)

But their escape from rules can only ever be temporary. They are stopped by the field's grounds man. 'I suppose you know that this is private property,' he says.

Norm realises they are missing and blames John. The manager seems on the point of a breakdown and claims John enjoys torturing him. We can see here that John is the person whose image in the band is as the most subversive. John, of course is The Beatle who famously made the comment relating to royalty 'rattling their jewellery' in the Royal Variety Performance and this rebellious image is played upon throughout the film.

When the band returns a woman stops John in a corridor and a mock conversation on his identity begins. This conversation of confusion and façade serves several purposes in the text. The woman's recognition of John relates to the idea of fame and public familiarity with celebrities. The woman is, like many of those shown at the theatre, superficial and quick to judge on appearance as well as being pleased when linked to a person of notoriety. Her fickle attachments, however, are revealed when she turns cold at John not being the person she has mistaken him for.

Thus, while the band is depicted as genuine, fame works against their being able to form normal attachments – which bring them closer. The potentially duplicitous nature of John is emphasised by the *mise-en-scéne* as he is shown next to a mirror but this is, of course, symbolic of the film itself in its construction of the band.

IMAGE

George, meanwhile, is looking for the canteen but accidentally goes into a production office. The woman is pleased to see him, also mistaking him for someone else.

'Oh there you are,' she says and when George points out the error, she talks at cross purposes. 'Actually I think he'll be very pleased with you,' she says.

Picking up her phone she reports her find. 'Hello, I've got one,' she says, to George's bemusement. George watches her putting on her shoes. 'Yes, he can talk. Well I think you ought to see him.'

From the outset this scene, which is arguably the most condemnatory of the London media scene, George's behaviour shows him to be completely bemused by the outlook of those he meets. This serves the purpose again of distancing The Beatles from calculating industry figures and though he is being portrayed as ignorant to their ways, he is not easily manipulated. The girl in reception is attractive but she is a product of the industry and is aloof and distant.

The girl presents him to a man behind a desk. 'Simon, will this do?' she asks.

'Not bad, darling. Not really bad,' Simon, another camp media 'type' replies, inspecting George. They tell him to turn around and look at him approvingly stating that he'll look good alongside Susan. It is a mystery as to what they wish George to do but their treatment of him as an object is apparent.

George apologises again for the misunderstanding but the man thinks his manner is an affectation:

'Oh you can come of it with us. You don't have to do all the old adenoidal, glottal stop and carry on for our benefit.'

'I'm afraid I don't understand', says George.

'Oh my God, he's a natural.'

'Well I did tell them not to send us real ones', she replies.

'They ought to know by now the phonies are much easier to handle. Still, he's a good type.'

Talking louder, as though he thinks him a simpleton, he asks George to give his opinion on some clothes for teenagers.

George's role in this comic encounter further emphasises The Beatles' down to earth, unaffected nature as the media industry workers recognise his 'real' credentials. Their calculating reproduction of fashionable trends shows the industry's view of young people as a burgeoning target market. Simon has no use for the 'authenticity' of The Beatles; in fact he simply doesn't understand it, showing the insularity of the industry in which he works. His interpretation of a working-class accent is that it is just a transient fashion. His recognition of the dangers of working with someone who is not just adopting mannerisms to advance their career shows his limited outlook.

George mimics their way of talking and says 'By all means, I'd be quite prepared for that eventuality.' But the man doesn't want his real opinion and says it will be written out for him and he'll read it:

'Can you read?' he asks.

'Course I can.'

'I mean lines, ducky, can you handle lines? he asks, in a line that cheekily hints at The Beatles having to act.

'I'll have a bash,' George answers.

The representation of the two characters emphasised in their use of language, shows that The Beatle is able to feign ignorance due to his social background while making fun of the oblivious Simon, whose superior attitude is based on snobbery. He clearly looks down on George but despite his apparent advantages of class and education, he appears wary of the changing times, rather than someone who wants to embrace it. Like the director he is scared of the threat young talent poses which, though he tries to control it, is clearly something alien to him.

Simon tells an assistant to give him a drink of what ever it is 'they' drink and comments that 'at least he's polite', clearly expecting bad behaviour from this social inferior.

He gets one of the assistants to show him some shirts. 'Now, you'll really like these, you'll really dig them,' he says emphasising the fashionable words in a display of contempt. 'They're fab and all the other pimply hyperboles.'

Simon's derisive manner suggests the contempt with which young people are viewed by an industry keen to make a profit from them and the conversation shows his assumptions that young people will wear anything if they believe it to be fashionable. George, however, speaks for the young and shows that young people are not so easily manipulated: 'I wouldn't be seen dead in them,' he says handing them back. 'They're dead grotty.'

'Grotty?' the man says before telling his secretary to make a note of the word and to give it to Susan. 'It's rather touching really. Here's this kid trying to give me his utterly valueless opinion when I know for a fact that within a month he'll be suffering from a violent inferiority complex because he isn't wearing one of these nasty things. Of course they're grotty you wretched nit, that's why they were designed. But that's what you'll want.'

The duality of the film can again be seen here, as George, though bravely embodying the young as thoughtful and resistant to manipulation, ultimately is a figure that shows the extent to which the public can be manipulated. 'Beatlemania', itself a mass phenomenon, shows the reaction that can be elicited and encouraged amongst impressionable consumers. Simon, despite being a comical figure, demonstrates this to be the case.

When George disputes that he'll want one of the shirts Simon's response is instructive regarding the nature of fame and the industry outlook:

'You can be replaced, cheeky baby.'

'I don't care.'

George's indifference to Simon's threat reinforces his lack of interest in fame and again underlines his credentials as a real person, whose entry into the media profession is a complete accident but Simon is oblivious to George's outlook and again mistakes this for a superficial posture.

The final conversation emphasises the transience of fashion and the insincerity of an industry that tries to schedule change. Their chosen representative of the young, Susan, is exposed by an audience quick to appreciate the 'fakes' that the industry uses to attract audiences but also shows the gulf between the young and those older figures who try to control and manufacture new trends.

COMIC

Back in the studio the producer, a self-important prima-donna, is panicking and threatening trouble if the band don't appear soon. He complains that TV is a 'young man's medium'. Marching back to his sound booth the band, having arrived, ridicules him. As The Beatles sing 'And I love her' their place as industry products to be mediated to their audience is once again emphasised as this time we watch their images through numerous monitors, the choice of images at the director's disposal there for us to see.

Back in the changing room there is a series of quick, madcap sketch-style jokes such as Ringo sat under the hairdryer wearing a bearskin. When asked by his manager what he's up to he responds, 'Page five'. This zany humour which incorporates references to eclectic sources reflects changing times. Paul quotes Shakespeare: 'Oh that this too, too solid flesh would melt,' he says, looking in the mirror before turning to the camera and shouting, 'Zap!,' at once combining the British historic traditions of literature and theatre, before undermining it with comic book language and the breaking of the fourth wall.

John accuses Paul's grandfather of being sex-obsessed and reverses the complaints of the older generation by accusing them of leading the country to galloping ruin. He asks his manager if he bought his suit at Harrods before telling a girl that he can get her on stage and merely gives her the directions. Grabbing the make-up girls they run to the stage where Lionel Blair is dancing with a showgirl troupe.

These conversations, though light-hearted and trivial, are reflections of the times in their content. A changing British identity is apparent and a willingness to make multi-layered, self-referential comments shows that through the medium of film The Beatles are able to express their place within this change. In a modest way they are confronting social status, sexuality, class and commercialisation.

They grab their instruments and in another moment of gentle subversion, John shouts, 'Why don't we do the show right here, yeah!' as he knowingly references the traditions of Fifties-style musicals. The band laughs and starts another song. Once again the TV studio is foregrounded and we look straight down a camera. This time it is the make-up girls who are substitutes for the usual female audience and they are chased away by their older supervisor, another parent figure.

While John walks away with a dancing girl, Ringo is told to look after John McCartney. In the canteen Ringo tries to read a book but ever the trouble-maker, Paul's grandfather extols the virtues of 'parading' and tells him he should be living his life. John McCartney is a traditional character who is able to see through the trappings of the media-generated life, not unlike Maxine in *Peeping Tom*. His criticism of the band is that their experiences are not actual experiences but a substitute for them, a fabrication, like the photographs and the autographs, merely reproductions. Although he is labelled a mixer, someone who

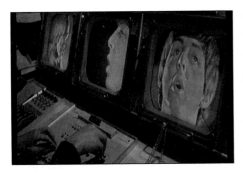

deliberately causes trouble, perhaps it is his role to stir up the trouble that The Beatles cannot for fear of ruining their image.

Persuaded by John McCartney's arguments, Ringo leaves the canteen telling him he's going parading. George explains that Paul's grandfather has 'stirred him up'. They chase after him but trying to split up they all walk in the same direction. 'We've become a limited company,' comments John, again knowingly, recognising their inseparable commercial worth.

Ringo is on a street, still taking photographs as though trying to capture real life, but is soon chased by girls. His real escape begins when he goes into a junk shop and comes out wearing a long trench coat and hat. Initially he is pleased at his new anonymity but he soon becomes a lost and lonely figure and re-discovers his place is with the band.

Ringo's escape owes much to Chaplin and he becomes a comic character through his tragic mishaps. He meets a boy truanting from school who says he is 'deserting' and tells him about his friends who obviously parallel the band. This is enhanced as Ringo says he's a deserter too and without the others he is truly lost. The sentimentality of Ringo's adventures are a strange contrast with much of the postmodern feel of the film and separated from the rest of the band it is as though he loses touch with the contemporary world.

PERFORMANCE

After a Keystone Cops-style chase in which Ringo is rescued from the police by the rest of the band they make it back to the studio in time to perform.

Hysterical fans inevitably greet their appearance on stage for this final performance as narrative equilibrium and the band's place and purpose are restored. This celebration of the band and the finale shows their unifying effect. After getting to know them as individuals we also recognise that their strongest impact can only be a result of their collaboration. One song blends into another in a final medley and even the begrudging director is seen enjoying himself. Dressed in their stage outfits they are the polished commercial product, the outcome of the industrial process and the creators of Beatlemania.

The television crew is still seen but they are now peripheral to the performance and the band is seen more as a unit against the backdrop. The shots from behind the band show the audience and its connection with the performance. The excited and hysterical reaction is shown by a fast moving camera which blurs the audience into a mass but also often zooms in on individual members in various states of excitement.

At the close of the gig the band exit the stage, coerced into another gig by their manager. They run out to a waiting helicopter as *A Hard Day's Night* plays again. Hand-held camera work communicates the energy and the helicopter is shown from below as it rises and they throw out John McCartney's signed photographs.

SUMMARY

The Beatles' film provides a connection between early Sixties and 'swinging Sixties' cinema. It demonstrates a change in outlook and shows the possibilities of this new exciting time. Ironically while the film focuses on the band's lack of freedom, it provides a greater idea of liberation for a wider audience. While it retains some of the characteristics of realism established by the British new wave and even retains the representational hope of down to earth integrity, it then adds stylistic and ideological experimentation which shows that anything is possible and that proposes the idea that we shape our own reality whatever our class origins.

The film's lack of a structured narrative and tenuous plot with its mish-mash of comedy sketches, light-hearted banter and musical interludes, could perhaps be considered as not much more than an early pop video or promotional film but therein lays its appeal and classic status. It is a film that recognises exactly what it is and in so doing, like The Beatles themselves, expresses the conflict of the age:

'The Beatles sent the class thing sky high; they laughed it out of existence and, I think, introduced a tone of equality more successfully than any other single factor that I know.' (Richard Lester in Walker, 1974: 236)

CHAPTER 5: SPIES LIKE US — *GOLDFINGER* (COLOUR, GUY HAMILTON, 1964) AND *THE IPCRESS FILE* (COLOUR, SIDNEY FURIE, 1965)

Films to watch: *Khartoum* (1966), *Zulu* (1964), *Damn the Defiant!* (1962), *Lawrence of Arabia* (1962), *Dr No* (1962), *Modesty Blaise* (1966), *Thunderball* (1965), *You Only Live Twice* (1967), *On Her Majesty's Secret Service* (1969)

NEW HEROES

Britain's collaboration with the American film industry is one which has often seemed to thrive on a shared outlook in terms of military imperialism and a sense of heritage. While the British new wave wished to escape the retelling of war stories, America continued to find the cliché of Britain's indomitable character attractive. Though the country was beginning to modernise, it still had a rather traditional role to fulfil from an American perspective.

However, in an age which would go on to espouse the wonders of peace and love, war did not have quite the same appeal as it once had and now:

> 'It was becoming clear that the empire's days were numbered and, after World War II, the dismantling of the British Empire — as former colonies became nation states — was one of the most visible signs that the nation was no longer a world power.' (Leach, 2004: 219)

It was against this background, of a changed geopolitical outlook that Britain's onscreen representation had to change:

> 'Then you were able to be more critical and less patriotic, to show that war was filthy and degrading...The flag waving and the patriotism was [sic] beginning to taper off.' (J. Lee Thompson, *Hollywood UK* BBC4)

No longer were the dutiful officer class heroes to characterise Britain. Films such as *Ice Cold in Alex* (1958) began to portray the war in a more ambiguous manner, with

John Mills playing an English captain vulnerable under pressure; while in the first of the new wave films, *Room at the Top* (1958), Joe Lampton makes it very clear to his former commanding officer that the war is now over.

It was time for a new British hero and James Bond, like The Beatles would become a link between the old and the new:

'One might see the early 007 adventures as providing a transition from British New Wave Cinema to films like *Darling* (1965) which reacted to the bleakness of social realism, for Bond's espionage missions caused colourful images of the international jet set to be imported into the Mother country.' (Baron in Lindner, 2003: 135)

Bond was a figure who could revitalise and reinvent an idea of Englishness for the rest of the world, with, of course, the help of his American chums. Here, in these times of confusion, came a hero for whom there were only certainties. Bond was, in the manner of those heroes who had come before, a military man; but unlike his stiff-upper lipped predecessors, Bond would present someone of the same level of bravery but without the uptight attitude so out of place in the Sixties.

He presented the audience with a devil-may-care bravery which still epitomised the belligerent bravery and civilised ideals for which Britain was known but combined it with glamour and charm:

'What the Bond films present is an image of Britishness carefully packaged for the international market. Bond is a modern, virile, classless character who combines the suave sophistication of the traditional British gentleman hero with the toughness and sexual magnetism of the Hollywood leading man. He is very much an Englishman abroad, a professional tourist whose job takes him to exotic foreign locations which are presented with all the glossy sophistication of an upmarket travel brochure.' (Chapman in Lindner, 2003: 97)

Bond was a figure of bravery and loyalty without being weighed down by the hardship often associated with service, a man for a new age who could fit in fighting evil between drinks, gambling and womanising. And in these times of Cold War espionage, the villains were not nation states but secret organisations or maniacal individuals whose enmity was aimed against 'the free world' whose values were that of America's.

'In all cases the, villain's conspiracy constitutes a threat to the peace and security of the "Free World", usually represented by Britain or the United States.' (Bennett and Wollacott in Lindner, 2003: 18)

Bond, then, in this new world order is a figure who though British, represents the free world, not just Britain, and a transatlantic hero who battles for principles of the west against paranoid delusions of Cold War enmity. In this age of political stand-off, of ideological change there was a need for someone who could still provide audiences with adventure and bravery while not subjugating themselves completely to the authority that they represented. This was, after all, a new Britain and although audiences still craved action, the conventional heroics of soldiers at war had lost their lustre.

But Bond is not the only espionage figure who could lay claim to being the hero of this new age. There was a different spy who more closely embodied the rebellious attitude of the times, one for whom the enemy was not quite so clearly defined and it is in the contrast between Bond and Michael Caine's Harry Palmer that we can see once again the contrasts of the age. Each character reflects a different reaction to a time which was provoking new ideas and new ideals and in so doing they are almost inseparable despite their differences:

> 'One of the critics called it the thinking man's Bond.' (Sidney J. Furie, *The Ipcress File* DVD commentary)

While Bond defended Britain against the threat from the outside world, Palmer defended *himself*. His individual outlook, his refusal to defer to his superiors, showed a figure with some of Bond's rebelliousness but less willing to conform. While Bond revelled in his role as Britain's all-action ambassador, Palmer eschewed responsibility:

> 'Looking after number one was Ipcress Man's motto… The notion of serving oneself first – and only then Queen and Country was one that touched a responsive nerve in a nation so firmly in the grip of a consumer boom….' (Walker, 1974: 304)

It is Palmer, then, who is a more readily identifiable figure particular to the age than his smoother compatriot, James Bond. While Bond was an amalgam of British archetypal qualities built up over a number of decades, Palmer was a figure who seemed very much of the Sixties. And yet their similarity is undeniable and illustrates how both engendered Sixties values.

REACTIONARY

> 'Connery and Caine could adapt themselves precisely to playing a neutral "meritocrat" who didn't owe his allegiance to a class system, but to his own abilities and to the job he was paid to do.' (Walker, 1974: 304)

Bond and Palmer's attitudes are a reaction to the changes that were sweeping society. While Bond gloriously exploits them Palmer's more working-class hero is the more reactionary. There is more resentment in Harry Palmer than there is in Bond and while 007 revels in the freedoms his job brings, it is freedom *from* his job which Palmer seeks. While Bond has faith in his country's moral right he gives off no sense that he has any morals himself, while Palmer has a sense of decency his officer-bred leaders lack:

> 'Caine's Palmer stands out as a human being, while his superiors are puppets.' (Nowell-Smith, 1965: 70)

Both Bond and Palmer inhabit an uncertain world where self-reliance is the key to survival, but it is Palmer's lack of patriotism that makes him more of a product of post-war Britain and a reflection of it. He is caught in the middle of greater powers and has to survive by choosing the right alliances, ultimately trusting no-one:

'…in the end the Bond of the movies believed in his job because he instinctively believed his country was in the right. Not so Caine's Palmer, who makes no bones about the fact that all he is out for is himself. At the end of *The Ipcress File*, he doesn't gun down Guy Green's traitorous Dalby because he has been betraying his country but because as Palmer puts it, "you used me"'. (Bray, *The Ipcress File* DVD programme notes, 2005)

Each character's views are reflected in the respective film language employed and it is the insularity of *The Ipcress File* that is striking. While Bond films are a glossy travelogue of adventures, with sweeping vistas of glamorous and exotic locations, *The Ipcress File* is very firmly grounded in drab London streets and claustrophobic interiors. Even those scenes which are shot outside are somehow limiting, shot through imprisoning framing devices.

Bond would provide succour to a nation whose world importance was greatly reduced, a fantasy figure that would both perpetuate old stereotypes of Englishness as well as providing a new way in which Britain could dominate the world and Bond's appeal became itself a tradition. Its visual and spoken motifs became a means of pleasure and ritual in which the mass audience could participate, enjoying a sense of security and safety in uncertain times. While 'the bomb' remained a threat in real life, in the cinema Bond diffused it through escapism.

For Palmer, however, there was no escape. His life is the opposite of Bond's, his job is something that does not provide freedom and he has been coerced into his role. Both characters are individuals employed by secret government organisations but, while Bond is irrepressible, Palmer is merely oppressed. While Bond provided escapism, it is Palmer's character that is a more accurate depiction of the lives of many, his actual occupation notwithstanding, and it could hardly be less 'swinging':

'Connery's Bond motored on the consumerist fantasies of the Sixties – effortless sex with fun and sand thrown in for good measure. Caine's Palmer chugged along in the down-at-heel reality of post-imperial Britain.' (Bray, *The Ipcress File* DVD programme notes, 2005)

Palmer has an appeal that is borne of ordinariness. The world he inhabits is one in which espionage is mundane, it is of beaurocrats and red tape, one that resembled many of the lives of those who worked in the growing white collar sector:

'The blueprint of "ordinariness" was followed sedulously in the look of the film – natural locations instead of superman sets – and the overall colour was restricted to the grey-green-brown hue of London.' (Walker, 1974: 305)

Despite this, a feeling of fantasy, of a dreamlike reality can still be discerned, but it is not the exotic fantasy of a dream lifestyle; rather it is a nightmare vision of a society out of kilter. It conveys at once both the familiarity and strangeness of the time and the unease which permeated it. *The Ipcress File* featured a uniquely experimental style of film-making by the director Sidney J. Furie, who deliberately broke with the by-then conventional style of a Bond movie. *The Ipcress File* shows a variety of locations as they have never been seen before and in so doing communicates a sense of discomfort and imbalance that shows a darker side of the Sixties revolution.

INSOLENT

While Bond encouraged a blithe and cavalier attitude which showed no fear and suggested that Britain could and would survive as a world power, *The Ipcress File* spoke of paranoia in a time where Britain was under threat. In this way, Palmer's character became a different sort of hero, someone who was facing a fear that came from the unknown and a threat which may not come from outside but inside, reflecting a society growing suspicious of an Establishment which was self-serving. Palmer's character displayed a functional and detached attitude, which was not deferential to his superiors:

'Ipcress Man cultivated the dumb insolence, as the Army would call it on the charge sheet, of an Other Ranker – the kind who forgot to say "Sir", or left the office door open behind him.' (Walker, 1974: 305)

Palmer's working-class foot soldier was going to have to be incorporated satisfactorily into society. The importance of the widespread changes in the Sixties had yet to be realised but there were issues still to be resolved from within. *The Ipcress File*'s vision is far from a comfortable one and it shows an Establishment that has survived society's post-war upheaval and continues unabashed.

Bond, however, focuses our attention on the positive changes, showing a revolutionised society through fetishising technology. While the Establishment still exists, it is a comforting and, although rather outmoded, still supportive family, embodied in familiar *mise-en-scène* of the Houses of Parliament combined with images of spectacular gadgets. Bond was able to reconcile the past with the future and portray this Britain as one very much at the forefront of exciting change:

'The pivotal historical period of the Bond series was the 1960's…when Bondmania was at its height. The films featured certain aspects of the "cultural revolution": the new vitality of British popular culture, the prominence of science and technology, and the increasing permissiveness in sexual attitudes and behaviour.' (Chapman in Lindner, 2003: 97)

Goldfinger shows how Bond presented ideologies of masculinity, patriotism and Empiric glory, reasserting Englishness and, while this was out of step with much of the swinging cultural scene to emerge in the decade, depicted a discernible shift in values that try to adapt dominant values of the Establishment into something more palatable for an adventurous age. Bond is not a character who is fashionable – in fact he eschews fashion. He is, instead a character who demonstrates many of the more conservative values of mainstream middle-class Britain:

> 'In the Connery and Roger Moore films there is no sense of moral confusion about either Bond or the Britain he represents. In place of confusion, there is a certain self-deprecation, but it is far from enervating or crippling. The films offer a moral universe in which reliance on Bond representing a reasonable moral order was total and did not need to be stated.' (Black, 2000: 99)

Bond films do the same for the idea of Englishness, reinforcing Establishment values that were being questioned and through brute force the character tries to reinforce Britain's status. In this vision there is no need for Britain to change, due to its inherent superiority and thus must remain a defiant figure, cementing standards of behaviour and etiquette. The Sixties may have been a period of experimentation but the outcome would be an amendment to tradition rather than a whole-scale revolution.

Goldfinger begins with a shot of what looks like a power plant shown from a high angle. The camera tracks outward and down to a small jetty, where we see a lone bird making its way through the water toward the quay. A close up reveals the bird to be false and Bond emerges from underneath and out of the water, throwing his comical disguise away.

He quickly makes his way toward the perimeter wall of the plant, past South American signifiers such as palms and rough hewn walls. He shoots a rope from a long barrelled launcher. Inside we see a guard turning around as he hears the sound. The claw has hooked over the wall and the guard comes to investigate but Bond appears from the side, disposing of him with a swift kick to the head.

The introduction of Bond in this pacy opening sequence is a good example of classic Hollywood narrative. Studio based, it is economic in its style and shows a huge difference in the production values and attitude of the British movies we have discussed so far. This is a big budget, Hollywood-backed film, aimed at a large mainstream audience, showing a character that would not only provide a template for action heroes to come but who could redefine the British character and identity. As Bond attacked stereotypical foreigners, so the audience was reassured of stability. There was no need to worry about changing attitudes when Bond helped to reinforce so many beliefs:

> '…the text's racism actually serves to legitimise Bond's role as imperial policeman, and Britain's place in a post colonial world.' (Baron in Lindner, 2003: 144)

Meaning in Bond is explicit. There is little of the interpretive style that we associate with Sixties cinema. In this way it echoes Bond's character, the masculine narrative shows a masculine man, who is decisive and violent. The representation shows little need to explore differences in culture. Bond acts as a penetrative assault on any society which dares to have its own values and instead deals cultural differences a swift kick to the head, dismissing any need for exploration or acceptance.

After descending the outside wall he takes off his wetsuit to reveal a rather elegant white tuxedo. Ever particular of standards, he places a red carnation in his lapel. Beneath the exterior of a new Americanised deadly killer is a suave and sophisticated English gentleman with an appreciation of tradition, of the proper way to dress and present oneself, whose superiority to those foreign threats is proven with decisive force.

The film introduces Bond as a figure of deadly effectiveness, a trained killer who can replace all those rather dull and staid British archetypes of the war films, whose adventures are not borne of arduous duty but still retain loyalty to the crown. Bond works not as part of a team but is an individual, working alone in the foreign darkness. His spirit of independence and adventure show self-preservation to be an admirable quality in a capitalist world opening up new pleasures. If the future was uncertain for Britain, Bond showed us we could survive and if the outside world was threatening the country, we could still depend on our resourcefulness and ability to adapt.

The interior of a Latin nightclub contrasts the foreign culture with Bond's suaveness. A dancing girl is attracting a lot of male interest but their crude leering is in opposition to Bond's civilised demeanour as he enters, pausing to take out a cigarette. He looks at the girl who is passionately shaking her chest in front of her male clientele. She immediately returns his gaze, Bond, an irresistible alpha male. He, though, has other concerns and checks his watch by the flame of his lighter. As he lights the cigarette, there is a cut to a large explosion at the plant. While those in the bar scream and try to leave, Bond, unaffected calmly makes his way in the opposite direction. The dancing girl looks bemused as her audience leaves.

Bond, in this opening, has introduced himself in no uncertain terms. He has established his sexuality, his masculinity and his superiority. His domineering male power is concealed by sophistication and playboy elegance.

A suited man at the bar, without looking at him, congratulates Bond in a South American accent, telling him that a Mr Romales will be out of business. Bond explains in simple nationalistic terms that he won't be able to 'finance revolutions with heroin flavoured bananas'. The girl walks angrily out, flicking her dress in a fit of temper showing her to be – of course – a passionate Latino, who has little control over her temper. Bond has thus dealt with South American culture and its threat of drugs while managing to impress its most attractive inhabitant. It only remains for him to soothe her Latin temper with his irresistible charm.

IMPERIAL

Bond's good manners and ironic understatement are the marks of good breeding and identify him as someone special, reinforcing ideas of old-fashioned standards as still relevant in a time of change. This is a consistent theme that runs through Bond movies, as he makes his way across continents and into countries which have different customs which are viewed as strange or bizarre, and by inference inferior. Bond is from the west and as such is civilised; as he is from England he is well bred and knows how to behave even in the most inhospitable surroundings. As such, while unmistakably English; he reinforces values of western cultural imperialism.

Bond's appeal to a predominantly male audience is well documented and reflects male superiority as well as a cultural one. This overt masculinity is apparent on entering the dancer's dressing room, his domination reinforced by his being clothed while she is naked, and therefore vulnerable. But there is more that implies characteristics of civilisation against primitive. This dancer is rather animal-like and her dark stare is suggestive of aggression. Though Bond can therefore appeal to her sexual instincts, he does not appeal to her on any other level and Bond does not even attempt to communicate with her in any other way. And despite her passion, she is scared by the gun which further reinforces Bond's superiority both in terms of masculinity and of race.

In a time that was producing pop stars with anti-Establishment values, Bond adapts the Establishment's values to something more appealing for traditionalists. While this was the decade that would see youth culture taking a stand against violence, he does not deny or feel ashamed of his use of a weapon, though he has incorporated the fighting skills of other cultures. But Bond's treatment of the dancer is dismissive and misogynistic. He will not hesitate to avail himself of the new morality to get sexual satisfaction and, though he is an English gentleman, this will not get in the way of pragmatic killing. In short, he is adapting traditional British Establishment values to a new age. However, this age is not one of British colonialism but American global imperialism, which would affect British character:

'This matched a shift in British, American and global culture. In Britain the 1960's, with growing individualism, social change, the Beatles, the decriminalization of homosexuality and many other shifts, were challenging the traditions, certainties and myths of Britishness. The notion of the swinging Sixties was intended as a reinvention of Britishness, but it necessarily involved a criticism of what had gone before.' (Black, 2000: 102)

PARANOIA

The opening scene of the *The Ipcress File* is memorable for its use of film time and immediately introduces the distinctive style of filming employed throughout the film. Viewed from inside a car we see two figures emerge from a hotel escorted by the porter. The use of a long lens stretches the hotel into the distance, exaggerating space. Two men get inside the car and while one reads the *New Scientist* the other looks nervously around.

The monotonous music builds tension, creating unease, and there is already a feeling of a world within a world. The view through the front window sees them arrive at the train station. The station porter collects their cases and the dialogue explains that there is a compartment reserved for a Dr Radcliffe on the 7.55 to Nottingham. They walk down the platform and again the long lens stretches the distance and a low angle looks upward creating a rather strange view of events.

There is a feeling communicated in these early shots that all may not be what it appears on the surface raising the idea of the illusory nature of the Sixties. This is not the crazy fantasy of Sixties frivolity, rather it is a feeling that real life may in itself be not quite as palpable as it seems. The everyday is taking on an appearance of strangeness that is quite disconcerting and unnerving with space being either stretched or condensed.

This representation, of course, can be linked to the developments of individual perception, psychological exploration and recreational drug use that were developing as trends but can also be interpreted as reflecting the world in a way that communicates the paranoia and danger inherent in espionage.

The doctor thanks his escort, Taylor, who tells him that he is to be met at the other end by someone called Henderson. Returning to the car Taylor finds the doctor has left his camera and runs back to the train. But when he gets back to the compartment, someone else has taken the doctor's place. The tilted camera shows a confused Taylor who asks, 'Where's Dr Radcliffe?' The train pulls away from the station, revealing Taylor's dead body on the baggage trolley.

The unusual use not only of space but time is noticeable in this sequence as the film's narrative style immediately introduces a sense of uncertainty and instability. The doctor is present in the carriage seemingly until the last moment and it is impossible in real time for him to have been replaced by the mysterious figure. Instability, insecurity and paranoia dominate *The Ipcress File* and give the opposite impression of the soothing confidence of Bond. The narrative style too, leaves questions and there is less explicitly explained for the audience.

Serving to reinforce the notion of personal perception, the next scene begins with an eye and the camera pulls out to reveal Harry Palmer in bed. He switches on his lamp and feels next to him; rising when no-one is there. He looks around but everything is blurred until he reaches for his spectacles; his glasses are perhaps an indication that help is needed to make sense of this new world. Looking around the room we see his small flat. His alarm clock which has been ringing continuously is shown in the foreground while in the background we see him opening the curtains. Two empty wine glasses give information about the previous evening.

This is not the glamour of Bond, though certain attitudes remain the same. Palmer, from his behaviour, is clearly reflecting the mores of the new lifestyle of the young single male, whose sexual relationships are fleeting. He is not a figure of fantasy, however; this bespectacled figure shows that the sort of attitudes we may have associated with Bond have now filtered down to the every day man. You don't have to be an international playboy to now enjoy the freedoms of the time:

> 'Ipcress Man needed to wear spectacles: Bond could not have admitted even to the fractional reality of contact lenses.' (Walker, 1974: 304)

The iconic glasses of Harry Palmer seem to separate him from the other characters. It is after all his unique perception of the world which gives him his strength. Palmer has a distinctly different outlook than those around him, but it is Palmer's world that we see and it is his alternative outlook to those in authority which is emphasised.

Palmer makes himself coffee and gets dressed before having breakfast and making notes on the horse racing in the paper. His demeanour and leisurely approach to life reflect his anti-authoritarian character. Pulling on his suit he checks in his bed to try to find something, first a necklace and then a gun. All the camera work gives the impression we are peering into the scene and watching surreptitiously. He is clearly no Bond figure. In fact he resembles a local government bureaucrat and the mundane is emphasised rather than glamour but nonetheless there is attraction in this independent, modern figure:

'The Ipcress File put deliberate emphasis on those bachelor habits that make a man independent of girls, yet don't interfere with his bedding them down in his pad. Ipcress Man prepared his own meals, whereas if Bond shopped at all, it was at Fortnums and Mason's.' (Walker, 1974: 305)

TRANSATLANTIC

A sign reading 'Welcome to Miami Beach' is pulled behind a biplane and an aerial shot of Miami's white buildings and palm trees is shown, introducing a glamorous location typical of Bond's lifestyle. This is America in all its aspirant luxury. The camera closes on one of the hotels and moves to the pool area. A man dives from the top board and then is shown underwater. A girl also underwater swims by and smiles through a window at the base of the pool. An incongruous man in a grey suit watches her before turning away and walking past a couple ice skating. He walks through the pool area before finding Bond being massaged by a glamorous girl.

Bond can thus be seen to offer a new role model for white middle-class and middle-aged males in this period of historical transition. His character plays upon the fantasies of this demographic group, as Bond is found attractive to younger women as a playboy and though he is often conservative by appearance, he is certainly not conservative in his behaviour and is ready to indulge himself in exotic pleasures.

In this new age of transatlantic tourism, Bond is someone who, while embodying many traditional English qualities, is adopting many American values. The conventional thinking behind Bond is that he is a representation of English values, but as we have seen he is very much a transatlantic creation, someone who represents not only the Empiric values of old England but the new populist values of America. He is a product of new global attitudes and though, like The Beatles it seems that British culture is being exported, Bond's values are shared values while some reject Bond as a British figure at all, considering him a product of America globalisation:

> 'Lee Drummond reacts against those critics who have seen Bond as an essentially British ideological construct and claims him instead for American popular culture. "The story of Bond, his geste or saga has become fully incorporated into the larger, ongoing story of America, The Dreamtime chronicle of that rich, gimmicky and bizarre land that is less a place than a state of mind", Drummond writes. The essence of his argument is that the Bond films were the first truly international media phenomenon of the modern age.' (Chapman in Lindner, 2003: 96)

Bond is an international figure, whose work for the government often takes second place to his own pleasures and adventures. What he shows us is a lifestyle, one of wealth and privilege. While Bond is not himself wealthy and is still an employee – to which his audience can relate – he is someone who lives the lifestyle of a rich playboy and thus demonstrates a dream of wealth, a very American dream.

Thus the film product of James Bond has a strong ideological message, promoting not only American-style wealth but also close ties forged between America and Britain. In this time of growth of global communications and entertainment, Britain actively participated in a partnership with America, sharing its values and outlook, often forged against a common enemy. In Bond films, of course, Felix Leiter is Bond's American friend, reliable, trustworthy and admiring; in real life, America was by the mid-Sixties very much the senior partner.

Britain, cowed in the wake of the Suez crisis, in world terms was now defined largely in terms of its 'special relationship' with America. Wilson's British government was seen as tacitly supportive of America's decision to attack Vietnam (although Wilson successfully kept Britain out of the hostilities) and, though the roles are reversed in Bond, the Anglo-American ties are central to the portrayal.

Bond introduces the masseuse, Dink, to Felix before instructing her, 'Now say goodbye.' The girl looks puzzled but Bond turns her around and slaps her behind, sending her away, explaining that there is 'man talk' to be had. His treatment of the girl is inescapably sexist. His total authority over her is assumed and their relationship, again only implies that Bond is interested in her as a sex object. Her name, and the way she behaves, implies stupidity, this is someone who is not privy to the important conversations of men.

Felix and Bond share some banter revolving around their professional rivalry before Felix puts an end to Bond's holiday with a message from 'M' instructing him in his next mission. He reads the name Auric Goldfinger, commenting that it sounds like a French nail polish. Felix explains some of his profile then points to a large man in a yellow shirt descending a staircase to play cards.

Bond' dismissal of Goldfinger's name demonstrates the sort of rampant anti-European sentiment and prejudice that Bond can reflect in his worst moments. The stereotyping of nations and national characteristics can seem extremely defensive and reflect Britain's uncertain attitude to its place in the world:

> 'Bond's anti-democratic style, that made him ill-suited for life at home, was emblematic of the image of masculinity frequently offered by 1960s films. The imperial/modern heroes were consistently positioned in opposition to the effeteness of the times.'
> (Baron in Lindner, 2003: 144)

Goldfinger is apparently a British capitalist but, even if this is the case in the story, the actor cast (Gert Frobe) was German and almost stereotypically Germanic in look. (Is the suggestion that Goldfinger has adopted British citizenship to 'buy' respectability?) As in the Second World War, it would seem that Britain and America have a common enemy and like most Bond villains, he is 'continental'.

Bond meanwhile makes his way along a corridor of the hotel and without consulting her grabs a young, attractive maid's keys and uses them to open a door. She protests that 'it is Mr Goldfinger's suite' but Bond merely comments, 'I know', and dismissively dispatches her with 'you're very sweet'. Bond does not want her opinion and does not wait to ask permission.

Once inside we hear the voice of a woman, calling out the names of cards. Bond goes out onto the terrace, where a young, slim blonde woman, laying face down on a recliner in a black bikini, is looking through a telescope, helping Goldfinger cheat at cards. Bond turns off the transmitter and the girl turns, and angrily asks his name.

'Bond…James Bond', is the reply as the Bond signature music starts up. The girl, Jill Masterson, tells him that Goldfinger likes to win. Taking an interest in her, he asks whether that it's only helping Goldfinger cheat that she gets paid for and she says vehemently that it is. 'I'm so glad,' Bond says.

Bond turns on the transmitter again and after flicking the speaker to cause Goldfinger some discomfort through his earpiece, he instructs him to start losing or face the authorities. Jill is amused as an irrate Goldfinger snaps his pencil. Switching it off again, Jill tells Bond how much she likes him. She refers to him as 'Mr Bond' but in typical fashion he tells her to 'Call me James'.

Bond's irresistible attraction for women is often questioned by feminists as it plays upon male fantasy of the availability of attractive women. Women are objectified in Bond and though today, he has to some extent become a figure of postmodern irony, at the time of *Goldfinger*'s release Bond could have been seen as reflective of a culture in which women were becoming more sexually active and he a reaction to this. His predatory attitude signals a need to dominate – which repeats itself in *The Knack* – a presumption that all young and attractive women are objects of desire.

Cut, to Bond's hotel room. A telephone call interrupts their (implied post-coital) embrace. It's Felix who wants to have dinner with Bond but he excuses himself telling, him that 'something big's come up'. Jill meanwhile plays with her hair behind him, tickling him, much to his irritation. He agrees to breakfast with Felix, but Jill whispers 'Not too early'. Bond playfully pushes her backward by the head and Bond moves over her and fondles a bottle of champagne next to the bed, telling her it's lost its chill. He holds it above her before getting out of bed, to fetch a refill.

Bond has conquered again. The woman who was previously cold has been won over by his charm and has agreed to sex. The sexual wordplay in this scene reflects how much times had changed since *Peeping Tom*: sex is now fun rather than something to feel ashamed about but it is very much to the male's advantage. While Bond refers to the bottle as having lost its chill, this applies to Jill, who has been seduced, she has now become attentive and compliant which Bond, with his streak of English sadism, seems to find irritating. He has had his fun.

Dressing in a robe he informs her that '…some things just aren't done, such as drinking Dom Perignon '53 above a temperature of 38 degrees Fahrenheit. It's as bad as listening to The Beatles without earmuffs'.

Bond's outlook, then, is separate from the new pop culture age and is delineated as such by his disapproval of The Beatles' music, which is nonetheless considered sufficiently embedded in the culture to be dropped into the dialogue of a mainstream film (how often do real-life figures actually get mentioned in fictional screen texts?). Though he may like sex, he is not to be included in the sexual revolution that confuses male and female roles and this can be seen in his dominance over Jill. There is no pretence at Bond being interested in equality but rather his insistence on certain standards, such as the temperature of champagne, indicates that he has a clear set of values which are based on class certainties and 'breeding':

'An intelligent male hero who does not follow the rules of the Establishment but is an Establishment figure, Bond reflects the way in which many men liked and like to project themselves. He competes with sinister organizations and is a gent with a taste for the high life.' (Black, 2000: 102)

As he looks in the fridge, sinister music begins and a hand appears in the foreground. Someone gives him a chop to the back of the head, causing him to fall unconscious. A shadow of a man in a bowler hat is cast against the wall. When Bond awakes sometime later to emerge groggily from the kitchen, he finds Jill dead on the bed, painted gold.

The iconic image of her painted body has become synonymous with the Bond legend, perhaps due to its literal embodiment of Bond's values. The image combines sex, wealth and power, objectifying woman and perhaps providing us with an insight into Bond's way of seeing the world. The woman becomes a literal trophy and object of male desire.

SUBVERSIVE

While Bond's adventure has begun in a world of glamour, with exotic locations and beautiful women, Palmer walks down the street on a sunlit morning, dressed in grey. There is no sense of escapism with *The Ipcress File*. Palmer is an anonymous figure who would not turn heads. He then goes into what looks like a deserted house and surprises one of his colleagues who is on a stake-out by kicking the door open. Palmer's sense of humour, like Bond's is to treat his work in a less than serious manner but whereas Bond inhabits a world of champagne and hotels, Palmer's posting is distinctly more down at heel. The man upbraids him on his lateness and his lack of tidiness, telling him he should remember that he is still in the army but Palmer, grinning wildly, is unperturbed.

Thus Palmer's character is not as mundane as he may first appear. Interestingly for this post-war time, he is ex-army and reflects a shift away from militaristic attitudes of the war film. He is still involved in activities one may associate with enmity and it seems still providing a role for the armed forces but these are no longer transparent battlefields, they are the now the subversive activities of the Cold War. More significant, however, is his anti-authority attitude. His disregard for his colleague, his untidy and unpunctual habits make for a contrast with Bond's suave and debonair style and cut him out as a more rebellious figure.

Palmer is a slacker and not only does he reject the importance of his work, he recognises himself as a cog in a wheel and actively undermines the significance of his duty. His behaviour is deliberately questioning in a role where unquestioning obedience and loyalty are expected. However, where once such a personality would have been viewed with disdain and even shame, his dissolute behaviour is now more charming (aided by Caine's persona) and it is in fact the regimented characters which have become comical stereotypes, unable to function in the civilian world.

Palmer enters the Ministry of Defence, and walks down a long corridor before showing his ID to gain entry to an area of high security. He enters Ross' office and once again the camera gives a sense of unease by marginalising him and showing the room from odd views, enhancing Palmer's alienation from his surroundings. Ross tells him to stop slouching in typically upbraiding military style. He is a figure of traditional, public school-bred authority, dressed smartly in a suit with a striped tie and, not for the first time in Sixties film, there is a photograph of the Queen on the wall as an image of outdated patriotism. While his back is turned, Palmer reinforces his role as a rule breaker by surreptitiously checking an envelope on Ross' desk.

Ross, an archetypal military man, tells him to stand at ease and Palmer asks him whether the envelope is his B107. Ross tells him that it makes awful reading. 'You just love the army don't you?' He says to Palmer and he responds with a marked difference in emphasis, 'Oh yes sir, I just love the army'. Ross is dismissive of Palmer's sarcasm, telling him it may be appreciated more where he is being sent as he is being transferred to 'Major Dalby's outfit'.

He asks him what he will be doing and whether the move is a promotion, quickly using it as a chance to ask for more money. Ross drolly warns him that Dalby doesn't share Ross' sense of humour. Palmer dryly comments that he'll miss it.

Palmer's irreverence bears similarity to Bond's attitude but there is a difference. While Bond accepts his place as part (and to some extent a tool) of the Establishment, there is a real sense of Palmer's detachment from those for whom he works. There is a younger attitude to Palmer which is much more in tune with the feeling of rebellion in the age. In fact, his character is more reflective of the average worker, who resents his job, looking for additional pay and longing for his return to leisure. Palmer is not committed to a sense of duty but rather tries to find any fun which can be had in his mundane world.

His desire to buy a grill with his increased expense allowance, a domestic appliance associated with women, also shows a shift away from Bond's attitude, closer to the feminine consumerist attitude for which Sixties film is known. While Bond may be able to identify a fine champagne, Palmer's readiness to look after himself and take an interest in domestic matters such as cooking separate him from his adventurous contemporary. Technology for Palmer is something that will make his life easier.

Ross takes Palmer to an imposing building claiming to be a domestic employment bureau and inside is an old lady in a cardigan who is interviewing another old lady, presumably for a job as a cleaner. However, she clearly recognises Ross and calls him 'sir' and tells him that the butler he has asked to interview is waiting upstairs.

The cover of a domestic agency reinforces the impression of this work as drudgery and that, rather than seeming like a clever subterfuge, this world is actually just as dull as that which it pretends to be. The conversations about coded paperwork and forms only reinforce the day to day, cloying routine of Palmer's work.

Ross goes into a large room where he meets Dalby who, standing immediately to attention, has the stereotypical appearance of an ex-army general (short hair, well-tended moustache). The wide expanse of the room contrasts with the narrow claustrophobia of the staircase, as use of space again creates a feeling of strangeness. There is an apparent rivalry between the men and they vie for superiority. Dalby has issued paperwork by which he says he expected to speed Ross' arrival, while Ross says pointedly, 'It was a pity you lost Radcliffe' and claiming that he expected something of 'that sort'.

Ross explains the 'brain drain' of government scientists leaving their jobs at the peak of their careers. He outlines those who left and those who defected 'to the other side' but there are still those who he suspects have been 'lifted'. He thinks he has a lead and instructs Dalby to get Radcliffe back, with the threat that his department may be closed down by 'the people upstairs'. Dalby disputes Ross' authority distinguishing between War Office and Home Office but Ross imposes himself revealing that it is he that set up Dalby's office and telling him he has a 'very good job for a passed-over major'.

This scene, with characters shot from low angles or positioned at the edge of the frame, depicts a warped, antagonistic representation of the politics of espionage and strengthens Palmer's indifference to his supposed superiors, whose status is reflective of an undeserving officer class whose self-serving attitudes and schoolboy rivalries are of a world alien to Palmer. The Cold War is one of hidden hostilities, but moreover the internal wrangling shows discord and discontent in those who have responsibility for the security of the nation. These are changed times and loyalties are less distinct with personal perceptions playing a larger part as the age of the individual has arrived.

Ross tells him about his replacement for Taylor and hands him the paperwork on Palmer, calling him 'a little insubordinate but a good man'. Palmer's character as a cheeky fun loving youth is reinforced as he is then shown smiling to himself, as he watches three young women crossing the road as he waits for Ross. Ross returns and wishes him luck, dryly telling him not to 'forget his mop'.

By equating Palmer's duties for Dalby with the domestic cover of the operation, Ross is perhaps putting Palmer in his place. Or maybe it is Ross' way of telling Palmer to be careful. Whatever, Palmer clearly has his mind on more civilian interests. The fashionable girls who he watches represent the outside world of fun he yearns for. Persistently throughout the film, the sights of London which we may associate with the swinging London films are shown from a distance and Palmer often views them from a dark interior. But once he steps outside, the grey of the city is re-established as though the idea of this 'swinging London' is a dream, a dream not accessible for Palmer:

'Grey, gritty…that's the effect we are seeking. The film is being shot in colour but so monochrome you'd hardly notice. This is meant to be spying for real, whereas the Bond films are for glamour pusses and jokes.' (Furie in *The Sunday Telegraph*, 29 Nov. 1964)

ESTABLISHMENT

Like Palmer, Bond is back in London. And, again like Palmer, Bond has his superiors to answer to. Bond tells 'M' that he knows who Jill's killer is but 'M' reprimands him for allowing his personal interest to interfere with work, threatening to replace him with 008. He goes on to criticise him for becoming involved with Goldfinger's girlfriend.

Bond is bridling at being upbraided and it is apparent that he finds being lectured to difficult. Bond's relationship with 'M' of course is part of his appeal to the audience as he, like the action heroes he gave rise to, has many of the problems we all encounter at work. 'M' is unappreciative and treats him as a naughty schoolboy, often seeming deliberately to avoid praise even though he is not part of the youth scene nor is he part of the older generation, who often disapprove of him. This gives him appeal, not just for downtrodden office workers with difficult bosses but also to the younger generation with strict teachers. Moreover, 'M' is a symbol of the Establishment:

'…007 did not critique Britain's welfare state or class system, but instead implicitly attacked Britain's older generation's "liberal" complacency and inveterate mismanagement. These "blunders" in the mind of young reactionaries were the reason that the Empire was lost.' (Baron in Lindner, 2003: 136)

Bond exits 'M's office into another room, where the secretary, Moneypenny, is filing. Taking his hat from the stand, he asks her what she knows about gold, which she associates with a wedding ring. She invites him to her house and offers to cook him 'a beautiful angel cake' before taking his hat and throwing it back onto the stand. He looks momentarily disconcerted before telling her he has a business appointment. She assumes it's a date with another girl and asks him who it is before she is interrupted on the intercom by 'M' who corrects her. 'So there's hope for me yet', she says. Bond leaves the room telling her, 'Moneypenny, won't you ever believe me.'

This exchange tells us much about the gender conflict of the 1960s and the way in which Bond films show the difficulty for women at this time of changing values. Moneypenny's behaviour is that of the adoring housewife. She is the loyal home-loving woman that would have been a common representation during the Fifties. Her 'angel cake' remark connotes her goodness and domesticity. She is tolerant of Bond's attraction toward other women, knowing that she offers something that he will eventually need, stability. In this scene it is noticeable that she replaces Bond's hat on the stand as a symbol of her preference for him to stay. She also offers to cook for him. Bond, however, must be free to retain his masculinity and Moneypenny is a threat to this.

Bond's place as a virile man is emphasised by his refusal of domesticity and, though he always returns to Moneypenny, he constantly leads the fight against female independence through his sexual conquests.

In a scene of the Establishment at leisure, Bond and 'M' are having dinner at the Bank of England, which could almost be a scene from any time in the last 100 years. Bond is being told that it is the Bank that is the main depository for gold bullion in England. As the camera tracks backward, it reveals the length of the table and the opulence of the room. A waiter is serving them. The man at the head of the table, the stereotypically named Colonel Smithers tells Bond how through estimates of gold reserves, the two governments of England and America are able to decide the true value of the pound and the dollar, which is why they are concerned when there are 'unauthorised leakages' which are being linked to Goldfinger.

This, of course, is a representation from the heart of the Establishment, something that was increasingly being questioned during the Sixties and it is why a Bond film differs from many of the Sixties texts discussed herein. Bond offers support for the Establishment and though it is presented in a rather traditional, not to say clichéd way, it is something that Bond is an integral part of. He is not disapproving of wealth or privilege but rather is a figure who understands how this world functions. Bond is an intelligent man and though he breaks rules when he chooses to it is the rules off etiquette and breeding to which he pays most attention. This can be seen as he samples the brandy and exposes 'M's ignorance on the subject:

> 'Bond was a dream figure in a traditional mode, not a social rebel like the screen figures at war with the reality of society around them. Unlike them he was not aggressively youthful… He was not anti authority… Bond served his country at a time when the country's confidence in its old imperial potency had been shaken by Suez and the retreat of the old certainties.' (Walker, 1974: 191)

Bond suggests that he should meet with Goldfinger socially and in another reference to war time enmity the Colonel provides a rare engraved gold bar left over from a Nazi hoard as bait, which Bond is instructed to collect from 'Q' branch.

If 'M' is comparable to Bond's headteacher, then 'Q' is his housemaster, and again Bond the rebellious youngster has little time for his superior attitude, although he respects his talents. 'Q' lacks humour and is diligent, the very opposite to Bond.

Bond asks to see his Bentley but 'Q' tells him that it's to be replaced by an Aston Martin DB5 on 'M's orders. The car he explains has been specially modified:

> '…the Bentley has had its day. The Aston Martin symbolized the style and the speed that that the 1960s were held to represent. It was fast, stylish, British and deadly, an enabler for Bond's potency.' (Black, 2000: 119)

'Q' explains the changes made to the car ('Windscreen, bullet proof… revolving number plates, naturally…') which will feature later in the film. He asks that the equipment be returned, 'intact for once' and tells Bond that he won't keep him for more than hour if he pays attention but Bond again looks rather intolerant of being lectured to. His fondness for the 'toys' Q supplies, reinforces his childlike quality. It is relative to those around him that he becomes a figure of youth but nonetheless his enthusiasm and cheekiness give him a certain schoolboy rebelliousness. Also evident here is his association with modernity through technology. Bond embraces technology, and his love of 'boy's toys' and gadgets add to the fun of his character.

> 'Despite "Q"'s crustiness, which possibly, in part helped some viewers to soften the potential conflict between traditional Britishness and high technology, the technology associated the Secret Service with the "white heat" of change that the new Labour prime minister, Harold Wilson, had advocated and sought to embrace.' (Black, 2000: 118)

INDEPENDENCE

The Ipcress File, while undermining some of the Bond clichés, also retains many of the features associated with Bond. Walking along a corridor, Palmer shows the same flirtatiousness as he bumps into a secretary and laughingly quips, 'Thank you for a wonderful evening', but Dalby tells him to 'spare the jokes Palmer. I don't have Colonel Ross's sense of humour' in the same way that 'M' might rebuke Bond. Palmer's eye for the ladies, however, has no guarantee of success and he seems often limited to admiring glances.

But Palmer, too, is granted entrance to a room full of secret weapons. Dalby informs him that he is replacing a man shot that morning (Taylor) and allows him entrance into a room with a sign that claims to contain fireworks but contains firearms. Dalby tells Palmer to give his gun to a man in an overall working at a machine, and in return is issued with a Colt 32. Palmer signs for the gun but says he's rather have an automatic but Dalby tells him he'll use the gun given to him and Palmer comically repeats his new boss' wish.

Both Palmer and Bond's actions are persistently free spirited and they define their individuality in their requests for personal possessions; but Palmer's contempt for this unquestioning aspect of his duties is abundantly clear. He has no wish to follow orders as this is the result of a culture bound by the old values of the Establishment.

Dalby takes him to a room which claims to be for a commercial television, perhaps an ironic reference to the manufacture of spies for entertainment. They enter a cinema projection room where Dalby briefs those inside. He introduces everyone to Palmer before showing them all footage of a man named Eric Ashley Grantby, codenamed 'Bluejay', from Albania who he suspects of 'marketing' Radcliffe. Palmer meanwhile is enjoying sitting next to the only young lady in the room (a low angle provides a revealing view of her legs). Dalby instructs them to try and contact Blujay and let him know they are in the market for Radcliffe.

Unlike Bond, Palmer's adventures are far from globe-trotting and on a typically drab, wet London day, he drives toward Nelson's Column. He runs inside an anonymous looking building which we find out is Scotland Yard before asking his friend, Pat, for information on 'Bluejay'. He complains about Palmer's one sided requests for favours and in return he asks Palmer for the number of a 'little blonde' called Rita. Palmer puts on a display of mock shock and tells him he should be locked up. Pat gives him the file and asks him for Rita's telephone number but Palmer, laughing, tells him it's 'disconnected'.

Once again, Palmer's frivolous approach to work is emphasised and, though the swinging London of famous landmarks can be seen in the distance, Palmer has to enliven his day by taunting his jealous colleague who connects him with the behaviour of the sexual revolution.

Palmer watches Grantby's parked car from across a road. A shaven headed man finally arrives and looks around suspiciously before putting another coin in the meter. Palmer follows him past the Albert Hall and into a library. He walks along one of the walkways above the man he has followed before looking below to where 'Bluejay' is sitting. He commands the shaven headed man to fetch some scientific books and Palmer descends the steps, shot at an off-kilter angle, to sit opposite him.

Palmer tells him that he is looking for an important piece of scientific equipment that was lost on a train and asks him to help him get it back. All the while they are watched by a man with broken spectacles. Palmer offers Grantby/'Bluejay' a deal and he hands Palmer a phone number, telling him to call after six. Palmer leaving the building goes straight to a phone box and calls the number only to find it is discontinued. He sees Grantby and his henchman pass by and calls after them. In a scene memorable for its originality, Palmer fights Grantby's protector on the steps outside the Albert Hall while once again being watched by the man in the broken glasses. Palmer is tripped and the shaven headed man uses this as a chance to run to the waiting vehicle.

The presentation of *The Ipcress File* is understated; even the fight sequence is filmed from afar, inside the phone box, giving distance to even the most dramatic action. Director Furie creates a world of quiet tension and underlines the ordinary nature of even the most unusual and dangerous of professions:

> 'I remember when Sidney Furie directed that fight scene outside the Albert Hall… I mean it was like two ants on a mound fighting and Salzman went crazy, he said, "you don't shoot a fight scene like that, you've got to get in there", and Sidney said, "No, that's how you shoot a Bond fight sequence."' (John Barry, *Hollywood UK* BBC4)

TRADITION

While Palmer hasn't strayed far in his adventures, Bond is living a playboy existence at a private golf club. Bond offers to play golf against Goldfinger for a 'shilling' a hole. As he steps outside he sees Goldfinger's caddy, a small Asian man in a bowler hat. The dangerous music sounds again as we recognise the silhouette who knocked Bond unconscious. Goldfinger introduces him to Oddjob, his manservant from Korea.

Oddjob's nationality also outlines him as a villain. Communist North Korea's invasion of South Korea in the Fifties led to the intervention of America and many Americans died in the subsequent war. Though he is dressed as a gentleman his silent, inscrutable demeanour conveys his threat, his foreignness. This threat to the English way of life is shown by the villains' demeanour on the golf course, with Goldfinger and Oddjob conniving to try and cheat Bond out of the gold bullion.

The game of golf is employed to establish the two characters' identities and their differing standards. One thing consistent in the traditional portrayal of Englishmen in largely American-backed films of the time is that they uphold certain standards and Bond is no different. Though he has shown himself to be ruthless, there are certain standards of proper behaviour to be observed. Goldfinger's obsessive desire to win, and compulsion to cheat (we have already seen him undone at cards), make him ungentlemanly:

> 'All was not well with traditional Britain. It was not losing only gold. When Bond played Goldfinger at golf at a luxurious, traditional style club and….having Oddjob decapitate a statue with his flying hat, Bond asked what the club would say. Goldfinger confidently replied that he owned the club. Britain was being taken over, prefiguring 1970's concerns about Arab prestige purchases, and those in the 1980's that focused on the Japanese.' (Black, 2000: 119)

The constant reminders to the threat of freedom posed by other cultures expose the xenophobic aspect of Bond films. His role as international policeman shows a disregard for the decline in Britain's position in the world. He himself is the embodiment of the pleasures that freedom western society offers:

'…the representation of games and sports has less to do with either the older public school ethic or the stereotypes of national character than with the new ethic of consumption and leisure. For the games Bond plays, like the liquor he drinks and the automobiles he drives are a guide to leisure. The sports represented…are the consumer sports of golf, skiing and casino gambling.' (Denning in Lindner, 2003: 63)

As Goldfinger's car is loaded onto an aeroplane the airport PA announces it to be a flight to another glamorous destination, Geneva. As Goldfinger mounts the steps to the plane Bond sits in his car watching from a distance. He is told by one of the flight staff that he has him booked on the next flight out, in half an hour. In a dramatic change of scenery, Goldfinger's car makes its way up a mountain road followed by Bond who is still monitoring his progress via the homing device he placed in the car at the golf club. In a Sixties vision of freedom, a girl in a sportscar, Tilly Masterton, sounds her horn and overtakes Bond, who initially reacts by accelerating after her in a typical show of male bravado but then slows down, repeating to himself that he must show discipline.

Goldfinger's car stops at a bend in the road as he buys some fruit. Bond watches him from above but as the camera tracks back, it shows that he is being watched through a rifle viewfinder by the girl, who shoots at him. In the chase that follows, Bond runs her from the road using retractable blades that extend from the wheels of his car. Feigning ignorance at the cause of the accident he goes to her aid, but she blames him, ignoring his patronising comment that she doesn't look like a girl who should be 'ditched'. She cuts off his attempted introduction and demands to be taken to the nearest garage.

DOMESTICATED

Palmer, too, in a scene worthy of any Bond film, finds a glamorous woman awaiting his return home. However, unlike the itinerant Bond, whose home is never shown, Palmer's meeting takes place in the domestic setting of his apartment. Noticing the light inside his flat he takes out his gun and moves stealthily inside where he finds the female colleague he has taken so much interest in, Courtney. She has his gun and tells him that it is unauthorised. 'My mother gave it to me for Christmas,' he replies cheekily. Dalby has sent her to gain information on Palmer but he is unconcerned and stands over her while replacing his gun. Their physical attraction is clear and she watches him closely before he tells her to use the information she has to find the whisky and fix them both a drink.

Like Bond, Palmer is unfazed by this independent woman but his reaction is not one we would associate with Bond. Palmer defies the stereotypes suggested by his character and profession. As Courtney pours them both a drink he tells her to put a record on while he cooks; surprisingly it's Mozart, which, again, does not conform to the stereotype of the single or working-class man. In this sense Palmer shows the possibilities of the new culture, that behaviour does not have to be limited or defined by gender or class. Palmer does not dominate Courtney but rather shows a welcoming and domesticated side and his taste in music reflects a sensitive and mature nature.

This aspect of Palmer is spelt out in the text as he asks her what she'll tell Dalby. She answers that she'll report that he likes girls, which he confirms, but also that he's not the tearaway Dalby thinks he is and that he likes books, music, cooking. Reasserting his heterosexuality Palmer answers that he likes 'birds better' but tellingly he does not deny his enjoyment of other, less typically masculine past times which in itself serves to reinforce his rebelliousness.

Palmer's capacity for boundary stretching is confirmed by Courtney. 'You were bailed out of detention barracks,' she states, matter of factly. Palmer explains that he was stationed in Berlin where he made a lot of money out of the German army before being made an example of. Quite what Palmer did wrong isn't expanded on but it is clear that he has exploited the situation for his own gain. It has, however, meant that he is indebted to Ross for his freedom.

He asks her to join him for dinner but she says she's not hungry, looking seductively over her glass. There is a reversal of roles here as it seems Palmer in the domesticated role is being seduced, albeit willingly by the widowed Courtney. Michael Caine recalls in the DVD interview how studio executives were concerned that his cooking for Courtney would be construed as effeminate behaviour ('Michael Caine is Harry Palmer' documentary, special feature, *The Ipcress File* DVD). However, far from being effeminate, Palmer is in keeping with a new style of Sixties masculinity that is neither afraid of women nor of appearing unconventional.

There is a dissolve back to the office, where the less organised Palmer is being helped with his paperwork by Jock (Gordon Jackson) when he is phoned by Pat who tells him that Shoreditch police have captured someone codenamed 'Housemartin'. Palmer tells him he'll be right down. At the station, however, intrigue grows as someone has posed as Palmer to visit the prisoner and has just left.

Palmer is taken to cell where the shaven headed associate of 'Bluejay', codenamed 'Housemartin', has been murdered. As with the fight scene earlier, this shot is obscured, this time by the grille of the cell door. 'Looks as if Bluejay beat us to it,' comments Jock and Palmer asks for the prisoner's charge sheet. 'Charged with unlawful possession of

a suitcase', he reads but is informed that the other gentleman took it. Palmer asks the policeman if he saw the contents of the case and he tells him it was 'electrical equipment'. The man was arrested near Sanderson's, a disused factory, and Palmer makes a telephone call to arrange for a police raid ('a TX82') at the factory, only to find it deserted, perhaps very recently.

The police inspector criticises the raid as a waste of time, but Dalby upbraids him by telling him his men were late. When Palmer thanks him for his support, he too is criticised for using the clearance code without permission. 'You know it's funny,' Palmer muses. 'If Radcliffe had been here, I'd have been a hero.' 'He wasn't and you're not,' Dalby tells him curtly, almost pointing out Palmer's difference to Bond.

Palmer looks around the factory and finds a piece of recording tape hidden in a still warm stove. The tape reads 'Ipcress'. Back at the office they listen to the tape but it is just a series of strange noises. The examiner, Chico, asks for more equipment and is told to 'open a file on it'.

Dalby's dismissal of Palmer as failing to make the status of hero once again shows that in these times, perceptions of 'right' and 'wrong', tied up in nationalistic ideas, have been blurred and with them the idea of the hero. While the Bond films perpetuate this ideal, the Harry Palmer films recognise that the military man is more often used by his country:

'Bond was the spy as a hero; *The Ipcress File* was the spy as victim.' (Michael Caine, *Hollywood UK* BBC 4)

MENACE

Bond too makes his way to a large industrial building, this one sitting at the base of a Swiss mountain, with the sign Auric Enterprises before positioning himself to watch the building from the mountains above. A long dissolve indicates the change to night time and Bond enters the plant. He climbs a ladder and looks though a ventilation grid, seeing uniformed Asian workmen inside taking Goldfinger's car apart.

Goldfinger appears with an Asian man who he refers to as Mr Ling. He explains how he uses his car to smuggle gold. Mr Ling encourages him to stop all his other activities in light of their current project but Goldfinger reassures him that 'Operation Grand Slam will have my undivided attention.' Goldfinger's cooperation with Mr Ling reflects a contemporary western perception of China as threat:

'In October 1964 the Chinese exploded their first atomic bomb, ending the monopoly of such weapons enjoyed by "European" peoples. Concern about China was far stronger in the United States than in Britain and can be seen as an aspect of the Americanization of Bond in the films.' (Black, 2000: 95)

Making his way back into the woods above the plant, Bond encounters Tilly, her rifle ready to shoot. She tells him that she wants to kill Goldfinger for killing her sister, but her previous ineptness with the rifle, having nearly shot Bond instead, undermines her independent behaviour. He realises that it is Jill Masterson's sister. Pursued by some of the workers from the plant they run back to Bond's car. In the subsequent chase Bond uses the gadgets in his car to waylay his pursuers but he is forced to halt at the edge of a precipice. Bringing up a bullet proof shield at the rear of the car he then gives Tilly cover as she runs for the woods. Oddjob, however, brings her down with his hat, killing her:

> 'The theme of oriental menace, which both recycled treatments in earlier treatments such as the Fu Manchu stories, and drew on their continual impact, is underlined in the film *Goldfinger* by the large number of blue-uniformed Orientals who seek to capture Bond in and near Goldfinger's Swiss factory.' (ibid.)

Bond is escorted back to his car by gunpoint and forced to drive in the middle of a small cortege which stops at the gatehouse to the plant. The gatekeeper is a kindly looking old lady. As he moves through Bond veers away from the first car and then using the ejector seat throws the guard from his car. Another chase ensues, during which the old lady proves to be very handy with a machine gun, and he is finally caught when tricked into crashing his car.

In a famous scene from the Bond canon, Bond wakes in the dark, strapped to a table. A light comes on and Goldfinger greets him as '007', his cover blown. He is in a large, high tech room, populated by scientists dressed in white coats. Goldfinger explains to Bond that above him is an industrial laser. It moves over him to the base of the table and then begins to burn a line through a layer of gold. Goldfinger explains his love for gold as it makes its way toward Bond, who is in danger of being bisected.

'Do you expect me to talk?' asks Bond. 'No, I expect you to die, Mr Bond,' Goldfinger laughs as the laser makes it way between Bond's legs, threatening the essence of his masculinity. Bond plays for time, telling him 008 will follow and finally persuades Goldfinger to turn off the laser by telling him he has knowledge of 'Operation Grand Slam'. Goldfinger tells him that he is worth more to him alive as another of the scientists comes closer and shoots him with sedating dart.

This landmark scene sets the tone for Bond's future, and much parodied, encounters with larger than life villains who employ high tech, over complicated chicanery as they bid to eliminate him.

UNCERTAIN

While Bond's battle is straightforward the narrative of the *Ipcress File* becomes more complicated and more labyrinthine, like the buildings in which the story primarily takes place. It is not clear who Palmer should be fighting against. When Ross meets with him in his local supermarket (can you imagine Bond doing his food shopping?) and begins to inquire as to how Palmer has settled in with Dalby, the extent of his knowledge is unclear.

Ross asks about the Ipcress file and when Palmer queries him why he doesn't ask Dalby, the relationship of mistrust between Dalby and Ross is apparent as he says he doesn't want him to know. He tells Palmer he wants to see the microfilm not the file and hands him a mini camera, Palmer stonewalls him and Ross threatens him with military prison before bidding him a polite good morning.

The internal conflict embodies a nation whose uncertainty is pulling it apart. The authority figures that do not trust each other represent a nation whose values are no longer clear and uncertainty reigns. Palmer is caught in the middle, out of step with the class-conscious, secretive hierarchy in which he plies his trade. Ross's appearance in the supermarket is incongruous and he declares his distaste for these 'American shopping methods' which Palmer is so at ease with.

Back in the office, Dalby hands Palmer Grantby's discontinued telephone number which is written on the back of an advert for a concert by the band of Irish Guards, and tells him he'll meet him there the following day.

Dalby sits listening to the band, enjoying the music which he describes as 'good patriotic stuff' to Palmer, while the man in the glasses is watching from the back. Grantby arrives and sits next to Dalby who asks him for the 'scientific equipment' again. They agree a price and Grantby hands him the arrangements for collection before leaving, followed by Palmer. As he does so, the man in the glasses also leaves. Dalby is left sitting amongst the empty seats in the park.

The contrast between the uncomplicated patriotism of the military band and the surreptitious activity between the parties in the sparsely populated audience indicates the change in times, and the uncertainty of who to trust is reinforced by the deal being struck with the enemy while being watched by yet another party, the purpose of whose sinister presence is not clear.

 An ambulance pulls into a darkened car park. Dalby is in the front seat. Another vehicle pulls in with Grantby in the front. Dalby nods to those in the back and Palmer and Jack exit with a machine gun to stand sentry. Their counterparts from the car also exit and do the same while a wordless transaction takes place where money is exchanged for the comatose scientist, Radcliffe. The car drives away but Palmer spots a figure in the shadows of the car park and begins firing. As Dalby checks the body, the spectacles on the floor indicate who has been killed – the mysterious figure from the previous scene – and Dalby 'congratulates' Palmer on killing an American agent.

The style of the scene is one of well rehearsed opposition, reflective of Cold War relations of mistrust. The canted camera work adds to the feelings of unease but the choreographed actions of either side suggest a well practiced routine in which money and people both become commodities. The business-like transaction takes place with one side's actions mirroring the other. However, Palmer is framed through the dead man's glasses so similar to his own and a reminder of the danger of this game in which Palmer is trapped.

There follows a curious scene where Dalby and Ross talk about the mistaken killing while, in stereotypical British fashion, enjoying tea. Dalby complains that the CIA should have informed them about the tail. Ross asks about Radciffe's health and tells him he wants surveillance on the scientist. Dalby says he'll put Palmer on the job.

Palmer leaves a building escorting Radcliffe. He accompanies him to a series of appointments and they are followed by a black, suited man smoking a pipe. As Radcliffe begins a lecture, he freezes mid-sentence seeming to enter a trance as a strange sound like that on the Ipcress tape plays on the soundtrack (it is not clear if this is diegetic sound as no-one else in the room seems to respond). The man exits the lecture but Palmer follows him and forces him against the wall at gunpoint. He reveals himself as another CIA agent. He reveals he is following Palmer after killing the man in the broken glasses. He tells Palmer he'll continue tailing him to see if he has anything to do with Grantby and if he does, he'll kill Palmer.

Unlike the friendly support offered by Felix Leiter in Bond films, the presence of America in the form of the CIA in *The Ipcress File* is far more threatening. The clever presentation of the agent in broken glasses as a sinister figure misleads the viewer in terms of expectations; but it also has the effect of presenting America as a threatening presence and one which should not necessarily be trusted.

But it is not just the American agent who Palmer cannot trust and his vulnerability is shown as Dalby meets Ross in the park (once again the soundtrack plays the music of the military marching band). Their presentation is far more predictably British upper-class, dressed as they are in bowler hats and carrying umbrellas. They talk about Radcliffe who is now suffering some form of amnesia and can no longer function as a scientist. They also discuss Palmer, who will try to regain the money from Grantby, and the American agent who is following him, agreeing that if he is found to be double-crossing them, the agent 'will take care of him'. The mounting conspiracies demonstrate the complexity of Cold War relations and Palmer's place as potential fall guy.

After failing to regain the money from Grantby and finding himself tailed at every turn by the CIA agent, Palmer returns to his office where Jock shows him the cover to a book which he claims contains the secret of the scientists who no longer function. The title reads, 'Induction of Psycho Neuroses by Conditioned Reflex under Stress'. Contained within the title is the word 'Ipcress'. Jock leaves, claiming he wants to see Radcliffe to conduct a 'wee experiment' and borrows Palmer's car. He leaves him with the book and tells him to lock it up afterwards but, while waiting at traffic lights Jock is shot through the head.

Pat phones Harry and gives him the news of Jock's murder. Palmer tells Courtney that it must have been the American agent mistaking Jock for Palmer, and Courtney tells him to move in with her for a few days. Harry locks the book away but returning home finds the CIA agent dead in his apartment. Returning to the office he finds the book has gone. He phones Dalby and tells him they must meet. Palmer tells the Major that someone is trying to frame him. He informs him of Jock's death and Ross' wish for the Ipcress file, implicating him in the theft of the book. Dalby agrees to 'clean' the flat but does not help Palmer ('you're just too hot'). Palmer bids farewell to Courtney – who, immediately after his exit, phones Ross.

The claustrophobic atmosphere, heightened by the camera work reflects the feeling of being trapped and the web of characters that surround Palmer increases the intrigue as their relations are not clear. As Palmer tries to abscond, catching the London–Paris train, Dalby meets Ross and tells him about the dead agent. Palmer's attempt to escape is futile and he is captured by someone posing as a ticket inspector.

Waking, without his spectacles, he finds himself in a cell and is subsequently subjected to a period of deprivation. To keep a semblance of time he begins to scratch a tally chart into the wall. After what appears to be a number of days – a passage of time depicted by the markings on the wall and the regular offering of food that is too hot to touch – he is visited by Grantby. Palmer tells him that starving and freezing him won't work and that he has read the file. Grantby tells him that's why he's there. After leaving the cell, Grantby tells the doctor that after a couple more days they'll begin 'the treatment'.

The guards collect Palmer from his cell and take him to see the doctor. He is strapped into a wheelchair and taken to the factory where Palmer found the Ipcress tape. They wheel him into a metal container where he is subjected to a battering of audio-visual torture, the sounds the same as those on the tape. He is watched on a screen by Grantby who discusses the advantage of this new form of torture which is more effective than a beating.

Grantby talks to Palmer through a microphone trying to hypnotise him, telling him to

forget the Ipcress File and his own name. Palmer, however, uses the straps with which he is tied to induce pain and distract himself from Granby's voice, twisting in the straps until his wrists bleed. Grantby halts the treatment and instructs the doctor to pad the straps. Grantby tells the doctor to intensify the treatment and to bring him to the container every time he falls asleep.

Palmer continues to keep his tally on the cell wall but is continually dragged out for treatment. Grantby again tries to hypnotise him and Palmer this time becomes calm, dropping the nail which he has been forcing into his hand to resist the treatment. Grantby tells him he is a traitor who stole and sold the Ipcress File to an enemy of his country. Grantby tells Palmer to obey the voice that says 'Now listen to me'. When Palmer comes round, he again feels pain from his self-inflicted stigmata and Grantby is convinced the treatment is progressing well. However, when the guards come to check on Palmer, he attacks them and escapes his cell.

COLLABORATION

When Bond awakes, it is to the sight of another beautiful woman who introduces herself as Pussy Galore. She tells Bond that they are on Goldfinger's private plane heading for Baltimore as Mr Goldfinger's guest. She introduces the stewardess, Mei-Lei and he asks her for his signature drink – a Martini, shaken, not stirred. He asks Pussy to join him for a drink but she explains that she's on duty, as she is Goldfinger's personal pilot. Bond looks taken aback and then asks her just how personal. She gets angry and tells him that she's a 'Damn good pilot. Period.'

Pussy is the strongest female character to appear in the film. She refuses to be patronised by Bond and shows, unlike Tilly, to be more than capable of looking after herself. Bond is shocked by her ability to fly the plane and he is unable to accept her explanation. Pussy's resistance to Bond's charms ('I'm immune') shows her to be not only to be an independent woman but also, in the Bond universe, implies her lesbianism, her 'deviance'. She presents a challenge to Bond's view of the world and the natural order he represents.

As Bond goes into the lavatory to change, a signal is transmitted to the cockpit. Pussy tells Mei-Lei to keep an eye on him. Mei-Lei, like Tilly, is easily overcome and in this comic scene Bond spots a number of peep holes and covers them before placing his homing device in the heel of his shoe.

After exiting the bathroom suitably attired Bond is met by Pussy who threatens him with a handgun. Bond tells her that if she shoots in the fuselage, they will both be sucked out of the plane due to the depressurisation. He sits himself down and picking up his drink, tells her that he wouldn't dream of refusing Goldfinger's hospitality. She strokes his face with the gun, saying, 'You like close shaves don't you?' Bond looks pleased as he drinks.

Felix Leiter phones 'M' and tells him that he has picked up Bond's homing device and informs him that he's on Goldfinger's jet. 'M' tells him not to intervene. Bond is thus the connection between two institutions and he is the means by which the countries communicate their shared values:

'…Leiter and "M" talk by telephone, offering contrasting images of their societies… Leiter speaks from a light office with the Whitehouse in the background, while "M"'s office is a dark, not sombre, wood panelled room. In one respect this is the future as opposed to the past, but this past is not presented in a hostile light, is open to new ideas.' (Black, 2000: 101)

Bond in fact exemplifies the qualities that each country must take from each other and points the way to a collaborative future.

The plane pulls in to a hanger adorned with a banner proclaiming Pussy Galore's Flying Circus. Bond descends the steps allowing Mei-Lei to exit first but as he tries to help Pussy Galore, she refuses his hand, pointing the gun at him. Her rejection of Bond makes her all the more attractive and he begins to charm her again before he is interrupted by Oddjob who ushers him into a car. Ever the gentleman he tells him he should take his hat off in the presence of a lady before warning Pussy that, '…he kills little girls like you'.

'Little boys too', she adds, refusing again to be patronised.

The car arrives at Goldfinger's stud farm and Bond is taken to an underground cell, but not before another offhand snobbish jibe (Goldfinger's horse is 'better bred than the owner'). Goldfinger meets with his guests, who are rival gangs of gangsters. He acknowledges that he owes each of them a million dollars but then shocks them by asking whether they would prefer ten million the next day. In what is to become a familiar Bond trope, Goldfinger now reveals his master plan ('Operation Grand Slam'), while his glamorous living room turns itself inside out to display aerial photographs and a scale model of Fort Knox and its surrounding area. Goldfinger reveals his plan to raid Fort Knox, which contains the entire gold reserves of the United States. Bond, who has quickly and predictably escaped his cell, watches from beneath the model of Fort Knox. As he does so he is captured by Pussy who again has the better of Bond, taking the gun he stole before escorting him away. Meanwhile all but one of the gangsters, Solo, are killed by invisible nerve gas. (Solo is later killed by Oddjob, thinking he is en route to the airport with a car load of gold bullion.)

Goldfinger is drinking with Pussy on the veranda. They discuss what Pussy will do with her share of Operation Grand Slam. Goldfinger strokes her hand but she moves it away and emphasising her character as a lesbian, she pointedly tells him that she'll have a house in the Bahamas with a sign that reads 'No trespassing'. Goldfinger is informed that two men are watching with binoculars. Goldfinger realises they may be looking for Bond and tells Kirsch to fetch him, instructing Pussy to change her clothing to convince them that Bond needs no assistance.

Bond is pictured in his cell, his superhero status now comically confirmed as he is watched by several guards. He is called up to see Goldfinger and offered a drink. Bond tells him his plan won't work and that it is impossible for him to remove the gold in the time he has. Goldfinger queries whether he actually intends to remove the gold. Bond then is left to conjecture and the plan to blow up Fort Knox with an atomic bomb becomes clear:

'China has provided Goldfinger with the device in what 007 terms "…an inspired deal…they get what they want. Economic chaos in the west."' (Black, 2000: 95)

Goldfinger leaves Bond on the veranda when Oddjob returns and tells Bond he needs to separate his Gold from the late Mr Solo. Goldfinger leaves Bond with Pussy who has now changed her manner toward him, suggesting getting to know each other socially. Walking to the barn, he tells her that Goldfinger is mad and this lifestyle will end tomorrow. The CIA agents look on in admiration, reinforcing Bond's role as a masculine role model.

Inside the barn, in another show of masculinity Bond makes a rough move toward Pussy but she rejects him. He drags her back again until she loses patience and showing her ability to defend herself, throws him to the ground. Some rough and tumble ensues but, this time, however, Bond is stronger and throws her into the hay. He then forces himself down onto her and she relents, embracing him in a passionate clinch. Her 'conversion' by Bond from lesbianism to heterosexuality, makes a 'real' woman of her and is central to the subsequent plot:

'Pussy Galore, is in a sense to Bond as Fort Knox is to Goldfinger, and his conquest of her is a recapitulation of Operation Grand Slam…it is when… she switches sides… James Bond and heterosexuality are able to carry the day.' (Ladenson in Lindner, 2003: 198)

The planes carrying the nerve gas are readied and Pussy instructs them to commence the maternally named operation, 'Rock a bye Baby'. The planes fly over Fort Knox and the soldiers collapse as the gas is released. On the ground, Goldfinger's gang put on gas masks, before they drive in a convoy toward Fort Knox. Bond is escorted by Oddjob. The convoy passes streets strewn with unconscious soldiers and when they arrive at Fort Knox the gate is detonated. Using the industrial laser they open a metal door and then Goldfinger arrives by helicopter. He greets Bond as the bomb is delivered, primed and the safe door opened. The bomb's activation, however, gives off a signal, suggesting that Goldfinger has actually been double-crossed – although this is unclear, as is exactly, for the moment, how Leiter and the troops surrounding Fort Knox are unaffected by the gas, instead pretending to be unconscious.

The finale sees a typical battle with Bond locked inside the vault and having to fight and eventually kill seemingly indestructible Oddjob while outside the American troops overwhelm the Chinese defences.

The American's bomb disposal man defuses the bomb with seven seconds left, the clock now reading '007'. 'What kept you?' asks Bond, coolly.

Leiter tells Bond that Pussy helped swap the gas canisters. He asks Bond what made her contact Washington and he tells him, referring to their earlier assignation, 'I must have appealed to her maternal instincts.' Bond, it seems, has successfully returned the deviant female to the role of mother and put paid to her threat to 'normal' behaviour.

INSUBORDINATE

Palmer, having escaped his psychedelic torture runs to the familiarity of a red phone box and contacts Dalby who is sitting with Grantby, revealing Dalby as a traitor. Dalby repeats the phrase 'Listen to me', instructing Palmer to contact Ross and to meet them both back at the factory. Dalby tells Palmer to forget what he has said and then instructs Grantby to evacuate the factory.

Even at this late stage of the film, uncertainty dominates as it is not clear whether Palmer has been able to have been strong enough to resist the treatment. However, when Dalby arrives at the seemingly deserted factory he finds that Palmer is waiting in the shadows with a gun. Much of this action is obscured as it is shot through shadows and from behind staircases, mirroring the obfuscation at the heart of the narrative. He frisks him and gets him to stand against the wall. Ross arrives and Palmer treats him the same.

With both held at gunpoint, on either side of a wall bisected by shadow, Palmer tells them that he knows one of them is a double agent. Dalby tries to convince Palmer that it is Ross, reminding him of Ross' request for the Ipcress File and accusing him of killing Jock, citing Ross' employment of Courtney as the means. Ross argues that he had suspected Dalby for some time. Dalby tries to use the phrase 'Listen to me' to instruct him to shoot Ross. Palmer struggles with the instruction, seemingly battling against the brainwashing. Palmer hits his damaged hand against the projector and regaining his wits, shoots Dalby.

Ross coolly tells Palmer, 'I was counting on you to be an insubordinate bastard Palmer.' Palmer complains that he was used as a decoy, that he might have been killed or driven mad but Ross merely answers 'That's what you're paid for' before handing him a dressing for his wounded hand.

While Bond's triumph is a triumph for Queen and country, for the joint forces of America and Britain and for masculine heroics, Palmer's is not. Palmer's work is reduced to his salary and it appears that it is only his belligerent resistance to be being told what to do that has kept him alive.

SUMMARY

Bond's adventures would go on for years afterward, reflecting different political situations and different attitudes but in the mid-1960s, he became a great stabiliser for a country whose suspicion of outsiders was at its height – and its influence at a new low. Bond was a reaction to uncertainty, sexual, political and racial. He provided national pride and reinforcement of familiar values while encouraging a new outlook:

'This new sensibility focused on "style", Bond's version of "modern" Britishness, however, rather than being defined by individual "style" or Mod clothing, entailed the licence to kill...007's stance represents a popular, and very troubling British response to the unprecedented immigration from the West Indies, India and Pakistan.' (Baron in Lindner, 2003: 138-9)

Bond embraced technological change, validated old values and welcomed America's support but more significantly thrugh its global values of capitalism and consumerism Bond showed that there was nothing to fear from the future, that the empire still existed and that Britain was still powerful:

'...the Bond films work, creating a fantasy world of beautiful women, easy sex and consumer affluence, and moreover, one in which the decline of British power never took place.' (Chapman in Lindner, 2003: 97)

Despite his distaste for The Beatles, Bond played a similar role in welcoming American values and providing a stepping stone between the old and the new. Though he too rebelled against the Establishment he was instrumental to its continuation, reinforcing Britain's role within a new ideological framework while simultaneously retaining much of Britain's historical identity:

'Far from being a world superpower, Britain had lost its empire and discovered nothing to replace it, bar a leadership in "style", music, clothes and certain films, such as those about Bond.' (Black, 2000: 128)

The Ipcress File, however, is not a Bond film, and Palmer's credentials as a hero though questioned by Dalby, are established by the end of the film. But he is a new type of hero that, like Bond, echoes the age but in a completely different way. It is his refusal to conform which is his strength and his resistance to the system. In this sense he is far more in tune with Sixties ideals:

'For the first time in a British film heroism is no longer the tight-lipped prerogative of a tight-lipped aristocracy imbued with a public school ethos. Nor is it seen as patriotic abnegation, the sacrifice of the individual to the nation. The cockney joker, a classic anti-hero if ever there was one becomes a true hero through his will to survive. And his power of survival resides not in class conditioning…but in the assertion of his own individuality.' (Nowell-Smith, 1965: 70)

The Ipcress File deliberately undermines the conventions of Bond and deliberately situates itself in polarised opposition to its presentation of the world. In its narrative, its style and its characterisation it seeks to separate itself from Bond-style espionage and present a complicated world that can no longer be understood in simplistic terms of good and evil. The political manoeuvring, as well as the portrayal of class, social and gender shifts, show a changing world, not a static one.

Palmer is a figure who seems to inhabit the real world of the Sixties and perhaps that is why the films did not move successfully beyond the decade (unlike Bond). His working-class roots are made for a time of exciting opportunity but, ultimately, he is too individualistic to embody Britishness. He is not a national figure; he is a figure of a time and a place.

CHAPTER SIX: SEX AND THE SIXTIES
— *DARLING* (B/W, SCHLESINGER, 1965)

Films to watch: *The L-Shaped Room* (1962), *Alfie* (1966), *Georgy Girl* (1966), *Here We Go Round the Mulberry Bush* (1967)

LONDON

> '...for Philip French, the ending of this film [*Billy Liar*] epitomised a major shift in British culture: "When Liz caught the midnight train to London at the end, the camera may have remained to follow Billy…, but spiritually the film-makers had a one way ticket to ride south with Miss Christie."' (Leach, 2004: 129)

While The Beatles played their musical interlude and Bond began his missions, Billy Liar's Liz made her way south and this passage to London was being copied by many other young people looking for a good time. The focus for British film would reflect this movement and would now turn its lens on the young 'swingers' who recognised that London was the place to be. This would not immediately halt the emphasis on class but the social divisions would no longer be as black and white as in the gritty realist dramas and Leach points to two films of the mid-Sixties, *Darling* and *Alfie* raised new themes alongside the old, illustrating not only 'social division' but also 'ambiguities in practices and duplicities in behaviour' (Leach, British Film, 2004: 124).

Transients such as Liz would become the focus figures of the second phase of British film which would try to capture a new and exciting modernity and Julie Christie would come to embody this new spirit. Her next role would enhance the public's idea of this new bright star. In *Darling*, her image would be cemented as inseparable from the ideas of glamour, beauty and excitement that came to embody swinging London:

> 'The narratives of these films heralded a new feminine perspective marked by the importance of sexual expression to self-identity; the centrality of individualized forms of glamour to a more female-oriented public life, and London's structural role in enabling and authorizing this glamour and agency…This feminine archetype contrasts with the New Wave's masculine-oriented dismissal of the false pleasures of mass culture.' (Luckett in Ashby and Higson, 2000: 233)

Despite the film's intention to condemn the excesses of the new freedoms, the role of the liberated female would be the identifiable image of the time and Christie herself 'the chief symbol of liberated womanhood in Swinging London' (Leach British, 2004: 103).

Thus it was those who were willing to embrace the new freedoms, were not contained by the old traditions and would explore their own identity that became the centre of attention. As *Peeping Tom* had foreseen, film became a medium that was no longer looking outward but became something more concerned with the self. Image and identity became the themes that dominated. In an age in which celebrity culture grew, what better character to express such themes than someone obsessed with themselves? Diana's picaresque adventure would also be a journey into the self.

As *A Hard Day's Night* shows, film language was becoming increasingly self-conscious, self-reflexive, aware of its role as a medium and its power. Not surprisingly then with the growth in attention on the self, the increasing popularity of psychology, and the impact of celebrity culture and the media, Diana Scott, a self-publicising, self-absorbed socialite, actress and model would become a defining, Oscar-winning role for Christie:

> 'The success of *Darling* was to be the start of a virtual cult of Julie Christie.' (Richard Lester, *Hollywood UK* BBC4)

If Christie was an actress who radiated the excitement of the times, it is her own rising celebrity as a film star which helped Diana Scott's character to be viewed more as a strong and independent female, who, despite her lowly position refuses to allow men to subjugate her and actually achieves her goals by the end of the film, albeit shallow, materialistic goals. Christie was becoming the glamorous star of the time. Here was the new face of the new media age whose liberated success was being held aloft to the nation as an example of a new type of woman:

> 'Julie Christie was to become the cinematic face of the Sixties and as such was the embodiment of what was now being called swinging London.' (Richard Lester, *Hollywood UK* BBC4)

However, while even today the Sixties is still associated with this glamour, most of the films that explored the swinging lifestyle actually showed this hedonism to be shallow and hollow. Despite an acknowledgement that young people were choosing to forego the values of the previous generation, many of the films focused on the dangers of following this kind of life. The morality of the Fifties could not just be disregarded wholesale. There would inevitably be a struggle and this was reflected in film.

Christie would star alongside matinee idols of the Fifties, Dirk Bogarde and Laurence Harvey. Harvey, the star of new wave forerunner *Room at the Top*, and Bogarde, the pin-up boy of many Rank productions, may have been the bigger names but their characters, possibly due to their world weary nature, seem from a different age. Bogarde, playing Diana's reliable boyfriend Robert, was beginning to branch out into more challenging roles in films such as *Victim* (1961) and *The Servant* (1963); but Harvey who would reprise his role as Joe Lampton in *Life at the Top* (1965) would not revive his earlier success. It is Christie's character who is the most colourful in this monochrome world, exuding a new attitude. The middle-class sophistication of the older male stars seems pale in comparison and Diana's lust for life and excited ambition capture the moment:

> 'People were not yet talking about swinging London and though we were all more relaxed about sex, the pill wasn't widely available. But the city had become a magnet for a new generation of affluent young people and was attracting back the independent film-makers who had spent the beginning of the Sixties up north.' (Richard Lester, *Hollywood UK* BBC4)

ZEITGEIST

Darling shows, in Diana Scott, a sexually active character who uses sex and beauty as commodities and in so doing confronts the age's changing moralities. This was particularly important in examining the attitudes toward women whose role in society was evolving more rapidly than those of men and around whom many of the films of swinging Britain revolved. *Darling*, in focusing on Diana Scott's adventures, highlights many of the conflicts of the age.

There is also a multi-layered complexity to *Darling* that revolves around the theme of celebrity and star image. If Julie Christie embodied the zeitgeist of the Sixties in her first appearance in *Billy Liar*, then, in *Darling* this role is developed in the glamorous figure of Diana Scott. However, whereas in the earlier film she was the spiritual embodiment of the naïve and guiltless pleasures of the Sixties, here she represents the cynical exploitation of such liberation and through the exploration of such excesses she falls to her inevitable demise as she first enjoys, manipulates and then falls foul of the pleasures which she endlessly seeks.

The development of the idea of sexual liberation inevitably led to questions concerning the freedoms allowed to women. If sexual emancipation led to a questioning of conventional morality then it also provoked a debate about the accepted roles of men and women. Women, as can be seen in *Goldfinger,* were still being promoted as figures of sexuality, as objects of desire or regarded as housewives and homemakers.

The plight of women was becoming ever more problematic. The theory that the contraceptive pill would free women to sleep with whom they liked ignored the reality of the way women were subjected to society's double standards. The new morality was creating an ideal of freedom but refusing to acknowledge that women could also be the victims of this.

The objectification of women became a central theme of many of the films of the time. In *Alfie,* the lead character often refers to women as 'it' and he uses them for his own convenience, showing little ability or willingness to engage with them as people. *Darling,* however, is a film which shows a woman whose outlook is probably ahead of her time as she 'enjoys' the freedoms and liberation to the full. While the country embraced Alfie for his cheeky charm (in large part due to Michael Caine's charismatic performance), a character who became symbolic of the freedoms of the Sixties, Diana Scott, the central character of *Darling* has since been rather overlooked due to the differing moral standards for men and women and this has resulted a rather male-centred view of the times:

> 'It was seen from a male point of view. She was seen as mercenary and selfish. And it could have been, if you looked at it from a women's point of view, the only way out or brave actions, she took but it wasn't…she was condemned in the end so it wasn't quite as generous as we might have imagined it was.' (Julie Christie, *Hollywood UK* BBC4)

The sexual liberation was heavily biased to benefit men and it is clear in *Darling* that this is a morality tale which punishes Diana for using sex to advance herself in a male-dominated society, where women are judged on appearance, which is itself a saleable property.

CELEBRITY

But *Darling* is also interesting for other reasons, a film that, more than any other discussed in this book, seems to locate and identify many of the changes that the Sixties brought about and would carry forward into the future. It identifies the growing importance of the media in the contemporary world and identifies the cultural capital of celebrity. The appeal of a media-generated status is highlighted and it also focuses on many of the conflicts produced by society's change. A tale that is unusually pertinent today, it can still be seen as a damning indictment of a culture that values the shallowness of fame and, thus, serves as a precursor to the sort of celebrity culture we have today.

Julie Christie may have been embraced by the nation for her beauty, style and poise; however, in *Darling* she may often be seen as a scheming, duplicitous money-digger whose every move can be explained in terms of her as a commodity. While *Billy Liar's* Liz is idealistically indifferent to the commercial world, Diana as a character is inseparable from the idea of women's commodification:

> '…like the working-class youth of the 50s, the 60s girl was placed firmly within the context of consumption. She was a figure around whom the wheels of marketing were spinning and liberal commentators worried about how far a desire to conform lay behind her purchases, making her prey to the designs of big business and the media. Nevertheless, in some senses the attempts of advertising, magazines and television to appeal to the young woman reinforced the impression that she was exercising choices which she could willfully withdraw.' (Geraghty in Murphy 1997: 157)

The story then can be viewed as a morality tale, with Diana subsumed by her indulgences which are the result of the changes in culture. Diana while striving for happiness is completely absorbed in the sins of the age which though alluring, are ultimately empty and facile. She is cast in the Dorian Gray mould as a victim of her own beauty whose portraits of happiness hide an ugly monster produced by sin. However, viewed by those who themselves were becoming enamoured by the new entertainments of which Hoggart had warned, she was still irresistible:

> 'Diana Scott's story was intended to reproach the vanities of the new Sixties acquisitive society…But social comment is not normally a recipe for a successful film. What Schlesinger and Raphael offered as well was glamour, set in the new world of the 60s media scene.' (Richard Lester, *Hollywood UK* BBC4)

As she reflects society's conflicts, Diana may be viewed in more than one way. She can be seen as a helpless victim of her own fate; she may be viewed as someone who precipitates her own decline; but perhaps more interesting is the way in which Diana's character is represented and received in terms of our understanding of Sixties woman.

She contrasts greatly to the women shown in most films of the time, which even in the latter part of the decade often conform to ideas of women's predominant role of mother or lover. She is certainly a world away from the largely subservient women featured in the new wave, whose traditional roles reflected the limited expectation of women in the Sixties:

> 'I suppose it was something to do with wanting not to be curbed, wanting not to obey the sexual mores of the generation previous to you, wanting to feel there was nothing you couldn't do, that includes sexual and that was absolutely true of us in real life.' (Julie Christie, *Hollywood UK* BBC4)

ADVERTISING

The film's title sequence features a billboard of an image of third world hunger over which is pasted the magazine cover image of Christie/Scott with the words 'My Story'. The magazine, entitled *Ideal Woman* gives us, right at the start of the film, an ironic representation of public image and the conflict between Diana's image and her reality. Diana is thus immediately positioned as a product and her 'story' will become the theme of the film. Her character throughout the film displays little in the way of self-knowledge and it is this lack of self which causes her to be shaped throughout the film. Diana's appearance on the front cover of *Ideal Woman* immediately raises expectations of how she is presented to the public and introduces the idea of an image sold to the public.

The decision to film in black and white suggests a cynicism that would have been alleviated by colour but there is still the influence of the new wave here as the story is not actually about glamour, though it features the trappings. The dominance of glamour over real life issues, introduces the intertwined themes of superficiality, celebrity and status. The viewer is involved in Diana's tale (which is voiced-over by Christie) in the form of an interview where the interviewer is keen to get Diana's own story; but more subtly, we may wonder how far the narrator can be trusted. The duplicity of the subjective narrative, as in *Alfie*, calls into question the idea of reality, which would be further deconstructed in this period through the more experimental films to come, but here Diana's version of events foregrounds the importance of representation.

The montage that follows introduces her rags to riches story as she looks back over her early life and we see flashbacks to her childhood and her formative years. Her friendly and affable tone has the effect of making her seem very credible and during the glimpses of formative moments in her life she is self-effacing and charming, in reflecting the down to earth nature often used in magazines to portray the 'real person' behind the star. The experimental nature of Sixties film-making is to the fore as the narrative communication of thought and the images on the screen are merged, showing a freeze frame of Diana as a young girl in school uniform, but this is not representative of the film's dominant style which is generally more formally conventional.

'I do remember how I was always the sort of child who got picked on to do things,' she relates, as her starring part in the nativity play highlights her angelic looks. 'You must be very proud of her Mrs Scott, she's darling', says one of the audience to her proud mother. 'She's going to go a long way, you can see that.' The words of the admiring parent are, of course, an example of dramatic irony, indicative of Diana's fate and whether her 'long' journey actually takes her anywhere will be questioned by the end of the film.

The next shot, another freeze frame, plays on Christie's role in *Billy Liar* reprising the scene where she walk changes the mood of the movie. She is pictured insouciantly walking along, swinging her handbag. 'This is me aged twenty,' she says. 'I don't know what I was wearing. Terribly Chelsea, I thought I was. Really I suppose I was as square as an ice-cube.' The music that accompanies her is upbeat, up tempo and captures the carefree mood of the time but also locates the real swinging lifestyle specifically in West London affluence in its reference to Chelsea. It is almost as if 'Diana' is looking back at 'Liz' and judging her naivety.

The difference in the two characters is highlighted as Diana, very much a product of the time and place, is spotted by a camera crew conducting vox pops. She is shown to be extremely excited at the prospect of being 'on the telly' and when interviewed she views herself as a rebel:

'Oh yes I hate convention, you have to breathe, you have to break away.'

'But isn't the breakaway of yesterday the convention of today?'

'Well then you have to break away again,' she replies, pleased with herself.

Diana, however, seems to miss the interviewer's point, that fashion is transient and that in following it, far from being rebellious she is actually conforming and it is her willingness to conform to others' perceptions of what she is that proves instrumental in her downfall. Throughout the tale Diana bends to other people's expectations as she shows herself to be a social chameleon altering to suit her surroundings.

The continuation of the interview is, in a scene reminiscent to *A Hard Day's Night*, then seen in an edit suite as Robert watches himself on multiple screens, questioning Diana about the young people's conformity to conventions in dress, dancing and talk. Like the Beatles' film the mediation of events issimilarly highlighted with the media trying to make sense of the latest trends. Diana vehemently denies being conformist despite being dressed in what he describes as the height of fashion, her superficiality indicated from the outset.

Robert leaves the TV studios having shown the edited programme to Diana. It is clear that she admires his intelligence and thinks that he has an exciting job, which he modestly dismisses as being a 'professional question mark' whereas she is dismissive of being a 'professional bosom' having modelled for *Bride* magazine. Ironically she is modelling a domesticated lifestyle, one that she herself will never accept. Diana is ambitious for more than being someone's wife and sees fame and wealth as being the keys to her happiness. She is shown in close-up, impressed when Robert walks to a Jaguar car in the car park —although it turns out not to be his.

INDUSTRY

The voice-over then describes how 'we just sort of started to meet...There was nothing deliberate about it at all'. The camera pulls out from the car park to reveal the industrial landscape surrounding the TV studios thus positing it very much as an industry. There is little glamour and it highlights the construction process of the product, the fiction and the reality. The next shot is similar as it shows a river, where the lovers are meeting and throwing stones in the water. 'Heads we do, tails we don't,' Robert says, enigmatically. Diana looks at the dilapidated cottages on the riverside and expresses how much she'd love to live in one. They are being refurbished and their dialogue shows how they are being sold to a new type of customer, as a 'home of distinction'. There can be no doubt that while society is definitely changing, much has to do with packaging, image and the way in which the product is sold. The difference between Diana and Robert can be seen here. While he laughs at the way the houses are marketed, Diana sees them as an ideal, something to aspire to and which potentially could make her happy.

It is now becoming clear for the viewer that Diana too is very much like a product. Her interview with the magazine interviewer is not as dependent upon substance as it is in the way in which Diana conveys the story. We are becoming aware of Diana, not as a person, but more as an image, a character representative of the commercialisation of women in the Sixties and the underlying problem of selling an ideal.

The next scene shows Diana's husband sitting and learning Italian from a tape; although he encourages her to join in, she clearly isn't interested. 'Oh it's so boring',' she says. He argues that it was her idea in preparation for a holiday and that he will continue. This further use of dramatic irony prepares us for Diana's ultimate fate as later she will agree to become an Italian princess, the hollow victory in her rise through society.

A tape recorder is rewound and it appears it must be the language tape but in a deft edit it turns out to be one of Robert's, as he interviews Walter Southgate, a famous novelist who refuses to be part of the establishment of 'literary lions who constantly lick each other'. This character is set in opposition to Diana, a man with talent and integrity whose success is not built on self-aggrandisement, fashion or superficiality. He is also, contrary perhaps to appearance, an actual rebel, someone who will not conform and, in this aspect too, he contrasts with Diana, who is so easily influenced by others.

This is made transparent as Diana, who has accompanied Robert, is shown seemingly listening to the interview with interest before the voice-over reveals the extent of her interest is confined to admiration of Robert. She describes the writer as '...a funny old bloke, spouting his head off. I'd never met anybody like Southgate, suddenly one felt madly *in*. I mean, this is one of the great writers of the century and here I am. It was extraordinary. I don't really remember much anyone said. That wasn't really the thing. The thing was they accepted me.' Diana's response to meeting Southgate is not to learn from him but rather only to bathe in reflected glory. Her fashionable language of being 'in' exposes the superficiality of both her character and the nature of celebrity. Diana's admiration for Southgate is not for what he has achieved but for his notoriety.

The next scene shows the lovers kissing passionately on the train back to London, where they then telephone to say that they won't be able to make it home that evening. They purchase luggage before going to a hotel room together, where they masquerade as a holidaying couple. The suitcase is filled with newspapers (the headline speaks of 'All Hope Lost' for buried miners, which may remind us of the now unfashionable working-class lives of the early new wave).

'The thought of breaking up someone's family was absolutely repellent to me,' Diana continues as she relates her story. 'If anyone had told me I was doing something like that I'd have been absolutely horrified.' The camera, however, reveals Diana looking from a telephone box across the road from Robert's house watching his domestic life. Diana is then shown around a large tenement flat, and the voice of the estate agent continues over an image of Robert leaving his wife and children, suitcases in hand. A letter to his wife, Estelle is left on a table as Diana achieves what she wants.

Jazz music introduces the lovers' new found freedom and a montage sequence shows the accumulation of messages, trinkets and photographs on the mirror and on the mantelpiece indicating the passage of time. Diana sheepishly introduces Robert to her goldfish, a symbol of domesticity. At Christmas Diana is writing cards and interrupting Robert's work. She hears noise from the flat above and as she steps outside the flat she sees two black men before returning excitedly to tell Robert that she has seen 'two of the most delightful looking negroes' going into the flat above and wondering what could be happening upstairs.

Robert suggests having their own party but the next scene shows Diana in the bedroom with the bed covered in coats wishing that everyone would go. A jump cut later and the coats have disappeared and now Robert and Diana are lying on the bed. The lively jazz music that accompanies this sequence seems to convey the free spiritedness of the age and the combination of Diana and Robert embodies new values of modernity. 'Your friends are so pretty,' comments Robert. 'Yours are so intelligent,' replies Diana. However, the first signs that something is wrong in this dream relationship begin to appear when Diana gets jealous of Robert spending time with his children (despite the voice-over's assurances to the contrary).

Robert proposes marriage but Diana refuses, claiming that she is happy as things are; but as he begins to make love to her she watches herself in the mirror distraught. There is a conflict here, as Diana, an example of new, liberated womanhood, seems to show self-loathing, perhaps reflecting contempt at not being able to fulfil the role of housewife. This ambiguity in the text illustrates the problem of Diana's role as an independent, modern woman. It is not clear whether she should be considered a success as such, or whether she is presented as a failure for not conforming to society's expectations of domesticity, demonstrating the conflicting ideas that the Sixties presented to women.

The next image, however, is of Diana, ecstatically happy in a pose as the 'Honeyglow' perfume girl, the contrast between the idealised Diana and the actual person immediately evident. The illusion of this advertisement is reinforced as we see where it is situated, next to row upon row of rail tracks, as a train lumbers noisily by. Robert is on the train, on his way to another report, clearly symbolising an imminent parting of the ways with Diana. This time he is inquiring as to 'the state of the nation' and asking whether Britain has grounds to feel ashamed. In a series of vox pops (which, appear to be 'authentic' and not staged with actors), Robert asks the public about what makes them feel ashamed of contemporary Britain. The answers are various, citing traffic problems, a lack of hard work and the prevalence of homosexuality – this a presumably unintended irony of the text, given Dirk Bogarde's own off-screen sexuality, at the time a well-kept secret.

As Robert types up his notes, he attempts to phone Diana but she isn't home. Her interest in domesticity has waned and she is at a charity gala in aid of 'world hunger'. 'Normally I don't do charity work, it's terribly draggy,' Diana says, but as the camera continues to explore the opulent building holding this grand event, she reveals why she has attended. 'But Robert was away and Miles Brand just happened to phone the same day.' While Diana describes how she came to be at the party, we see Miles, dressed in dinner jacket, greeting guests. Diana explains that it was he that he had chosen her as the 'Honeyglow' girl, and future scenes vaguely suggest Miles indeed works in PR or corporate marketing.

In the now familiar voice-over we can begin to interpret Diana's actions and see her motivations. Clearly not an altruist, Diana is attending the charity event for her own advancement. The introduction of Miles as her employer demonstrates her relationship to him is based on her commercial potential and infers his ownership of her.

As Miles vainly checks his reflection in a large gilt mirror, Diana explains how he was not a part of her private life. A guest approaches him and accuses him of admiring himself 'as much as ever' and being a man after his own heart. The verbal duel that follows between this pair demonstrates their competitiveness and casts Miles as a womaniser. Their barbed comments are designed at one-upmanship and though they kiss each other it is with no impression of actual friendliness. The society Diana is now entering is a competitive one, where there are no real friendships but rather relations are based on mutual advantage.

Miles approaches another acquaintance called Shaw, a film-maker. Miles is concerned that he won't want to make commercials for the Glass group but Shaw reassures him that 'a lie can be told with integrity, like anything else', once again reinforcing the importance of image construction. 'Who's the crumpet?' he asks of Miles, nodding to Diana.

Miles introduces Shaw to Diana. A Member of Parliament is speaking on the stage, praising the generosity of private benefactors to charity. As we see a shot of the well-dressed crowd, he comments how he has never seen a group of people so clearly with their hearts in the right places. The subsequent shots show women bedecked in jewellery, one checking her own reflection as he speaks about their understanding of the plight of people in the third world. The black serving boys are shown as he talks about fellowship with different races, creeds and colours and a rather plump woman is shown eating sandwiches as she gambles at a roulette wheel, while the speaker talks of the agonies of malnutrition.

Diana's access to society has been enabled by her beauty and she is now swiftly using it to her advantage. Her ability to adapt to new surroundings is apparent and she makes contact with Shaw who can put her in the movies but she will have to be ruthless if she is going to succeed with people whose lack of humanity is highlighted while the MP makes his speech. Miles' ironic reference to Pepsi-Cola and crisps highlights the changing tastes of an increasingly Americanised Britain but also his distance from this new mass-culture. There is very little of the 'new' Britain in this gala except the relentless consumption of an over indulged elite who continue to exercise their influence in society.

Miles greets one of two men who are seated on a couch at the top of the stairs. One man, a rather effeminate character, Alex, comments on the black serving boys who he says he would like to wrap up and take home, as they, like Diana, are treated like objects. Alex, whose manner indicates open homosexuality, highlights the differences in standards between mainstream society who, as seen in the vox pop would see this as unacceptable and the type of high society who set their own standards.

As they walk to the library, the MP comments how the only way to preserve a library these days is to build a gambling den around it, reinforcing a common contemporary impression of moral decline. Alex watches them with disdain, before beckoning to his companion and walking down the stairs, looking intently at one of the black servants. As he does so the camera tracks in to a large picture of the Queen on horseback, saluting, while Diana is heard reciting Shakespeare – '...this royal throne of Kings, this sceptred isle, this earth of Majesty...' – to the MP, who looks on lasciviously.

The *mise-en-scène*, similar to that used at the prison in *Billy Liar*, emphasising the Queen as symbol of the country, reflects a growing critical view of monarchy which would not have been seen in British cinema prior to the Sixties. The Queen is here shown as a figure symbolising the Establishment, full of repellent, selfish and greedy people who make their own rules and thus the very fabric of society is being questioned. No longer is the Queen a representative of *all* her people but rather she is a symbol of a very few wealthy people whose place is at the top of society.

ADVENTURE

That evening Diana and Miles are walking outside a new office block, with a modern sculpture on the terrace. Diana enquires about the statue and Miles says it is known as three couples taking their pleasure while a fourth looks on. Diana's successful progress into society is continuing, but as she walks past the statue with Miles, her position can be inferred. Of course sexual freedom is something associated with the age but here is not being linked with ideas of freedom but rather with ideas of power and commodity.

Entering the building and exploring the suites, Diana, in an indication of the sexual adventures to come, wonders what life would be like if it took three sexes to make a child. Miles, hinting at his own love life, answers that matters are complicated enough with two. She asks about the safe in Miles office and puts on a mock spoilt voice as she quizzes him on the contents. She tries to make him open the safe but he refuses, then she tries bribery, asking him whether he'd do it if someone made it worth his while. Miles sits shaving and shaking his head, puzzled, before asking him whether he has ever been 'really afraid'.

For Diana, Miles is a mysterious and attractive figure. His wealth, power, good looks and confidence make him seem as if he has everything and contrasts with her own insecurities. Her question about the sexes indicates that to get what she wants from Miles she will have to do so through sex and experimental sex at that. He is clearly not easily manipulated and Diana's good looks are not enough to give her control. As she continues to quiz Miles a conversation about takeovers ('how do they know when you're interested?') clearly becomes a metaphor for sexual interest and when Diana can't get Miles to open up emotionally, he becomes even more alluring.

At a casting session, Diana sits as Shaw and two other men scrutinise her. After subjecting her to close inspection they give her the title role in Shaw's new film. They explain to her that she will be playing 'Jacqueline'. Shown the book Diana nods approvingly. This session, probably arranged by Miles, shows that he is granting her what she desires in Mephistophelean style but in this we also recognise the power that males traditionally have over females in both industry and society as Diana is once again regarded as an object, exposing the Sixties myth of the new liberated female.

At the film's premiere, there are more indications of Diana as a victim of male-dominated society, as we see her in the role of 'Jacqueline' chased down the staircase of a Gothic mansion. Screaming in horror she is shot to the ground by an unknown assailant with a pistol after which the titles appear and we realise that this is the opening scene. 'So much for me', Diana comments to Robert in the audience, 'that's me lot'. Robert sits in disbelief as she explains that there was another scene that was cut. 'From now on it's just about who did me and why,' explains Diana in dialogue which seems to be mocking Diana in dramatic irony. She turns around seemingly seeking someone and then sees Miles with another woman. He smiles but she looks jealous while Robert seems to understand what is going on.

Returning home, Diana asks Robert what he thought of Miles and is pleased when she thinks him jealous. Diana tells him that she is pregnant. Robert is pleased but there is an underlying tension brought on by mistrust.

Though it is not clear whether Diana is sleeping with Miles, Robert is convinced that Diana's motives are self-seeking and he coolly accepts that she may want to sleep with others or manipulate their sexual interest. Therefore there seems little chance that the arrival of the new baby will indicate a happy ending.

The noise of squeaking toys begins the next scene. A shop window displays fashionable clothes but then the camera moves down to a display of toys and dolls. A hand reaches down to grab a teddy and it belongs to a delighted looking Diana who shows it to her friend. She wants to wear a maternity dress to a party that night, although it is too early in the pregnancy, showing how she craves attention.

Diana's voice-over explains how she hadn't thought of the consequences of being pregnant as she walks in carefree fashion down the street with her friend. As she walks she progressively becomes unhappy as the voice-over describes how she realised it would ruin her career and mess up 'everybody's' lives, including Robert's and how she couldn't then go through with it.

Diana's attempts at shopping for baby goods aren't enough to persuade her of the appeal of motherhood and it is noticeable in the dialogue that she refuses to take responsibility for her decision to terminate the pregnancy. Instead she views herself as the victim as she connects her own situation with her new friend Heather's miscarriage, but with a cold lack of empathy.

Diana books herself into an abortion clinic, a contrast to the depictions of abortion shown by the earlier new wave texts, where back street abortions were linked with shame, deprivation and degradation. With abortion soon to be legalised but clearly accessible to some with the means, Diana is pictured handing over a large wad of notes to a doctor, in a commercial transaction. A cross dissolve shows that time has elapsed and she is now lying in post operative bed feeling 'empty'. When Robert visits her she tells him she will be staying with her sister and not returning to the flat ('don't forget to feed the fish').

In a brief interlude Diana is seen at her sister's house, playing in the garden with her nephew. From this we see Diana's background and the contrast between her suburban middle-class roots and the metropolitan life she leads in the city. It is apparent that Diana's sister lives a suburban life outside London and the way in which her sister's life is portrayed is something more akin to the Fifties. At a dinner party she is introduced to a rather upright character named Rupert to whom Diana clearly isn't suited. Her sister and her husband discuss her that evening in bed and it is apparent from their conversation that they are trying to match-make her with Rupert, who they see as a potential husband.

There is a clear lack of understanding of Diana and they cannot fathom why she has turned out the way she has but it is in this rather short sequence from the film that we gain a brief insight into Diana's reasons for living the life she does. The sedate lifestyle of her sister, though comfortable, lacks excitement, the very antipathy of Diana's urgent life. However, *her* attitude is seen as anomalous by her family and gives us an understanding of the limited expectations that women had at this time beyond getting married.

As the couple talk, we see Diana returning to London. They discuss her relationship with 'this chap of hers in London' and her sister is astutely convinced that the relationship is completely finished. This shows that although her sister shows no understanding of what Diana wants, she does have an idea of what she *doesn't* want. As they discuss her, she is shown on the train and when she returns to the flat, takes her coat off to reveal she is dressed in her night gown, explaining that she left without even getting dressed because it was so boring:

> '…since the film treats Diana as an enigma her family cannot be pinned down as the source of the problem she poses. Nevertheless Diana cannot ignore the family, and much of the of the film's narrative traces her failure to establish her own family.' (Geraghty in Murphy, 1997: 157)

TEMPTATION

Life seems to return to normal but Diana is restless and is shown disturbing Robert as he writes, bored and provoking a fight. He encourages her to an audition but she leaves it when she realises that she is in competition with much more experienced performers and gives in to temptation by going to visit Miles. She shows him that she is no longer pregnant and they return to his flat. Undressing, Diana, indicating her discontent tells him, 'I always feel that there's one more corner to turn and I'll be there.' As they strip the bed, Diana, as though trying to convince herself, still insists that she loves Robert while the parking metre outside is shown expiring and moving ominously to 'Penalty charge'.

Diana's behaviour has become indicative of the problems that come with the opportunities that new freedoms bring. Diana seems to have it all but as she is confronted with the seemingly limitless pleasures that are at her disposal, she cannot decide what to choose. Her visit to the theatre shows that her brief flirtation with acting is finished as it now presents her with the prospect of having to really work. The audition means that she will not gain the role easily as she did with the film and she doesn't seem to have the necessary determination to achieve this. Instead her liaison with Miles provides her with both sexual excitement and upward mobility but, as the parking meter indicates, there will be a price to pay.

She returns home to find Robert sitting in the dark, who listens to her excuses as to her lateness with clear disbelief. She tells him that she went to her agent and there is a chance of a job in Paris, to where we cut and see Miles and Diana driving recklessly. In the voice-over, Diana relates how Miles was able to introduce her to two sides of Paris: the tourist sights and how 'sophisticated' people live. She tells of how they went to a wedding, name dropping those who were wed and afterwards to a place where the guests revealed themselves as emotionally inquisitive. Becoming ever more superficial, she describes them as 'fabulous' and 'marvellous'.

Diana's narration continues to reflect her view of events and the way she describes the people at the party as sophisticated reflects their status rather than their behaviour. The scenes that follow illustrate a world only accessed by society figures but full of sexual impropriety. This time the scene is far more bohemian than the previous fundraising gala but it is still inhabited by the privileged rich who again dictate their own rules of acceptable behaviour.

The party is decadent and hedonistic, with guests who are very intimate with each other. Scenes of Paris nightlife are intercut with Diana's pained reaction as she witnesses something distressing at the party and the fact that we don't witness the sight makes it all the more disturbing. Later the group is gathered to watch a 'home movie', described as cinema vérité existentialist – but it isn't a movie at all. Rather, a projector illuminates a blank screen in front of which the group dance and strip to African-style music.

A black guest pretends to be Diana and, when questioned, he parodies her willingness to do anything to advance herself. Diana is bemused and disorientated but when she runs to Miles for comfort she is shocked to find he is kissing another girl. However, Diana is nothing if not determined and when it is her turn she parodies Miles and his selfishness, telling the assorted guest how vain he is. Diana is triumphant but only in the sense that she has identified Miles' characteristics. She has proven herself in his world but is still dancing to his tune and immediately runs to Miles and kisses him passionately. The scene ends with a guest raising a tribal mask to her face, another mask in this film of pretence.

The overtones of promiscuous sexual activity at the party are quite clear and though they are subject to censorship, the way they are staged make the inference of pornography, orgiastic activity and perverse performance strong. The use of tribal rhythms indicates unfettered physicality (perhaps stereotypically so) and the dense smoky environment has echoes of a sex club. This is the world that *Peeping Tom* peered into earlier into the decade but now it is apparent that such pleasures have become appealing for the thrill seeking rich. Diana is thrown into this debauched environment but again, she adapts quickly and establishes a foothold in this erotic group.

The scene carries with it echoes of the Profumo scandal, in which high society figures were exposed as mingling with prostitutes, which many took as the key point in the decade where the collapse of the Establishment took place (see Geraghty in Murphy, 1997: 158). *Darling* is not just a film that explores the liberated female central character but also shows the hypocritical ruling elite. This idea of corruption within the Establishment is steadily revealed to Diana and the further she moves up through society, the more debased the behaviour.

In an ironic repeat of the scene where Robert and Diana had phoned their partners from the train station, Miles now phones Robert, masquerading as a French telephone operator, from the airport having returned from Paris. Diana looks scared while her voice-over explains how her main concern was to protect Robert and that she expected her affair with Miles to burn out. But the juxtaposition of images against her commentary reveals the extent of her mendacity as she is then seen at Miles's flat eating and drinking.

Robert returns home to find an invitation to an art gallery and a message from Diana that she'll meet him there. The gallery is showing the work of Ralph Riggs, a former criminal whose work depicts scenes of violence in a pop art style. In another depiction of gossiping society, a woman asks if he is really a crook and another foppish guest confirms it, saying he's just interviewed him for television and that he has recently finished a five-year sentence.

Riggs meanwhile is happily signing autographs for a group of fans and the woman comments how he has a wonderful lean and hungry look. 'Is it true he's so tremendous in bed?' she asks. Diana meanwhile enthusiastically greets Alex, one of the guests from the charity function and now seemingly one of Diana's 'friends'. The words 'darling' and 'sweetie' are used and although they parody the greetings with fake kisses, it is exactly this type of superficial friendship that 'darling' Diana specialises in.

The inquisitiveness of the Sixties is shown as once again we see someone of lower status gaining entry to high society. Cockney Riggs, whose painting style is of the moment, probably owes his fame as much to a high society need to incorporate those from a different social status as he does his work. The character owes much to the real-life Kray twins, East End London gangsters who were mixing in higher social circles because of their notoriety and shows the Sixties fascination for criminal heroes whose tough upbringing and anti-establishment attitude gave them a dangerous charm to those outside that world.

Some guests are continuing to talk about the artist. interms that reveal their fascination with the working-classes. They describe him as having the 'sort of furious lyricism that one finds in Whitechapel'. The artist speaks with a cockney dialect and Alex introduces Diana to him. Robert enters and Diana greets him with her newly attained manner. She is full of praise for the artist and claims to have done a screen test for another talented film-maker. Robert mimics her phrase, 'Tremendous fire,' but Diana, too self-absorbed, doesn't recognise his barbed comment.

Outside Robert stops Diana taking a taxi and calls her a 'whore'. He knows she's been back from Paris for two days, as she carelessly left her plane ticket out with her luggage at the apartment. At the tube station Diana indulgently plays the role of a crude whore, shouting at Robert that 'a pound's not enough', trying to embarrass him. They play argue in front of commuters and this continues until they get home. Robert persists in calling her a whore but she argues that he doesn't have the right to call her anything, telling him that they're not married. She scoffs at his loyalty and calls the flat a trap, where she is imprisoned.

Diana's disregard for those around her on the tube is the best example of her formidable determination not to be judged by society's standards. When Robert tries to demean her by calling a whore, she does not shrink in shame but instead throws the term back at him. In a demonstration of defiance at patriarchal society she accepts the fact that she is bought and sold but instead argues over her value. If she is going to be a product she lets him know that her value is high. She has not accepted his proposal of marriage which she knows will reduce her value and instead has chosen to remain an individual.

The inference is that Robert is no different to the rest of the men she sleeps with who wish to control her. Robert, in making her the proposal of marriage, simply seeks another means by which to gain control and instead of money it is the monogamy of marriage.

Diana throws Robert's books to the floor and he goes to the bedroom to pack. She then pleads for him to stay and after he has left we see a lingering close-up on a reflective Diana. It seems at this point that she might change, but the voice-over calls the scene an unnecessary drama and Robert 'unreasonable'. Looking at herself in the mirror she is cleaning she describes how she flung herself into her work.

The difference between Diana's public gaiety and private unhappiness is seen again as, having her photograph taken at a studio, Mal, the photographer, encouraging her to be happy, calls on her to be 'the happiest girl in the world'. As she swings her hair in voguish poses she breaks down and bursts into tears.

These photographs are inspected at a boardroom meeting for Miles' German clients, who agree that she should be the 'Happiness' girl ('Buy her then, do you, Kurt?' asks Miles). Some of the businessmen blow up a balloon adorned with a picture of the Happiness girl and throw it around the table – before Miles bursts it.

No matter how far Diana's fame spreads, albeit as the face of another product, the pattern repeats itself that she is controlled by men. The visual metaphor of the balloon, empty on the inside, toyed with by the men around the table before being destroyed by Miles is a powerful one.

Diana is out shopping with her new friend Mal, the photographer. They go into Fortnum and Mason, the very embodiment of respectability, where Diana proceeds to go on a shoplifting spree in front of some shocked older customers. Laughing as they reach Diana's flat, Mal sings 'Rule Britannia' as she tips a selection of stolen goods from her bag and even from her bra. She opens a letter from her husband, Tony, who is requesting a divorce. The pair sit laughing and gorging themselves on the fine foods they have stolen. Diana asks why life is such a cesspool. Mal sarcastically blames 'the bomb, the great big nasty bomb', the perennial excuse for the younger generation's behaviour. Diana invites him to Italy where she has a job next month, and the scene ends with a shot of Diana's dead goldfish, which the pair have drunkenly mistreated.

The dead fish connote the death of her partnership with Robert but more to the point it is also the end of Diana's attempt at domesticity. She has rejected convention, as she said she said she would in her first interview with Robert and has broken away again. Her one-woman crime wave through the traditional British shop and the ironic singing of 'Rule Britannia' is Diana snubbing her nose at British society.

DECADENCE

In Italy, Diana is filming a ridiculous commercial for ironically named 'Cupid' chocolates on location at a lavish palace. She is dressed as a medieval princess and is accompanied by a jingle for the product which describes them as 'chocolates with the fairytale centres'. She once again represents an unattainable dream of femininity in an age that seems to be forgoing romance for sex. It is here, however, that Diana will achieve the fairytale she has seemingly dreamed of, though the disparity between reality and image will again be significant.

Diana walks around the palace in a break from filming. Looking at paintings, she finds out that the wife of the Prince who lives here had died. She latches on to a romantic idea of Italian life, family and countryside. She explains through the voice-over how her stay in Capri was a break to get away from it all but here we see that it is no escape from her decadent lifestyle. She talks with the photographer and watches an assortment of gigolos while admiring a good-looking young waiter. Mal tells her that he recently ran into Robert.

He tells her that he was with a young blonde before admitting that his story is false and that Robert was alone. This pleases Diana who still has some attachment to Robert referring to him as 'my Robert'.

Here Diana reveals her discontent and that far from the idea we might have of her as the epitome of the thrill-seeking Sixties, she admits that she doesn't even enjoy sex that much but uses it in her quest to fill the inner void. Here, in the beauty of rural Capri she initially experiences some sort of peace, though this soon wanes.

The Prince who she met at the advertising shoot proposes marriage to Diana, whose insincerity is apparent and in the morning after sleeping with a waiter turns him down. 'I thought about it all last night, Cesare,' she tells him. 'I hardly slept at all with thinking', Diana explains to the Prince in dialogue that emphasises her duplicity. She expresses her unwillingness to give up her life but she seems to be deluding herself. The Prince accepts her decision but tells her that he will not change his mind. Later, sunbathing with her new friends, she laughs and bids the Prince, departing in his yacht, a sarcastic goodbye, while they all except Diana mechanically turn over to ensure an even tan. Despite Diana's claim that she has found contentment on the island, and her attempt to adapt to Italian life, she has inevitably reverted to her decadent lifestyle, quickly finding like-minded people on the island.

Back in England Robert's voice is heard over an image of Walter Southgate, the writer he interviewed not long after meeting Diana. He has died, and in a TV show celebrating his life, he quotes Southgate's own opinion of London as 'a jam factory' and praises the writer's flinty integrity.

Having returned to London, Diana meanwhile is hosting a party for the London set at her flat. Miles sends her to the kitchen for ice but when she returns everyone has paired off and Diana is left with someone for whom she cares little. 'Proceed,' she says, 'amuse me', before locking in a violent but passionless kiss.

Robert calls to at the flat tell her Southgate is dead but when Miles comes out of one of the bedrooms, Diana is embarrassed and shamed. Robert leaves and Diana, recognising the emptiness of her life, shouts at her guests to leave, which appears to mark the end of her relationship with Miles. Her face is frozen at this moment in anguish.

This sordid scene shows how far Diana has fallen and that despite every opportunity given to her she has failed in her bid to become happy. The sexual revolution has given her nothing and her boredom with another new lover for whom she feels nothing is an empty experience. When Robert arrives, she blames Miles, for having led her astray and for having lost Robert but his scepticism highlights Diana's unwillingness to take responsibility for her actions:

> 'The film soared away and everybody said this is a new sort of film. And she was…it was the absolute pin, it was the pin down, of that boring, tiresome, throwaway lot, that disposable lot of the mid-Sixties. She was absolutely the epitome of it.' (Dirk Bogarde, *Hollywood UK* BBC4)

Diana is pictured against a number of photographs of herself in different pictures in fashionable poses that decorate the wall of her flat. The voice-over relates how the damage to their relationship is done but how she had to see him. She remembers thinking, 'I'll bet he'll be at that funeral.' Her lack of empathy and selfishness are demonstrated again – unable to feel genuine grief at Southgate's passing, she instead schemes to encounter Robert. Diana goes to the funeral but again is detached until approached by a reporter from the *Evening Standard*, she lies that she and Southgate were close. Still dressed in her funeral attire she goes to buy a number of copies of the paper from a street vendor.

There follows a curious scene when, returning home from the funeral, the phone is ringing. Diana answers what appears an anonymous call, and, unable to make sense of the caller, becomes increasingly agitated and upset. Feeling alone, she seeks help from Father Chapman, who she describes in her voice-over as being 'terribly human' – as if this were an alien quality – and who apparently wants nothing from her. She then tells of her belief in God and the supposed earnestness of her conviction that allowed her to get married.

Cut to Diana posing for her wedding photographs. As the camera tracks out she is revealed as having wed the Prince. A news show reel reports, 'New English Princess' and relates the tale of Diana's fairytale wedding to the Italian Prince. The news item draws attention to the mediated presentation of facts as a Diana takes part in a series of well-constructed photo opportunities that combine to portray her as a paragon of virtue.

The portrayal of Diana as a housewife and mother is significantly different to the Diana who appeared on television earlier in the film. Then she wanted to break convention, yet now she *embodies* it, adopting a traditional lifestyle. The media portrayal is one of a fairytale princess, betraying the fact that the media version of Diana is far from the truth.

Diana is a lonely figure as she walks along the balcony of the palace. Her footsteps echo and she even has the door opened for her by a servant. She eats at a long empty table surrounded by servants in the absence of her husband. It is clear she has become a prisoner as, in a single lengthy take she walks frustrated to her bedroom, stripping the glamorous clothes and throwing them to the floor before standing anguished in front of the mirror and collapsing on the bed.

Returning to England she is met by Robert at the airport. In bed together, Diana speaks of being a couple again and she seems happy for a moment. Diana begins to plan a future together with Robert – but this is no fairytale romance and he brutally dispels her dreams and phones to reserve a place on a flight to Rome. She accuses him of using her but he counters with the opposite. Diana pleads with him but he is resolute, although disgusted with himself. He drives her back to the airport where she is interviewed by a reporter. He asks her if she is happy and she claims to be as happy as one could possibly be. She watches from the steps of the plane as Robert, on the observation platform, turns and walks away.

The final shot shows Diana on the front cover of *Ideal Woman*, on a news stand with a singer in Piccadily Circus singing 'Santa Lucia'.

SUMMARY

Although sometimes heavy handed in the way it makes its points, *Darling* is as much a reflection of the problems of the Sixties as any other film. The dichotomy of Diana is a reflection of much of the confusion of the Sixties in relation to the advancement of a new morality. While Diana is an individual who lives for pleasure, she is punished in the text for doing this.

The film seems to be attempting a balancing act between presenting a liberated and assertive woman yet punishing her for being so. There are points in the story when she is genuinely rebellious in asserting her independence but this is often depicted as her being greedy and calculating. For a modern audience, however, Diana may appear trapped, rather than the author of her own downfall, as she cannot escape the control of men.

Despite, however, the way she is cast as being a shallow and self-seeking character, the combined appeal of Christie's star persona and a new attitude made Diana in some respects an irresistible character. If there was to be a sexual revolution, Diana showed that it didn't necessarily have to only benefit men.

This control equates to a new independence which made Diana a threatening figure for a male-dominated society. Unlike Michael Caine's Alfie who was considered charming despite his flaws, Diana was not embraced. She showed that while some women accepted their place as housewives and mothers, there was now a new breed of women that didn't have to. Thus, sex could be used to empower women and rather than being seen as connected to domesticity, Diana steadfastly refuses to accept it until she feels that she is able to dictate the terms and it benefits her.

Darling then prioritised women's need for enjoyment and in doing so, it came to highlight women's important place in society's revolution that these new ideas of freedom should not be monopolised by men and should be open to all:

> 'I suppose it was all to do with trying to be economically independent, trying to be sexually independent and to put it on the screen and not entirely to condemn it but then to make it the focus of interest rather than peripheral to a man. I suppose these were all quite 60's things.' (Julie Christie, *Hollywood UK* BBC4)

The charm and appeal of Diana, however, do not simply lie in her ability to use her sexuality to her own advantage. This would not have been enough to appeal to audiences had it not been for Julie Christie and the audience's prior knowledge of her:

> 'The emphasis on individuality and personal freedom is reinforced by Christie's star image, which built on her appearance in *Billy Liar* and emphasized her impulsiveness, her lack of calculation, her overwhelming desire for freedom. Like [Rita] Tushingham, Christie is approachable, "friendly but honest" and she has "real friends who are not in show business"; her middle-class origins (she was born in India) are disguised by her then "rather nomadic" existence – "I just dossed down in the flats of my friends."' (Geraghty in Murphy, 1997: 159)

This image of Christie as someone who is rather rootless, Bohemian and free, means that she escapes the ties of conventional British culture. She had a newness and naivety which the public could embrace. Her origins in India provided a genuinely exotic background which was appealing to some.

Darling is a film which also predicts many of the main features of our modern society in pointing out the facile and superficial nature of a society driven by fame, wealth and celebrity.

A recent advert for Dior perfume shows a model recreating Diana's lowest moment and tearing off her jewellery and dress in a recreating of this iconic scene. However, today the model is depicted as being strong rather than despairing, suggesting that Diana indeed has more in common with the acquisitive celebrity-driven world today than the Sixties' search for freedom. But *Darling* also shows that underpinning this society was an almost immovable male-dominated Establishment, that, despite any modernisation of Britain, was not going to disappear. This was the Establishment that produced Bond and now it was going to take the character of a free and liberated woman and use it for its own means.

CHAPTER SEVEN: LONDON LIFE – *THE KNACK...AND HOW TO GET IT* (B/W, LESTER, 1965)

Films to watch: *Georgy Girl* (1966), *The Pleasure Girls* (1965), *Here We Go Round the Mulberry Bush* (1967)

MONTAGE

If there is *a* Sixties film, that is to say, one which resembles the stereotypical notion of what a Sixties film is, or a film that in its style captures the mood and the essence of the Sixties, it is surely *The Knack... and How to Get It*. From the very outset it is a whirling, cavorting chaotic montage of 'cut up' imagery that could only have been produced at that time:

> 'Swinging London films pivot around young women... defying convention as they try to fulfil their ambitions and find romance in a modern and uniquely unconventional London. Many of the films are structured around the story of a single girl who arrives in London, a city that comes to represent a site of pleasure and autonomy.' (Luckett in Ashby and Higson, 2000: 233)

The film language *The Knack...* uses to communicate fun and freedom foregoes many of the conventions and rules upon which narrative film depends and throws in a lot of extra ingredients besides which are indicative of the way in which film was beginning to push the boundaries of its form.

Dick Lester's film style was reflective of pop culture in its widest sense and it was a product of Sixties culture in terms of testing the notion of what a film could be. This unfettered collage of images is not so far away from pop art paintings. Its use of repetition, of slogans, of sketches and of commercially inspired products, communicates a sense of not only the excitement but also the confusion of the period and its connection to the new pop culture:

> '…the celebrant of the Swinging London style was Dick Lester. Lester's films, particularly The Knack and Help, were mercurial, modish mosaics, his style fragmented and breathtakingly fast-moving, an amalgam of influences from television commercials, cartoon strips and Goon Show surrealism.' (Aldgate and Richards, 1999: 217).

Whether this makes for a jumbled mess or an avant-garde experiment in film language is debateable, and certainly reviews for the film are mixed; indeed it is often dismissed as being a misogynistic reflection of the worst tendencies of the age. But in our overview of films reflecting the age, The Knack does just that, and not only in the sense that its style is of the time. In substance too, it shows again the conflicts that we can now see are part of the Sixties revolution.

The film is a digest of Sixties attitudes, of excess and experiment, a willingness to try anything with a frivolity and joie de vivre that are the very essence of the time. It is nevertheless in the efforts of the film to use the unconventional in trying to communicate that spirit that makes it an interesting case study and it is perhaps even because of its failings it reflects the age.

HEDONISM

> 'The film Dick Lester made…reached the screen at precisely the moment when society was ready for its celebration of youthful hedonism. A new generation had come to earning and spending power and though "permissiveness" wasn't then in general use in Britain the extension of economic independence into the sexual sampling of experience was in the air and it was what the film caught and defined and welcomed.' (Walker, 1974: 263)

For modern viewers the movie presents a significant problem and that is probably why, out of all the films in this book it remains to a large extent hidden. The problem is one key term – 'rape' – and the context in which it is used. But that is exactly why it is such an important film to examine as it reveals much of the confusion of the time and consequently creates a problem for our perception of a time that is commonly associated with unadulterated fun and innocence.

At the beginning of this book, we commented on the Sixties image and how it made cohesion from disparate and competing forces. *The Knack* seems to achieve this on more than one level and in so doing describes both the problem and the joy of the period. This is apparent in the way in which the tale presents an awkward combination of characters which are thrown together in these changing times. The movement of people attracted to the capital by the supposed glamour of London led to the growth of bed sits and young people willing to flat share and it is this that is the premise of the film.

This new idea of 'living away' from the family led to a generation of individuals who would have to try to integrate with others on their own terms. They were throwing away old, established, shared standards and values. But in so doing they would have to invent their own to establish common ground and this would cause conflict. Indeed this was seen by many traditionalists as a sure sign of the decline of society, with the older generation suspecting all sorts of depravity in such dens of iniquity. The truth, however, would be far more mundane, of young people who were not part of any perceived 'scene' groping clumsily for a sense of identity and belonging.

The characters in *The Knack*, then, were supposed to be representative of a larger group of people who were all following the movement to London.

MICROCOSM

'The people we put into this house in Hammersmith…were meant to be a microcosm of London in its early swinging days. Something had definitely changed from the time when I was first trying to find accommodation in London. Whether it was the relaxation in our attitudes to sex or the relaxation in the laws of rented accommodation, for a young man, possibilities were definitely improving. What I remember as a dreary bed sit could be transformed with a lick of paint into…the pad.' (Richard Lester, *Hollywood UK* BBC4)

The 'knack' referred to in the title is the ability to attract women, an idea which may seem rather sexist by today's standards but in this decade of new experience, it describes an aspiration which young men perhaps feel they should aspire to in this new age and it is presented in much the same way as commercial product. The:

'knack itself is treated as if it were endowed with the aphrodisiac quality of a posh deodorant or bath lotion in a telly-commercial.' (Walker, 1974: 266)

The Knack explores the notion of a new male who can exert his dominance over women by means of his sexual attractiveness as was also seen in *Alfie*. This figure, which could attract women at will, was a product of a society whose expectations of manliness had changed and for which sex had become more important. However, despite this, the idea of this mythical male prowess is parodied and punctured and *The Knack* is not as sexist as it is often portrayed. Instead the film examines the pressure to respond to new times with new behaviours.

The film explores attitudes to sex and sexuality and the story, such as it is, explores these themes. There is tension between the main characters who seem to embody two sides of masculinity; Tolen, an irresistible new mod stereotype and Colin, a repressed teacher who desperately craves physical attention. Colin is drawn to Tolen but is also repelled by him as he tries to gain the elusive 'knack'. This is largely because to be like Tolen, Colin would have to adopt his beliefs and values, which he finds repugnant:

> '…one might suppose the film to be a male chauvinist fantasy about the opportunities opened up by the new climate of permissiveness. In fact the real hero is Colin, a shy weedy, schoolteacher who against all expectations wins the love of the innocent but canny country girl Nancy, who comes to London looking for adventure.' (Murphy, 1992: 136)

Aside from the film's tenuous plot and rather shallow characterisation, there is a more interesting aspect to the *The Knack* in the way in which Lester attempts to show attitudes reflected in the physical environments and the film language, rather than in the development of a structured story. There is little here that can equate to a logical narrative but rather it is the way the film tries to communicate through its form that makes it a more interesting reflection of the times.

The style of the movie is a development of fantasy employed in *Billy Liar* or *A Hard Day's Night* in that it completely forgoes any real sense of reality. Rather, the film language employed is the essence of the film. The viewer can never escape the knowledge that the events are not real and therefore the events are clearly representational and more open to interpretation. With the Sixties experiments in psychology, perception and drug use, this becomes a growing trend of the period as individual viewer interpretation becomes more crucial in the viewing of a film.

The Knack, though, is not completely free of structure but rather it is a deliberate, theatrical piece which draws on performance as part of its communication. Perhaps not surprisingly, it is based upon a stage play and never really transcends the confines of this. Much of the story revolves around the flat and the Brechtian devices of experimental theatre contribute to its stylised feel.

Despite this theatricality it does bear comparisons with the deconstructionist film work of the French New Wave, though it lacks the philosophical attitude of the more successful French directors, and instead employs the light-hearted whimsy of British Carry-On films. This combination of sex, slapstick capers and British pop music, make it a uniquely British Sixties film.

MINI-SKIRTS

The dizzying overhead camera work of the opening sequence is immediately unreal in nature and gives a sense of Sixties film-making as we might expect to see: the sight of numerous young women, all dressed identically in the height of fashion standing on a staircase. The girls with bobbed hairstyles and tight sweaters and mini-skirts stand in aloof poses, similar to the mannequins that appear in the shop window later in *Blow Up*. Similarly, Hammond organ music is employed on the soundtrack, which adds to the feel associated with times.

Once again, it is the association of young women with commodity that is noticeable. The portrayal of these mannequin-style women has echoes of mass production. They are characterless, lacking identity, merely being portrayed as objects of sexual desire, the bleached whiteness, heavenly but also fabricated, like the organised artificiality of a shop window display.

A young man, Tolen (Ray Brooks) playing a drum kit breaks up the heavenly chorus which opens the film and introduces the connected ideas of pop music and sexual freedom, as he gets up from his drums to lead another girl into his room. They all seem under his spell, hypnotised, but another young man, Colin (Michael Crawford) on the next floor down looks out of his room in panic at what he sees and slams his door shut. To some the Sixties is a sexual adventure, while for others it is a time of confusion.

While the girls come and go, Colin edgily peers through his door. The girls continue to make their way inside the room at the top, one girl welcomed again by the now familiar suited arm which is toying with her pendant necklace. This shot emphasises the woman's breasts and while Colin seems to want to speak to the girls and tries to impress them by exercising on the door frame, he is unable to.

As the credit sequence continues, the numerous girls are signing a guest book and are welcomed by the impassive Tolen. Another girl is shown by a tilted camera perfuming her ankle while Colin finally cheerily welcomes one of the girls inside his room. However, she merely looks about before picking up a chair and returning outside to wait her turn with the other girls. He, a solitary figure, sits on his single unmade bed, before the film cuts to a zebra patterned double bed where Tolen is throwing a boxing glove to another of the identical young women, signifying his aggression. Here we see the contrast in the two men's rooms, one a smart bachelor pad, the other a rather drab bed sit.

The opening sequence of *The Knack* shows how Sixties film began to test the boundaries of film communication. The narrative is no longer bound by the restrictions of realism that began the decade and the viewer is immediately immersed in a world where there is no demarcation between what is real and fantasy. Unlike the earlier *Billy Liar*, which uses fantasy to express the escapism of the central character, in which dreams spill into reality, here the fantasy is not delineated as being different from the reality and it is merely another form of expression. The contrasting characters of Tolen and Colin are established but quite how the viewer is to make sense of the events is debateable.

The disorientating blurring of the girls on the staircase appears to express the repressed insecurities of Colin, who fears his flatmate is having a better time than he is, but the new-found film-making freedom doesn't make the reality any more real than the supposed fantasy as, when the credits end, he breaks 'the fourth wall' and addresses the camera directly and immediately suggesting the unreliable nature of the events we are watching. ('It's not like that. It's an exaggeration. He's just got a certain success with the ladies, that's all.') This dialogue would seem to indicate the events are in Colin's imagination but this is by no means certain as in the opening four minutes, director Lester has used a variety of non-naturalistic devices to draw attention to the artifice of the film.

'Out', a tense Colin shouts up the stairs. He decides that what is needed is a 'steadying influence', such as a 'monk or an older man who's an accountant, poor old men in sexless professions'. He scribbles a 'to let' sign on a square of cardboard. If, as Lester indicates he desired to capture sixties society by presenting the audience with a microcosm, the neurotic, teacher Colin functions as an opposite tendency to the fashionable Tolen and his fears embody a repressive characteristic of British society.

While he dreams of monks coming to London with no place to stay, we see the rather unusual sight of a coach full of robed monks. The shot of the front of the coach reveals that it is coming from the North West. Perhaps even the most pious will be converted to the London life. Now in bed Colin talks of a young lady looking for a clean home with clean surroundings and back on the coach the camera tracks left away from the monks to reveal just such a young woman, Nancy (Rita Tushingham), reading *Honey* magazine. She is reading an article entitled, 'A Party is for Two', accompanied by a romantic picture of a man and woman holding hands.

YOUTH

Colin's dreams bizarrely become real as the coach party becomes exactly what he wishes for. Nancy is typical of a number of young people who are making their way south but, far from the fears of sex-crazed youth, her magazine reveals her dream to be rather quaint and old-fashioned, not unlike Doreen in *Saturday Night and Sunday Morning*. Her appearance, though somewhat fashionable, is rather vulnerable and childlike, hidden under a large hat and coat. She is certainly not one of the mannequin-like girls that appeared earlier and puts forward a different ideal.

This presentation of events highlights the fictional nature of what we are watching on the screen. The self-reflexivity which was a growing trend in film-making enables the viewer to confront the artificiality of the film and its 'story'. It is designed to make them think about its construction and how they, the audience, engage with it. Lester, an admirer of the French New Wave, was keen to explore this aspect of film. Though events at this stage seem to be connected to Colin's imagination, the film recognises that Colin himself is a fictional character and that the film can make anything 'real'.

As Nancy hurriedly tries to leave the coach she is told by an older woman to 'Just watch where you're treading'. Following this, there are a series of comments that seem at first to have no source but then it becomes clear that they are being spoken by the other coach passengers. These are a combination of hackneyed and well-worn expressions that may be voiced by a disapproving older generation, such as, 'after kicks', 'hoping to be debauched', 'heading for a fall', 'drugs', and 'it'll end in tears'. The music in contrast is light-hearted and comic.

'I know what she wants and it isn't the YWCA,' comments a woman to her husband, looking out the coach window at the young woman. The girl collects her case from the driver, 'London', she affirms, looking around both pleased and excited. 'Lovely', she comments.

Thus in this cacophony of comments the older generation provide a commentary on Nancy's actions and preside over her like judges. Just like the lead characters, the other characters are representative of wider society and the phrases used reveal a wealth of comments, mostly negative, which show the generational gulf. The older generation's version of the young girl's life is based on assumptions about what the young are indulging in. The comments show that while many are willing to make judgements most are without substance and based on their own prejudices. The words, spoken aloud are those that would often stay just as thoughts and demonstrate again a rather unreal quality employed by advertisers:

> 'Lester's television technique was never so appropriately used as in the Greek chorus of middle-aged "squares" photographed with disapproving expressions on their faces and one liners on their lips, after the style of a telly commercial for digestive mints.' (Walker, 1974: 265)

Nancy goes to the lockers with her cases but, in a comic sketch, as she tries to open one locker another flies open. As she struggles with both lockers the station attendant looks on disapprovingly and she flees. The interlude ends with the attendant closing a locker door by pressing a button on the drinks vending machine. This battle with the lockers is typical of the surreal comedy employed in *A Hard Day's Night* but in this case it emphasises the girl's status as a stranger in London. She is looked at disapprovingly by the attendant as she struggles with the impossible lockers, while he is able to make sense of the nonsensical rules of his environment.

Colin, meanwhile, is upset as he has lost his chair from his bedroom and he shouts out of his window to the road below, where Tolen is now starting his scooter. The fast, 'cut up' style associated with the period shows the young man call out, 'My chair', the young girl on the floor above shouts out 'My hair', and then he suddenly appears at the bottom floor window, asking what he is going to sit on. Tolen is dismissive and is too busy admiring himself in the mirror of his scooter to pay much attention.

Here we see the film language echo and enhance the events as narrative timing and the logical presentation of time and space are altered. Colin's appearance at two windows in a short time frame emphasise his panic and his nature, his appearance and dialogue being paired with the girl's to highlight his lack of masculinity. Tolen meanwhile exudes masculinity, his lack of concern showing his cool. But there is also criticism here of Tolen, whose vanity is obvious.

CUT UP

This cut up style, made so much of as a feature of film from the period is often seen as a rather flamboyant and unnecessary feature of cinema of the time. Another deconstructive technique, seen briefly in *Darling*, it has the effect of condensing time and is sometimes cut to music, giving priority to the beat of the popular music rather than expressive cinema but like the music itself it does communicate the vital energy of the times and a sense that anything is possible.

The experienced Tolen embarrasses Colin who comes over shy as his flatmate asks him whether he has a woman yet. Telling the girl, who begins to laugh, to shut up, he offers to show him how to attract one and remarks that they like to be dominated while the girl, now on the back of the scooter puts his gloves on for him. Colin tells him to keep his views to himself, slamming the window shut.

Tolen's domination over both Colin and the girl is typical of a certain type of masculinity and reflects the importance of sex in this age. If we think back to *Peeping Tom* at the beginning of the era (and this book) sex is private and secretive. Now, with Tolen, it is a public symbol of status and success, something to take pride in. He is in control because he understands the importance of image and it is his self-importance, his sense of the image he projects, that makes him a figure of the times and moreover gives him power.

Riding away, wearing dark glasses and having his hair stroked by the girl, he is the epitome of cool. The older generation's opinions are again audible and while the camera work emphasises the power and the dynamism of youth, the opinions are by contrast comical in their assumptions. The Hammond organ music is again reflective of the spirited Sixties and contrasts with the comments which seem very old-fashioned. Most are comments on freedom and regulation, while the phrase 'I'm bound' is repeated throughout the film, emphasising the rigid rules the older generation live by, consequently they talk in platitudes:

'It's merely high spirits really.'

'Every lane's a speedway.'

'They rule the streets.'

'I'd rule them.'

'Conscription.'

'She'll regret she didn't wear a safety device.'

'I feel for her chest, that's my feeling.'

'I'm bound.'

'Legs up, all up the road.'

'I'm bound by my age.'

'Skirts up showing everything.'

'Filth.'

'I think not.'

As the statements are made there is a montage sequence which focuses on the gloved hand of the rider on the throttle, pictures of older members of the community and the young girl's skirt and legs. The picture becomes increasingly blurred.

This sequence again expresses the generational gap. The young people's freedom and energy are contrasted with the older figures on the street that are excluded from their ideas of excitement and fun. Word association is used to expose the older generation's underlying fears. It also opens the same interpretive process to the audience as they create meaning from the juxtaposition of words in this linguistic montage. An example of this would be the association of speed with youth and a bound older generation who are set in their ways. This type of film dialogue has much in common with the word association poetry inspired by the 'beat' poetry of the late Fifties and reinforces the growing importance of psychology and the sub-conscious. While the older generation are 'bound', the young are freeing their minds.

The next scene shows an older woman complaining, 'That's no behaviour,' pointing to a large swathe of paint on a wall. 'Out,' she says to a young man, Tom (Donal Donelly), who is complaining that her house is too brown. The word association again condenses the text as the landlady repeats the word 'out' that Colin used earlier in the film to Tolen and there is a feeling that all the events are somehow deliberately interconnected and deliberately constructed. He argues with what is clearly a landlady that she would like his efforts when he's finished but she insists on him leaving and resolves in the same words heard earlier that she'll be looking for 'a young lady looking for a clean home with clean surroundings'.

Returning to Nancy at the bus station it is clear that she is being introduced as the girl who fits the bill as again the deliberate interconnectedness is apparent. To reinforce this, a voice-over from an older gentleman speaks the words spoken by Colin earlier, 'Just come to London with no place to stay and glad of it they are.' She sits in a photo booth having her photograph taken in different poses, manufacturing a new image for her new life as the Sixties obsession for image-making re-emerges. As she poses, she takes control of her own identity and becomes independent. However, she is again shown as an outsider, as Moya Luckett observes:

'Her tourist status is emphasised when she has a passport style photograph taken shortly after her arrival at Victoria coach station, suggesting her entry into the city....' (Luckett in Ashby and Higson, 2000: 238)

Cutting back to the recently evicted Tom, he writes the word 'Help' in capital letters on the wall outside the house which he has just left, perhaps a reference to Lester's work with The Beatles.

DISPLACED

All of the main characters have now been introduced and are beginning to be linked though most are experiencing some sort of displacement. Colin feels out of place in his own home, Tom has just lost his home and Nancy has just left home. Tolen, self-confident in his appearance and sexuality, and supposedly 'typical' of the swinging Sixties youth as perceived by the older generation, is actually the exception.

At the station a middle-aged man in a bowler hat pushes his female companion inside the photo booth outside which Nancy is awaiting her photographs. She watches as the woman inside the booth proceeds to hand out her clothing and we see her legs as she strikes a series of poses. There is confusion as they collect their photographs and have to exchange them with an embarrassed Nancy.

The superficial respectability of the couple is a reminder of *Peeping Tom* and yet now the sexual preferences of modern Britain are the stuff of comedy. There is no longer the terror of corruption that was such a feature of the beginning of the decade. A voice ironically declares that 'the streets are full of them', while another states, 'I blame the army' and 'it's all strip and look big'. The ideas of the Establishment and respectability being the backbone of the country, which could not be questioned when Powell's film was released, are now sources of fun as the country begins to take another less serious look at itself.

Nancy's journey looks closer at the Establishment. She is now stood watching the marching soldiers in Buckingham Palace Road and the comments centre around the army and the decline of standards. 'It was national service made a man of me, taught me the value of the belly laugh'; 'I blame the teacher's if you ask me.' Her face is one of amusement as the guards pass by. Her very Sixties make-up and hat mark her as a contrast with their regimented roles.

Despite its flamboyant style, *The Knack* is a film of everyday change taking place in the country. Unlike, for example, *Darling*, the film does not portray a privileged elite but instead chooses some very ordinary characters. These displaced young people are the future of the country and while the previous generation's views constantly are heard bemoaning the state of the nation, the young people who are going to change it are adopting new values.

Nancy continues to wander the streets and passes the horse guard barracks. She asks the soldiers for directions to the YWCA but the conversation is confused and makes little sense as Lester's surreal dialogue reinforces the strangeness of the world for this young girl. This continues when Colin, another innocent, arrives at school. He walks through a crowd of students, as the vox pops now discuss memories of school such as 'I walked eight miles', 'I walked twelve' and 'Can you wonder they're crying out for ruffage?' Bizarrely, there are children lying in beds outside.

Nancy's journey is one of exploration but her perception of the country in which she lives is very much that of an alien. Her innocent characterisation demonstrates her naivety but also her willingness to question what is around her. The images and voices which accompany her walk past Buckingham Palace show the divide between the ordinary person and the privileged and though she is British, this view of the country is just as alien to her and she differs from the tourists who are prepared to stand outside in the rain. The broken-down car being pushed by a chauffeur ('heritage in motion'), of course, symbolises the weakening of the country's place in the world and the monarchy. The word association here, though open to interpretation, is effective in expressing the decline of the nation's power.

Meanwhile Colin is teaching his class who, clearly bored, are obliged to merely repeat what he says. This meaningless repetition of facts by rote almost becomes part of the surreal dialogue as it seems senseless to those involved. He looks agitated by a group of girls outside playing netball. They are laughing and chasing the ball but the camera's low angle emphasises their short skirts. A crash zoom reveals a group of older men watching from beyond the school fence. Two of the girls pose provocatively for Colin before being guided away by their teacher. He looks away, only to see himself as one of the old men watching the girls. He stares out the window, his class laughing and then we see the gym mistress waving him away. One of the boys in his class blows a kiss to the girls and Colin throws chalk at him.

Colin discusses what happened with an older teacher in the lavatory, who has no sympathy for the boy, but Colin clearly feels guilty. When they emerge Colin becomes embroiled in a conversation about the rape of another teacher in Camberwell, which prefigures the later scene of rape. One of the teachers criticises him, saying he has no control over his class while Colin turns on the PE teacher, defending his class for being only flesh and calling her class provocative, much to the other teacher's bafflement.

REPRESSED

Colin's characterisation as sexually repressed exemplifies his containment within a rather traditional role from which he yearns for freedom. This perception that sex is all around is shown in his hallucination and his inability to cope in the way he lashes out. Colin's preoccupation with sex makes him a rather hapless character trapped between the standards of two ages and not able to fully embrace modern pleasures as he would like; but the way in which he is linked 'comically' with 'dirty old men' and the anecdote of a classroom 'rape' are unsettling undercurrents in what is so far an energetic romp.

Nancy, making her way along the consumerist Bond Street, finds a hole in her bag and goes into a shop. Her journey through the capital is now to a commercial centre but retains its focus on the Establishment, as Harrods can be seen clearly in the background. Going in she looks around before being accosted by an unctuous salesman whose smooth talk emphasises his knowledge of women and how they can be manipulated. He asks her to try on a dress which he has selected especially for her.

Nancy's visit to the shop again demonstrates her inability to fit in but also expresses her lack of a need to. The confusion over her coat shows the transience of fashion and the salesperson shows how women are exploited by this industry. Nancy's inability to slot into the idea of the 'typical' Sixties woman is shown by her inability to wear the hat, but it also emphasises her individuality. This is also indicated in the casting of Rita Tushingham, who was hardly a conventional mini-skirted glamour girl of the times:

'We were sort of oddities which is perhaps why we fitted into the Sixties cinema. There was also a rash of the long legged, mini-skirted, very trendy girls.' (Lynn Redgrave, *Hollywood UK* BBC4)

Colin is walking by a lake which, it transpires, is where Tolen works. He seeks his advice on how he can 'get' a woman. Emphasising his masculinity, Tolen tells Colin that he needs to consider his diet and that he himself, with his unusual demands, needs twice the usual amount of protein. He instructs Colin that he must look at women. While the inept Colin tries to write down his flatmate's advice Tolen looks at girls dressing for water sports and out on the lake.

The concept of 'looking', of voyeurism, as a means of control, has been explored in Film Studies through the idea of the 'male gaze' (Mulvey, 1975). Tolen objectifies women and as at the beginning of the film we see women made into commodities. As Tolen talks, some of his words appear on the screen, overlaying images of women walking in the street. Such phrases as 'Just Types', 'Free from Responsibility', 'If Pushed Man Must Dominate', 'Dominate…'. The word 'dominate' flashes on the screen as we see Nancy walking down the street, as if to identify her as a target.

Tolen's advice is based on his sexist attitudes and demonstrates that he is using sex as a means of control. The montage, which shows a variety of apparently independent women, suggests, like the film *Alfie*, that men are threatened by women's changing place in society, that sexual liberation must be something that is rigidly controlled.

Colin desperately tries to keep up with Tolen's advice but he cannot. As Tolen drives the boat away, Colin chases after him, grabbing some skis and water skiing behind the boat fully clothed before sinking into the water shouting, 'I've wet my trousers.' Back at the house he is a forlorn figure, wrapped in a towel and soaking his feet in a bowl of water. Tolen tells him that he needs help and asks how many women Colin has had and remarks that some have had more in two hours. Tolen tells him that he has an idea to help him, while Colin begins talking about the size of his bed, expressing his sexual inadequacy as he thinks he requires a bigger one.

Tolen begins telling Colin about his friend Rory McBride, hoping to persuade Colin to let him take the vacant room downstairs, little knowing that Tom has already taken down the to let sign and is busy making himself at home. He speaks of his plan to share women with Rory McBride but Colin refuses. Tolen tries to persuade Colin by telling him that he could share the women but he is adamant. Rory McBride is never seen in the film and it is uncertain whether he actually exists. Seemingly a mythical figure of masculinity he may be another illusion of the sexual sixties.

Colin goes upstairs and runs a bath, while Tolen tells him about another of Rory's girls, this one a Swede. Colin complains that with all these girls he'd never be able to get in the bathroom. As he does so he enters to find it full of girls, wrapped in towels, who turn to look at him. The scene is accompanied by heavenly music. Once again we seem to access Colin's thoughts, whose delusions of the availability of sex are preoccupying him.

The dialogue shows a trend that was developing in British film, to show women as sexually available for the purpose of male pleasure. In the wake of *Darling*, which reflected the idea of a new, sexually independent woman, this idea has been distorted to mean a sexually *available* woman:

> 'Christie thus added sexual power and confidence to the honesty and unpredictability of Tushingham and created a figure which was to be carried through in British cinema into the late 60s. But the difficulty in maintaining the possibilities of identification for young women can be seen in the rapidity with which it turned into a stereotype of what Robert Murphy identified as the late-60s figure of "a spontaneous, vulnerable, sexually willing young woman".' (Geraghty in Murphy, 1997: 160)

While Tom, who has found his way into the house, paints the room downstairs, an inundated Colin slams the front door shut, the action edited to repeat several times. He then proceeds to try to permanently seal the door by hammering a wooden baton across it. This is accompanied by the now familiar chorus; this time, however, the comments are DIY related and while Colin works with various tools the words describing them appear on the screen.

'That is indeed a job,' Colin says before realising that he now can't get out. Conversely Tolen, who has returned with another girl, complains that he can't get in. He is expecting his friend Rory but Colin discovers the new lodger, Tom, painting the room. Tolen is dismayed to find this new incumbent but much to his disgust Colin agrees to let the room to him. The impact of advertising, such an influence in this new age, is seen again as Tom sings a jingle for Windolene while attempting to clean the windows and expressing the desire to leave the white cream on the windows and advises Tolen to do the same – 'White reflects the heat, alright when the bomb drops.'

URGENCY

The mention of 'the bomb' again, which reoccurs in many of the films in this book, shows an undercurrent of fear that underlies many of the films of the time. Perhaps tellingly, it is never the main feature of the films but is apparent in many. The urgency of living for fun, such a feature of the Sixties films, is sometimes equated with the threat of the bomb, although as we have seen in *Darling*, this may be more an excuse than a cause.

An egg is cracked into a frying pan and we return to Nancy who is speaking to two Asian men through a shop window as they cook the eggs in traditional British butcher's aprons. She asks for the YWCA and after the footage of the egg breaking is reversed they direct her. She steps into a telephone box in another location and though there is a lack of continuity which has been apparent in her journey, she seems to have made her way through tourist London into rather more everyday surroundings.

The Knack's presentation of the world is perhaps what we most associate with Sixties films but the content too reflects changing attitudes. It is not merely a film of style; Nancy's journey is littered with the sorts of sights that both reflect and challenge the perception of our culture. Her journey has already featured sex, the monarchy, commercialism, multi-culturalism and class and though they are presented in a rather casual way, they are nonetheless a reflection of the times.

She, an independent female, travelling from the north like *Billy Liar*'s Liz has the same spirit of adventure and is associated with this shifting identity. The sights are new and fresh and it is as though, through her eyes, we see the changes in society taking place. This is quite different to the way the men are presented in the domestic setting of the flat.

Tom is continuing to paint the room white, giving it a stark, modern, minimalist look, while Tolen complains that the furniture, blocking the hallway is preventing his guest from leaving. Another fashionable young woman comes to the top of the stairs. Tom, however, is not impressed by Tolen's behaviour and distracts him with erroneous conversation. Tolen comments that 'after a girl has been with me she doesn't feel like clambering over furniture'. But Tom's bizarre, surreal answer ignores the point being made: 'After an elephant neither would you.' In a similar vein Tolen asks him if he is a homosexual but he answers, 'No. Thanks all the same.'

Tom adds a new dynamic to the relationships in the house. His refusal to be belittled by Tolen and his dismissal of Tolen's sexual prowess are admirable and even when Tolen tries to ask his sexuality he is non-committal in his answer, refusing to accept that it is important. This indifference to sex makes Tom a very modern character, a precursor to more enlightened attitudes to come and someone who can help Colin from his subservient position to Tolen, who measures masculinity in the number of girls conquered.

Tolen leaves and then returns (through the window) with yet another girl:

'How long?' Tom then asks Tolen. 'How long did you take this time?'

'Did you time me?' he replies.

'Did you time yourself?'

'No more than ten minutes.'

While Colin talks about the size of Tolen's bed and is clearly impressed, Tom's questioning of Tolen's performance is clearly an attempt to undermine him and his attitude towards women.

The comic way in which Tolen immediately returns to the house with yet another conquest emphasises the way in which he treats women and Tom's insistent questioning of the time he has taken highlights Tolen's adolescent attitude. While suggesting that to time himself would be crude and vulgar Tolen then confirms it was ten minutes. The girl in the background looks embarrassed and uncomfortable while Tom begins to deride Tolen's encounters and pushes him to improve his performance, saying ten minutes is not good enough and that he should strive to become faster.

As Tolen goes upstairs, taking the girls shoes off, Tom encourages him to try and 'get the time down' treating it as a record attempt. Colin meanwhile in an obvious *double entendre* that highlights his insecurities is becoming preoccupied with the size of Tolen's bed. 'Yours is quite big isn't it, Tolen. How big is your bed, Tolen?' When Tolen gets to the top of the stairs Tom is talking in a frenzied manner, talking of getting his time down to three minutes, like the three-minute mile and in the background, a screaming crowd is heard until Tolen's door is closed after dropping the shoes outside.

'Is it nice faster?' asks Colin. Tom points out that Tolen's treatment of women is based upon his own ego and begins to show his new landlord that Tolen's behaviour, far from being admirable or something to aspire to, may actually be a weakness.

Tom tells Colin that he knows where to find a big bed and we then see a crane in a scrap yard lifting a large cast iron bed. Colin protests that he wants something 'sexy, quilted, that makes a very loud noise'; but when he hears the sound the iron bed makes he decides to take it. He asks Tom whether he was promiscuous at thirteen but he answers that, 'we're all more or less sexual failures'. Tom's influence is having a positive effect on Colin who is growing in confidence.

INSECURITY

The attitudes of Tolen and Colin toward sex are both adolescent in nature and fuelled by insecurities which are not aided by this new age of 'freedom' and although it is an age of supposed sexual adventure, there is a naïve innocence about these new explorers who are seeing the world anew. Colin and Nancy in particular seem to be particularly childlike (not unlike *Peeping Tom*'s Mark, if less murderous), although the whole group behave somewhat childishly.

They discuss Tolen who Colin cannot believe is a sexual failure as he apparently needs sex five hours a day. Tom's silence seems to provoke Colin to question his perception of Tolen. 'He can't be a sexual failure can he?' Once again he refers to his bed being a bigger size than Tolen's but Tom is unimpressed. 'Is it?' he says seemingly disappointed that Colin should be concerned but at that moment, Tom spies Nancy, whose search for the YWCA has brought her to this site.

Tom encourages Colin to chat her up but he is again is too shy and avoids contact. However when she asks him for directions to the YWCA they connect briefly and the camera cuts between the two, their faces combining them. The transitions blend their faces and they are caught in each other's gaze, indicating their mutual attraction.

They decide to wheel the bed through he streets and the scrap dealer comments 'mods and rockers' as they take it away. The sequence that follows is a montage which follows them as they wheel it through the streets. Platitudinous comments from the older generation once again accompany the action: 'There's not a bus route in London free of it's share of youth, vice'; 'hand back the city to those with their fair share of legs'; 'they'll do anything but use the good feet they were born with'; 'anything but walk, mine's the same'; 'I mean, I'm broad-minded but a bed's place is definitely in the home, definitely'; 'we had our own sleeping arrangements'; and, again, the condemning 'mods and rockers'.

Throughout the sequence there is a focus on the social mix and class divisions. Where Nancy's journey began with Establishment and tourist sights, there has been a shift toward the everyday social change and her joining the young men from the house seems to have freed them from convention and care. Their behaviour, as is the case with young children, can be understood as them making sense of a changing world in terms of play. As the young people wheel the bed through the streets in carefree fashion they pass hotel doormen, a man in an expensive car and a parking attendant, people whose roles are defined by society.

The feeling of the sequence is that these youths are free from society's rules and regulations. They get the better of the parking warden by actually paying for their parking space; they get a lift from a lorry carrying cars, throw stones in a lake and jump up and down on the bed, appearing above a wall. Colin continues to bounce on the bed as they wheel it down the street, puncturing a large painting of a patriotic, historical war scene being removed from a large house ('there's no national heritage anymore', 'Ma it's all on the National Health'). Tom lashes the bed to the back of a car and they are dragged through a car wash. Colin and Tom are shown from a low angle surveying what's around them before the camera reveals that they are now on a barge, floating the boat down a river. When Colin falls in, the camera reverses the action.

This montage sequence is all about freedom and fun and though the older generation's voices are heard throughout, the young people's carefree exuberance and energy are expressions of a new attitude. The older generation may equate them disparagingly to mods and rockers, who are linked with social disorder, but their childlike innocence is reflective of a generation who want to enjoy life now.

They walk past the Royal Albert Hall and finally return the bed to Colin's house. Nancy, in asserting to the men that she has been picked up, reverses the seduction process. It is she who is in control and it is her choice to go to Colin's house.

When Tolen comes home he is angry. He complains about the mess in the hall but Tom is not intimidated. When Tolen refers to 'that bloody bed', Nancy tells him not to swear. 'Just come off the boat have you,' Tolen remarks, identifying her lack of urban experience. But it is exactly this that separates her from the less attractive values he embodies.

While Tolen goes to complain to Colin, Tom and Nancy, in a scene reminiscent of the later *If...* (1968) begin mimicking lions. When Tolen and Colin return Colin joins in, ignoring Tolen's orders not to be so childish. While they have fun Tolen tries to influence the girl, making it sexual – 'You're exciting him, don't you know he's a desperate man?' This play acting again links the young to more 'natural' uninhibited behaviour and though Tolen accuses the others of being childish he is no better.

When he finally joins in, Tolen takes a different role, removing his belt and becoming the trainer. His performance, like his character, is very aggressive and he backs the others into corners. Focusing his attention on the girl, he keeps shouting at her to get back until, upset, she runs out of the room. Tom is again quick to see what is at the root of Tolen's behaviour saying, 'Just think what you could do with a real whip Tolen, a real whip.'

Nancy goes to collect her bags and coat. Tolen, still brandishing his whip calls her like an animal. 'Come on,' he repeats as she backs into a corner. He begins a conversation seemingly specifically aimed at reducing her confidence, insisting that she's nervous and repeatedly badgering her, while Colin's eyes are shown in extreme close-up looking angrily on.

Tolen feels threatened. Nancy, Tom and Colin are beginning to enjoy themselves and have fun, which is endangering Tolen's dominant position in the house. Their youthful and naïve enthusiasm is in contrast to his mannered and superficial posing and in response he forcefully tries to re-establish his authority and his dominance through aggressive sexuality.

He begins stroking Nancy's hair and playing with her coat. 'Are you watching, Colin?' he condescendingly asks. He goes on to make her laugh and encourages her before brusquely turning away and saying, 'She's all yours, Colin,' encouraging Colin to behave toward the girl in the same way but bizarrely he asks her, 'Has Cardiff got big dogs?' assuming she is Welsh because of her surname, Jones.

Confused, she walks away, again asking for the YWCA and then angrily turns on Tolen. Finding he has her magazine she demands it back and slaps him. He, however, grabs her face and presses her into the corner and forces a kiss on her. Hurt, she turns her face to the wall. 'You see. It's not that difficult,' he says smugly. Angered, Tom storms out, and commands him to stay out of his room but Tolen merely repeats his request to have the bed moved. He asks Colin why he needs such a big one and Colin blusters some excuses before going to move it, leaving Tolen and Nancy together.

RAPE

The tone of the film now turns much darker. Closing the door, Tolen says to Nancy, 'No one's going to rape you… No. Girls don't get raped unless they want it.' Tolen begins to apologise for his behaviour, blaming the other two housemates for his clumsiness. He calls her 'sweet' before inviting her upstairs, repeatedly asking her. While Tom and Colin are struggling with the bed Tolen is walking the girl to his bedroom.

Tolen's views, of course, are by today's standards completely unacceptable and seem particularly out of place in *The Knack*, which has to this point been a film of light-hearted frivolity. It is at this point that the film's message seems especially confused in terms of sex but this is exactly why the film is such a good example of the times. *The Knack* comes at the precise point when liberation, permissiveness and promiscuity were new items on the country's agenda. Tolen's attitude is a reflection of this and the film, far from approving of his outlook, seeks to warn against a masculinity which is reacting against women's freedom by confusing rape with sex.

Throughout her journey Nancy has been a natural figure, she is unspoiled whereas London is a place of confusion and false values. She is not like the manufactured, mass-produced mannequins that follow in Tolen's wake and she embodies an innocence which is admirable. Tolen's need to dominate women reveals his self-loathing and it is this aggression against women which the film seeks to expose.

Tom realises what Tolen is up to, and he and Colin come running downstairs. Colin confronts Tolen and forbids him to take Nancy to his bedroom. He offers to take her to the YWCA but it seems Tolen has worked his magic and the girl seems intent to stay. Colin gives her a fatherly lecture telling her that he will not allow his house to be treated like a 'common boarding house' and finally Nancy leaves with Tolen. Tom instructs him not to let them get away.

Tolen and Nancy ride away on his scooter and once again the Hammond organ music, previously associated with light-heartedness, begins as a montage sequence shows Colin and Tom chasing the pair. They run past a typically *en vogue* fashion shoot outside some derelict buildings, get stuck in some tar, pull a rope across the road, and appear and disappear behind some temporary hoardings made of doors in quickened time, with one door revealing a front room of a house. All of this is accompanied by jaunty music and is redolent of the capers of The Beatles in *A Hard Day's Night*.

Tolen pulls up and walks the girl to a small fenced green. As he kisses her there is a freeze frame emphasising the two characters' emotions. Tolen is happy while the girl is uncertain. The music slows as Colin and Tom search the streets and Tolen repeatedly kisses the girl. The long transitions stretch time and Tolen walks the girl to the bushes but she is now pulling away. Soft focus blurs the trees as we hear the girl's voice, 'Stop it, you're touching me, keep off.' As we hear her voice the camera tracks down revealing her face. She is shaking as Tolen's gloved hand strokes her breast, moving down over her body to her legs. As Colin and Tom leap over railings we see Tolen's intent face. The music increases in volume and intensity, as does the pace of the editing, cutting quickly between shots of Tolen and the girl as he strokes her body and takes off his glove. A point of view shot shows her backing away as she repeatedly tells him to 'keep off'.

'Don't touch me,' she says as the camera tracks in toward her. She is puzzled. 'What is it?' she asks. 'What do you want with me? What are you trying on? What are you trying to do?' The camera is now close in on her face before starting again from a distance as the girl calls him names. The camera repeats this movement as the girl defends herself telling him not to come near her. 'Just you don't better come near me,' she says and as she repeats the phrase, it becomes shorter until, seemingly apoplectic with panic she repeats the phrase, 'Come near me,' before rolling her eyes and screaming, 'Come, come', before fainting.

The representation of this scene is particularly disturbing and, as with *Peeping Tom*, puts the audience in the position of the aggressor. This portrayal of such an ordeal arguably stretches the bounds of acceptability probably more today than at the time but also perhaps illustrates the innocence in which the topic was approached in a time when the subject was barely understood or mentioned. A period viewed as joyously sexual was also a time when a husband was allowed by law to rape his wife and thus, though clumsily handled by today's standards, it can make uncomfortable viewing for those whose notions of the Sixties as the 'fun' decade are exposed as, at best, stereotypical.

Tolen's attitude toward women blurs the distinction between consenting sex and rape. He sees women as objects and does not think females can resist him because of his 'knack'. This gives women no choice as he believes that sex is the inevitable outcome, giving him licence to do anything to persuade a girl to sleep with him. The text's disapproval of Tolen's attitude communicates a very modern message but it is not consistent. The blurring of the consent is extremely uncomfortable. As Tolen approaches Nancy, and her phrases of protest get shorter, there is confusion as to whether she is rejecting his advances or inviting them before she faints in what could be interpreted as a sexual frenzy. Yet this was dismissed at the time by many critics to whom it seems the subject could not be taken seriously:

> 'As the innocent who roams into their orbit and becomes the focal point for the testing of their abilities, Miss Tushingham is a dear – a grinning child who can credibly manage to concoct a rape from a swoon.' (Bosley Crowther, *New York Times*, 30 June 1965)

Tom and Colin discover Tolen with the girl collapsed on the ground. Tolen argues his innocence and puts her panic down to his knack. The men are terrified; in contrast, however, Nancy, sits up, puts on her hat and calmly announces, 'I've been raped.' The men are shown in different positions in the park in quick succession as though they have leapt backwards in shock and terror. 'Raped,' she repeats and they move back again as we see their shocked faces.

Tolen again denies it, using the queues of women outside his bedroom as a reason why he wouldn't. The reaction of the men is to group together: 'Lock her up,' says Tom '… because she can get into serious trouble.' 'A cup tea. Hot sweet tea. She'll soon forget this rape nonsense.'

As Nancy punctures a tyre on Tolen's scooter, Colin shouts, 'She must be stopped.' The men are shown trying to help Colin climb over the railings. Nancy looks pleased and some old ladies watch from across the road as if the men are animals in the zoo. She approaches a policeman and tries to report the alleged rape but cannot say the word. The boys retreat back into the park and, in a scene shot in reverse, are shown collecting rubbish (paper flies into their hands, rather than them bending to pick it up), trying to appear innocent before the police constable.

This satirical attempt at the portrayal of rape is grossly miscalculated. It may have been intended to break taboos at the time but it misfires in treating a serious topic in too light-hearted a manner and thus necessarily relegates the film's standing in modern viewers' eyes; but it is exactly this point that makes it such a key film. It shatters the Sixties illusion and exposes the myth of the time.

Nancy is then seen dancing down a high street, singing the word 'Rape' to a shocked real-life public. She stands in front of a building and sings the word as all the windows of the building are simultaneously opened. The men follow her but pretend not to. She calls at a house and sings the word to an older woman who tells her, 'Not today thank you.' The men chase her back to the house where she begins to throw Tolen's records out the window.

Colin offers to make some tea but she says, 'I can hear you, plotting who's going to be next on the job, aren't you?' Colin talks to her in a bid to rationalise the situation: 'Now then my dear girl. This all... This is all a fantasy.' His words are interrupted by her cries of 'rape' and then we see his class repeating, 'This is all a fantasy.' Colin opens the door to Tolen's room and discovers her naked. She is shown lying beneath a pile of magazines. 'Ten years and I could sue you for paternity,' she cries. Tolen goes to make tea but Colin disturbingly tells him to get in the room. 'Go on Tolen. Get in there and rape her... She wants you to rape her. That's what it's all about. Go in there, help her out of her little fantasy and all will be well.' Once again throughout their conversation, we hear the girl shouting 'rape'. Tolen is now reluctant but Colin is insistent. 'You have got the knack. Satisfy her. She wants raping so go in there and rape her.'

SHOCKING

While the film is attempting to expose masculine ideals, the context in which the word is used cannot be interpreted, especially by a modern audience, as humorous and Colin's theory of Nancy as having a 'fantasy' of rape is actually shocking. But, also, Nancy's portrayal can be read as instability. Her new behaviour seems irrational and bizarre, and does little to undermine male values, instead arguably reinforcing her claims as false and reinforcing the cultural stereotype that females are prone to overreaction.

Inside the room she is shown against a black background, holding a camera, 'I'm not being done twice.' Colin suddenly turns on Tolen, truly beginning to suspect him of forcing himself on Nancy. 'How do we know? You. Yeah.' 'Before we arrived,' adds Tom. Tolen, now visibly shaken, begins to make excuses while the girl inside is hitting the drums and talking of criminality and phoning the police. He says he has to be at the Albert Hall.

Colin tries to tell her off and tells her that he saw everything and that she wasn't raped but as she walks down the stairs, dressed only in her coat, they back away. But then Nancy accuses Colin. Sitting on the table she talks of prospective newspaper headlines. 'Little did his pupils realise that beneath the handsome exterior of their tall, fair haired blue eyed school teacher, there lurked the heart of a beast, lusting for the blood of innocent virgins.' Colin is amazed. 'Have I really...got a handsome exterior?' 'Lovely hands,' she replies.

'Alright now?', a returning Tolen asks and tries to persuade her to come to the Albert Hall where he and Rory are hosting an 'informal gathering' of women friends but as he tries to talk to her he is clearly flustered and she is not interested. Used to being the centre of attention he tries to stand between her and Colin but they move to look at each other as he continues to try to talk to her. Tom tells Tolen. 'Colin did her. Colin raped her.' 'He's a sexual incompetent,' Tolen argues. 'What's that?' asks the girl. 'Not good at it,' says Tom. 'No good? Get on,' she says, 'he's marvellous, he raped me.'

Tolen is panicked and insists she has not been raped as the girl goes on to describe Colin as rugged and handsome. Tolen has lost all confidence and he tries to encourage them to the Albert Hall but Nancy now only has eyes for Colin. 'Lovely hands and he raped me, marvellous, super.' Tolen disputes it again but Colin now, confident, says, 'Why not 'eh? You think I couldn't.' He waves a hand at a light bulb which immediately comes on.

If earlier application of the term rape was not disturbing enough, the confusion between sex and rape is bizarre while the intimation that rape has endowed Colin with power is intolerable.

Colin chases Tolen out telling him that he's not incapable. 'I'll show you.' He turns to the girl at the top of the stairs and says, 'I didn't really but I'd love to.' He says softly before correcting himself for Tolen's benefit. 'I mean I did, didn't I?' 'Yes,' she shouts. Tolen forces his way out the door telling Colin that he doesn't know women and asking him if he could fill the Albert Hall before leaving.

Thus Tolen's power over Nancy is lost – but so too is any fantasy that Sixties values were all about freedom and liberation. The 'swinging Sixties' become 'sordid Sixties': Colin has asserted his masculinity and through Nancy has become a strong and confident character and although the portrayal is obviously trying to indicate Nancy's consent, the word 'rape' is misused and associated with sexual competence.

Outside the Albert Hall are the identically dressed women, as previously, in sweaters and mini-skirts, holding placards with the legend 'Rory' written on them. Some get out of an iconic mini while others are queuing around the building. A poster proclaiming 'Tolen and Rory McGrath' decorates the wall and a girl stoops to kiss Rory McGrath's name. Inside organ music is playing. The line of girls stand in the sunlight keenly looking forward to entry but when Tolen arrives he cannot get through. The girls don't recognise him and trample him underfoot. He has lost 'the knack'.

Dishevelled he returns to the house. In a reversal of the opening scene in which Colin felt insecure, Tolen is now the same. 'It's an exaggeration,' he says to himself, 'Rory's got these friends, that's all.' Colin is smoking and enjoying a cup of tea with the girl. 'Don't you feel tired?' he asks her, 'After all that rape?' The girl seems pleased and contented and they are enjoying each other's company. Tolen, downstairs, asks Tom where Colin is. 'Upstairs,' Tom replies. Tolen asks whether the girl is moving in. 'I imagine so,' he answers. 'Do you approve of that sort of thing?' he asks dejectedly before leaving.

Colin asks her to laugh and says how lovely it would be to see her laugh, cradling her face in his hand. The soundtrack of strings builds to a romantic finale. They are then pictured next to the Thames walking under lights and fireworks hand in hand as was shown in Nancy's magazine, thus confirming her faith in a feminine view of the world.

SUMMARY

The Knack is very much a Sixties film in its style but also the mixed messages that it sends out gives us a much clearer picture of the confusion of the time. The film seems to reflect the maelstrom and excitement of change and portrays many of the issues that are at the very heart of the Sixties inherent conflict. It deals with the Sixties liberated attitudes to sex but also presents a rather conservative message in presenting the triumph of a conventional romantic conclusion.

Nevertheless at the heart of the film, as in *Darling*, there is the issue of men exerting control over women through sex, dispelling the myth of a sexual revolution that treats all equally. It is Tolen's inability to accept Nancy's refusal that is punished by her shouting 'rape'. This exposes men's insecurity and the notion of there being a 'knack'.

Thus despite its controversial presentation of the rape and being open to criticism of making it seem, if not acceptable, then not, *per se*, criminal, the film does seek to show through Nancy an independent woman who is the catalyst for change that future happiness lies in an equal relationship:

'To promote promiscuity among young people certainly was not the film's anarchic intention…But the film deflected attention from its preachy centre by the centrifugal energy it threw off everywhere around it.' (Walker, 1974: 263)

Despite all its conflicts, *The Knack*'s success seems to lie in communicating the exciting potential of the age. Even for those who lead quite ordinary lives there is the possibility of adventure, and though there is a fantasy of the swinging Sixties, it remains just that, elusive and ephemeral.

CHAPTER EIGHT: KALEIDOSCOPIC NATION — *BLOW UP* (COLOUR, ANTONIONI, 1966)

Films to watch: *The Caretaker* (1963), *Repulsion* (1965), *Deep End* (1970)

INTERNATIONAL

Part of the vibrancy of Sixties Britain was the increasing diversity of British society. The altered position of Britain in world terms and the impact of immigration were forcing the country to be more outward looking and more accepting of other cultures. This would never be a simple process and Britain's ability to redefine itself in a new international world would be a continuing problem into the next decade and beyond. But part of the process was Britain's adoption of artistic émigrés from around the world who would offer a different view of the country and who would during the Sixties offer their interpretation of the changing times.

The new British society would integrate different beliefs and values of its immigrant population and in turn these people would help shape a new perception of a country that had perceived itself in absolutes for many decades. This shedding of certainties produced not only excitement and variety but also uncertainty and self-questioning.

For some this was a period of instability, something to be feared, the beginning of the end, a shift away from morals and values upon which the country was built. But however defined, there was a distinct change in outlook from which the country could never turn back and part of this change would be wrought by those new to the shores. Karel Reisz, Joseph Losey, Stanley Kubrick, Richard Lester, Sidney Furie, Roman Polanski and Jerzy Skolimovski all made films in Britain during this period and trained their lenses on a country undergoing change. Some were attracted by the excitement and glamour of the times or puzzled by the rigid class system, while others were merely escaping from more oppressive cultures. Some were visitors passing through, others would stay.

Britain's new and very chaotic revolution was perhaps most effectively captured by an Italian, Michelangelo Antonioni, a now legendary, *auteur* film-maker known for his modernist style, whose movies repeatedly tried to capture the experience of the contemporary world and examined the problem of establishing an objective reality. His individual film language, which often featured slow camera movement and long takes, communicated the confusing nature of modern life in an often ambiguous style that illustrated an increasingly fragmented world. Rather more serious than that of *The Knack*, and not confined to the Sixties, in Antonioni's world confusion and incompleteness translate the alienation of the individual in a world without meaning.

It is apt that through this style Antonioni made a movie that is perhaps closest to communicating both the myth of the swinging Sixties scene but also the confusion of the time. *Blow Up* for many is the definitive film of the Sixties, its iconography more than any other from the period capturing the idea of a swinging lifestyle. The central character of the fashion photographer like model Diana Scott in *Darling* epitomises a figure able to live a glamorous lifestyle with access to the London 'scene' but for whom it is similarly empty and unrewarding. David Hemmings' character Thomas, inspired by photographers such as David Bailey, is a person who not only captures the moment but also embodies for Antonioni the alienation of modern times as he is a figure without root, purpose or attachment:

> 'I think London is the best place. Fashion photographers here belong to the moment. And they are without background: one doesn't know where they come from. Like the girl in the film played by Vanessa Redgrave – no-one never knows anything about her, not even who she is.' (Antonioni in Walker, 1974: 315)

It is perhaps also apt that a photographer, a creator of images, someone concerned with capturing the moment, should be the person to best reflect the idea of the Sixties. A mediator, someone whose representations of reality are shaping the world around him, Thomas is a fashion photographer partly responsible for creating the world he documents, and whose job is convincing the public that swinging London exists. It is this very illusory nature of communication and thereby existence with which *Blow Up* seems to deal. Thomas is at once at the centre of the so-called 'scene' but has difficulty connecting with anyone and is ultimately an isolated figure.

The film is experimental but does not have the frenetic energy of *The Knack* and the positive mood already seems to be dissipating as it has little in the way of quick camera work or tricks we may expect from a film of swinging London. It does employ narrative time and space to communicate its themes but not in the 'cut up' style popularised in the period. *Blow Up* is the opposite to frenetic; it instead deals with extended sequences, often featuring prolonged silences in which there seems to be little of significance happening, and yet it is in this presentation of nothing happening that our perceptions of this 'exciting' London scene are questioned. Moreover there is a gulf between the real and the perceived and a lack of understanding in everyday experience which Antonioni captures in the London of the time.

This is perhaps more in keeping with the perception of an age whose spirit is elusive and more a media construction than a reality. There is never any sense of permanence or peace in *Blow Up*. There is an edge of dissatisfaction and distance which pervades the characters and, as many critics have noted, many of the interactions between these people are subject to interruptions. Despite initial appearances that the film is showing a world of glamour, which for many is at the root of the film's appeal, it is clear that Antonioni's view of Sixties London is not wholly concerned with this. A film which has little in the way of conventional plot but plenty in the way of expressionistic and philosophical exploration does not completely immerse itself in the elitist scene of fashionable London and refuses to ignore the conflicts which are taking place in Sixties society.

ALIENATED

Even the myth of Sixties London as a place of fun is questioned. It may have been a place to which Antonioni was drawn, where though something was happening it is not to say that the much talked about changes were necessarily all good or even desirable. Moreover the film seems to question the substantive nature of the supposed scene, as much as what we take to be real is questioned. London, far from being an exciting place of new adventure is dulled by experience, the people incomplete, alienated and disconnected:

> 'Something is gone from London…innocence is too easy a term for it. Its loss replaced by something else, something that keeps going. Is it imagination? Is it activity: mockery and mime?' (Macklin in Huss, 1971: 37)

It is this disconnected feeling between the individual and his surroundings, this absence, which Antonioni explores through the commercially-driven environment of modern London where relationships seem forged by commercial transaction. This is reflected in Thomas, described by James F. Scott, in The Beatles' words, as a 'real Nowhere Man…' (Scott in Huss, 1971: 89). Someone who inhabits a supposed scene, which may be just a product of imagination, uses his camera to construct reality.

The character is a development of Mark in *Peeping Tom*, with Thomas reflecting this supposed reality in which the people seem to lack any real substance. The figures he meets, involved in London's fashionable scene, all appear to have lost something and show little in the way of identity. They are sad reflections of a world that has ceased to have any real meaning and when Thomas identifies something in the real world of the park, it is through his camera.

Thomas then is almost an amalgam of many of the characters we have seen in the book: while most obviously a development of *Peeping Tom*'s camera obsessed Mark, he also resembles the masculine angry young man, the fashionable Beatles, the disenchanted Diana Scott, and has the glamour of Bond and the cool of Tolen. He is the embodiment of many of the Sixties iconic attitudes and yet he is a figure who, in Antonioni's eyes, is lost, a characterless and aimless man who merely reflects what goes on around him without any point of view or judgement. He is dissatisfied because there is no substance to his life and like those around him he is looking for a way out, already signalling a disillusionment with the values of the new age which will continue to grow:

> '*Blow Up* must be seen as the interpretation of an era, an age that is carefree on the surface, but terrifying in its depths. The film is set in a city subject to the caprices of fashion, gaudy with "pop" colors and populated by crowds of young people who eagerly seek escape from the daily humdrum by getting "stoned" on LSD.' (Antonioni, 1971: 7)

However, from the very outset *Blow Up* seems to embrace the age. The vibrant colour, compared with magazine supplements, contrasts greatly with the films of the new wave and we are allowed tantalising glimpses of the glamour to which we will be exposed throughout the film as the titles of the opening sequence are transparent and reveal a fashion shoot taking place underneath. Antonioni actually painted locations such as Maryon Park in Woolwich, to give them their distinct look:

> 'A direction like "Thomas gets into his Rolls-Royce and returns to his studio" gave Antonioni the chance for literally scene-painting…one of the film's strongest links with the colour supplement world which the photographer serves and in which he is king…The whole film has the coloration of high quality advertising features.' (Walker, 1974: 325)

But the bright alluring colours of this world also convey its artificiality and the way in which it has been processed and mediated. How quickly the vibrant spirit of swinging London, communicated in *The Knack*, has once identified, been killed by its commercial reproduction.

IMAGINARY

As *Blow Up* begins it is not the collapsing Victorian terraces of *Billy Liar* we see; instead the exterior of a new, modern building is emphasised and the view of the modernist lines enhance it as a piece of modern sculpture. The 'towers' derided in *Billy Liar* here are reflective of modernity and a growing commercial environment – cold, clinical and dominating.

The entrance into frame, however, of what seems a student rag immediately suggests revolution, a different way of thinking. The liberated and excited revellers, all in white mime-style make-up and theatrical dress, care little for what is around them. They are a vision of anarchy and perhaps of an undercurrent of instability lying beneath this modern façade. They drive a militaristic jeep and though they are all high spirited there seems to be a sense of threat to their presence, a pre-echo of what is to come later in the decade in the form of student protest.

Mimes of course make something real out of something imaginary and their blank white faces may pose the question as to whether the people of this London inhabit an imaginary world rather than a real one, or perhaps the revellers are creating their own world.

This puzzling and enigmatic opening is indicative of what is to come and Antonioni's style of film-making which often shows a series of seemingly unrelated incidents and leaves the viewer to make sense of them has already had a disorienting effect on the viewer:

'My films are documents not of a train of coherent ideas but ideas which are born of the moment…As for knowing if it tells a story about our time, or on the contrary, a story without any relevance to our world, I am incapable of deciding.' (Antonioni, 1971: 11)

Many have tried to analyse *Blow Up*, to make sense of a film whose communication method is as incomprehensible as the world it reflects. Coming at the height of the swinging Sixties perhaps it is this that makes it arguably the film of the time. It has exactly the spirit of the age not only in its content but its style. Its very indecipherability captures the elusive moment, the space between the reality and the myth.

The antics of the lively revellers contrast greatly with the next scene of a group of homeless men, listlessly exiting a doss house. In this opening, there is a juxtaposition of two sides of London and how we are to understand it will depend upon perspective, reflecting Antonioni's interest in the impossibility of establishing an objective reality. This scene shows a Britain which is different from the wider perception of London. Thus a film which seems to embrace the vibrant and exciting world of fashion is not quite as straightforward as it may seem and although it is one that has become known for its portrayal of the swinging Sixties enjoyed by a privileged elite, it doesn't ignore other, more uncomfortable realities.

The camera returns to the revellers who are now running down the street. They are dismissive of two nuns and a guardsman, figures who seems to represent traditional beliefs or values which mean little to the young. This group seem to provide a threat to the old values and neither religion nor royalty stand in their way. The visual emphasis here seems to be on their clothes being merely an alternative costume to represent a different way of life.

Returning to the homeless, the camera draws attention to one young man, Thomas (David Hemmings). He is talking with a small group and then separates himself and after looking furtively around gets in a rather expensive car. It is clear that he is someone very different to the rest of the men, in that he is not down on his luck; far from it, he is very affluent. Here is the symbol of a new generation. He is someone who is not inhibited by class but who can move through social strata comfortably, seemingly attached to no-one. He neither feels guilt nor involvement. This creates an enigma that is one of the few in the film that can be solved, as it transpires that the man is a photographer.

Thomas and the revelling students briefly intersect for the first time as they surround his car to solicit a donation. In this way they provide bookends to the story and presumably provide comment on the story in between.

While Shadrack in *Billy Liar* is one of the few characters in a new wave film to embrace the modern age, using a CB radio but is ridiculed for doing so, here the young man uses the same from his car, reinforcing his vitality and modernity and reflecting a significant shift in values. Here is someone who is busy and dynamic, although restless.

Returning to his fashionable garret in converted buildings, our impression of him as being a success is reinforced. As he puts the camera away in the glove compartment, his role is defined. There is also evidence of the fashionable lifestyle that will pervade the film as, when he gets to the top of the stairs, two girls in another room beyond are getting changed, one topless. There is nonchalance about the presentation of these characters that show that this must be the fashionable, decadent London which has been so much talked of (not least by the chorus of disapproval in *The Knack*)!

The scene that follows has become one of the most iconic of all Sixties cinema, employed as it is on the movie's publicity posters, as Thomas takes photographs of real-life model Verushka in a series of poses. The editing here is typical of the Sixties and creates a series of still photo-like images by cutting from one pose to another, conveying the process of photography. The energy and dynamism of the photographer is clear in a scene which has much eroticism and sexual energy, the shoot concluding with the photographer straddling the model before collapsing on a couch while she rests on the floor before going to get changed.

The representation of the relationship between the model and the photographer in terms of sex gives the scene energy but also conveys the level at which these characters are able to connect. 'Swinging' organ music begins as the session commences while the editing becomes faster as the activity more frenzied. It is here and only here that the film employs the 'cut up' style, applying it in its context of the industrial manufacture of images.

The chemistry between the model and the photographer is apparent but it is for only as long as he needs her. It is a representation that is bound up in the virility of Thomas' character, whose aggressive masculinity is shown in his ability to make the woman bend to his will. Following the session he is as dismissive of her as he was before, having now served her purpose. Reclining on the couch his attention wanders and he takes a phone call from a junk shop.

Thomas moves quickly to another part of his studio and calls for his assistant Reg to 'bring the birds down'. The models all come to the window and stand in a line, ready to be selected. The idea of women as 'birds' in the Sixties parlance is a reminder of the attitudes toward women at the time which despite the new ideas of liberation, are not applied equally.

DISSATISFACTION

Thomas shares a similar demeanour as Tolen in *The Knack*, as both characters are detached and share the same overtly masculine passive-aggression toward women. However, whereas youthful fun and romance dominate *The Knack* it is this detached figure of cultivated cool who is the representative figure in *Blow Up*, the essential dissatisfaction of the character exemplified by his constant movement and inability to remain still:

'…He constantly moves from one context to another and is incapable of focusing his attention on a subject for very long, and this is partially expressed by the rapid succession of visual images. Not one single episode in the film is sustained: there are always interruptions.' (Kinder in Huss, 1971: 85)

The photographer walks into the stark white space of the studio. It has some black transparent square screens in the centre creating fashionable geometric patterns. This is his world, here he is god-like and he walks into the set to inspect it.

A female assistant uses clothes pegs to make the models' dresses fit and she hides the tags which are still attached to one. The commodification of the girls is emphasised, as in *The Knack*, and the models this time are like mannequins, made up in different ways but all devoid of personality, for all their fantastic outfits still industrial objects:

'The outfits Antonioni selects reveal to what tastes mod designers are appealing:

the taste for fantasy. The fashions H. (Hemmings) photographs belong to a science fiction world cut off from ordinary experience. As a fashion photographer, H. is an indispensable middleman. His job is to catalyze the imagination of the larger community and to induce women into mod's fantasy world…H. and his like keep the establishment imagination (inhibited by discipline) supplied with images of delight, abandon, passion, freedom; no matter that they are fantasy images.' (Slover in Huss, 1971: 111)

Thus what was for a moment rebellious and exciting has been immediately transformed into commodity and what was indicated in George Harrison's encounter with the trend setters in *A Hard Days Night* is repeated here as the industry kills the ideas of excitement and vibrancy by making them mass-produced products.

The photographer stops one of the models chewing gum as he controls their every move in what is a world away from the fantasy freedom they are selling. 'Not on my floor,' he commands militarily before ordering another model to lower her arm. He shouts at them to wake up and tells them to thank their lucky stars they're working with him. The women strike a series of ridiculous poses and though they are told to rethink, it is clear they are not expected to think at all and he vilifies them for not smiling. 'What's wrong with you? Have you forgotten what a smile is?' he asks, exposing the tragic lack of passion in this fashionable world. Finally he tells them to relax and close their eyes before leaving them like that in a childish prank.

Thomas' bullying behaviour not only shows someone who is arrogant, egotistical and uses his position to indulge his own self-importance but whose rampant masculinity is a reflection of an age, as illustrated in *Darling*, in which men are using and exploiting the glamour industry as a means by which to control women. The idea of glamour is extremely important and alluring but women have to subjugate themselves in order to achieve success. The fashion models all look underweight and are misused and abused. Despite the informal environment and modern music, there is a lack of happiness or even humanity. Annie Goldman points out:

'…the absence of all erotic value in these women whose skinniness is akin to the rigidity of dead bodies and whose pale makeup is responsible for their loss of individuality.' (Ross in Huss, 1971: 102)

DREAM

Thus the commercialised, mass culture is associated with passive conformity, even death.

Excitement and individuality, the domain of the young, have been packaged and sold until they become pale imitators of something that doesn't exist. The freedom they supposedly all symbolise, a manufactured dream.

Thomas next visits his artist friend Bill with whom he shares his rather bohemian work space. Bill talks about his abstract work, which, echoing Antonioni's own approach, he only can better understand by revisiting it, examining his own paintings for meaning that appears later. He likens it to an investigation in which the pieces fall into place. This self-reflexive dialogue is outlining how *Blow Up* and Antonioni's work should function for the audience as it is an investigation that follows. As ever with an eye on commercial transaction, Thomas immediately offers to buy another of his paintings but his offer is declined.

The painter's girlfriend, Patricia, played by Sarah Miles, enters and pours the photographer a beer. He sits and drinks it while she massages him. It is clear that she is attracted to Thomas and has genuine feelings for him, though he seems unaware, his disconnected demeanour apparent.

When Thomas returns to his own apartment, two young would-be models are awaiting his arrival. They look at him with doe eyes and try to persuade him to spare them some time but he is unsympathetic. 'I haven't even got a couple of minutes to have my appendix out.' He eyes the girls but does not talk to them and turns on the radio after playing with a coin, another symbol of commercialism. When they ask when they should come back he answers, 'don't'. He is disdainful of them and when his assistant returns he checks on the other models which are still waiting for him to return. He walks out without paying the other girls any attention other than to tell one of them that their bag is 'diabolical' and drives away as they chase after his car.

The desperation of the girls in trying to impress Thomas shows his elevated status as a creator of images. He is able to give these two rather insecure people affirmation through taking their photograph as though without their image being reproduced they do not have any validation in a world where image is all.

As the girls are left in the distance he turns the car radio on and listens to more of the swinging music with which he seems associated. As he drives, the camera movement and editing are fast, exaggerating the pace of movement. He drives through derelict areas where there is rebuilding in bombed out spaces. This less fashionable area of London is in transition. Pulling up outside the junk shop mentioned previously, a gay couple pass by, walking their poodle. Once inside, an older shop assistant is very unhelpful, seemingly taking an instant dislike to the self-confident young man. Returning to his car Thomas picks up his camera and, after taking some pictures of the shop, goes into a local park.

This journey outside of the glamorous, mod world indicates a change in the nature of the story as indicated by the environment. The bright colours of London give way to a space which seems untouched by the swinging Sixties and the park seems to have the peace which Thomas' life is lacking. He again tries to capture the moment, perhaps to make it into commodity.

The park is very quiet and the framing of shots emphasises these wide open spaces. The photographer runs around, chasing pigeons, looking for a shot. He spies a pair of lovers, who are making their way to the top of a hill. He follows them and takes surreptitious pictures. The girl, played by Sixties icon Vanessa Redgrave, seems distracted and keeps looking around, even when embracing her lover. (This sequence continues for four minutes.) The photographer takes some more shots before walking away.

Here as in many of the sequences Antonioni's style dominates, as the viewer expectantly awaits an event. There is a naturalistic feel and he does not employ non-diagetic sound to indicate to viewers when moments are of significance to the story, encouraging the viewer to find their own meaning. His very visual way of shooting and arranging shots encourages the viewer to experience the world in a different way and is at odds with the fast editing of most modern film, particularly those associated with the Sixties. In *Blow Up* there is a cinflict between the long takes, which slow the narrative, and the way Thomas leads his life.

The woman, noticing their observer, chases after him and seems fraught with worry. She offers to buy the photographs but he refuses as there are others on the reel he wants. Desperate she tries to wrestle them from him pulling the camera away until she falls to her knees. She appears absolutely distraught. He pulls the camera away, 'Don't let's spoil everything, we've only just met.' 'No, we haven't met. You've never seen me.' Turning around she suddenly runs away across the deserted park and Thomas takes some more photographs of her retreating figure.

This odd encounter builds up both tension and mystery, without any resolution. Their conversation hints at the lack of apparent meaning to their meeting and questions the significance of it. Her response that they haven't met calls into question Thomas' experience and is a precursor to the film's climax.

Strolling back to the junk shop, Thomas finds that the owner has returned. She is a young woman, who seems somewhat distracted (perhaps due to drugs). Telling her that his agent phoned earlier, she seems to have little recollection only conjecturing that money may have been a problem and that this is always seems the case, repeating the commercial concern that seems so central to relationships in the film. She tells him of her wish to leave the antiques trade and 'get off' to Nepal or Morocco. Seeing a huge propeller, Thomas suddenly becomes animated stating his need to have it immediately ('I can't live without it').

The sights associated with swinging London are seen on his return as he drives past numerous red London buses but there is also the contrast of affluence against poverty. Thomas, as we have seen, is a commercial figure and his role as middleman is again emphasised. Having been to the junk shop, he is acting as an agent and contacts a potential buyer via his car radio that the shop is worth purchasing. The buyer seemingly doesn't like the idea but the photographer tells him what he has seen. 'What about all the buildings going up around the place? Already there are queers and poodles in the area.'

He is an opportunist, an exploitative figure who is keen to avail himself of whatever the changes in London are. He is a character who wishes to capture the right moment in more than just his camera.

Pulling up outside a restaurant where he meets with Ron (Peter Bowles), his publisher, and shows him the photographs he has taken at the homeless shelter. Thomas tells him where he wants them positioned in a book they are publishing. He tells him that he has a 'fab' photo that he has taken at the park that morning that will finish a book otherwise filled with images of violence with one of peace. Ironically the picture he has taken will illustrate the opposite…

FREE

Once again we see Thomas' agitated manner as he quickly orders his food and peers outside through the blinds as though there is something better elsewhere. His comments that he has gone off London this week, reinforces his dissatisfaction. Nodding toward a fashionable girl, he comments, 'I've had enough of those bloody bitches. I wish I had tons of money then I'd be free.' 'Free to do what? Free like him?' Ron asks pointing out a picture of a vagrant against a background of squalor.

Thomas' discontent at his own surroundings and life shows a generation looking for meaning. Despite all the changes that have taken place and all the new supposed freedoms, Thomas like Diana in *Darling* searches desperately for happiness but it is always somewhere else, freedom an elusive concept.

The intrigue of the story begins again as Ron points out a man, peering through the window of the restaurant. This mysterious fidure goes to the back of Thomas' car before running away. Thomas goes outside, checks the boot before driving away. He briefly stops for 'ban the bomb' protestors, one of whom he allows to plant a placard in the back of his car. Looking behind him he sees he is being followed. The placard ('Go Away') falls from the back of his car. Though these are the elements of a chase, this is not emphasised in the narrative and it is not clear who is persuing who as again conventional spectatro pleasure is denied.

Thomas' brief involvement with the protestors shows how easily he ingratiates himself with the 'moment' and yet remains utterly uninvolved. As the placard falls from his car, he is unconcerned, a further sign of his lack of engagement. He pulls up outside his studio, making a brief phone call. The girl from the park, Jane has presumably followed him with the mystery man and wants to retrieve the photos. Inside, she looks around his flat, inquisitive and clearly anxious. He asks her why the pictures are so important and insists that he wants some of the shots. 'My private life's already in a mess it would be a disaster if…'.

'So what?' he answers, claiming it could help sort out her mess. Like so many of the conversations in the film it is disjointed, marked by its interruption and ambiguity. The inability to communicate is demonstrated by the characters which seem lost in this world.

She paces uncomfortably up and down and though he tells her she could be a model and stands her in front of a backdrop, she is not interested. Unlike the other women in the film, his control over her is not through her own desire to be captured by the camera; it is through her being reluctantly captured. He puts on music again as the sexual tension increases.

The phone rings and Thomas tells Jane it is his wife, but it isn't clear what Thomas' actual relationship with the caller is, if indeed there is one. When he begins to tell her about his 'wife' he is vague and keeps changing his story. The dialogue is pointless as though there is little difference whether he tells her the truth or not. This has the affect of calling into question the reality or how the ability to communicate can undermine what we think we are seeing and hearing.

Thomas expresses his dissatisfaction again, petulantly complaining that he is bored with the beautiful girls that he has to photograph all day. However he then becomes briefly animated when a modish track comes on his record player. Handing Jane a joint, he instructs her how to smoke it but though she tries to relax she is unable to. When he leaves the room, she steals his camera and tries to get away but he intercepts her. Returning upstairs, she questions what it is he wants and then strips and stands topless in front of him, assuming it is sex. He, however, tells her to get dressed and that he'll get the negatives she wants. In the darkroom, though, he merely picks up a replacement roll of film. When he returns, however, she hasn't dressed and they go to the bedroom.

If the Sixties visions of A Hard Day's Night and The Knack communicate energy, the relations here are drained. There is little in the way of any life, the dope smoking and their unspoken agreement to sex seem borne of boredom and a routine aspect of their lifestyle rather than any desire:

'As defined by Hemmings and Redgrave in their hurried meeting, the sexual attitudes of all the characters tend to be unromantic and coolly sardonic.' (Ross in Huss, 1971: 103)

The need for escape is a motivation for the characters and this is reflected in their behaviour. This, however, is denied them and, yet again, there is an interruption. Before they begin their love-making the doorbell rings, indicating the delivery of the propeller from the junk shop. 'What's it for?' she asks. 'Nothing, it's beautiful,' Thomas answers, their disjuncture evident. They sit and smoke until she realises the time and gives him her telephone number before hurriedly leaving.

Thomas goes straight to his darkroom and begins the process of developing the negatives. He blows them up and hangs them on the beams of his loft. He inspects the photographs ever more meticulously, blowing up some of them to poster size to try to make sense of what he has seen. The camera moves backwards and forwards from print to print as the photographer interprets that something out of view is having an effect on the events in the pictures.

He tries to phone Jane (aptly enough for this fashionable girl, it is a Knightsbridge code) only to find the number doesn't exist. Turning back to the photographs he sees something significant. Blowing up a part of the undergrowth he sees a figure holding a gun. Each still image is pictured and retells the (hidden) story of what was actually happening that afternoon as though in a film narrative.

This process shows the construction of a film itself and provides another self-reflexive aspect to *Blow Up*. Thomas' means of communication and his ability to understand the world around him come through his camera.

MEANING

As he looks at the image it reflects the director's choices in constructing a sequence that makes sense. In an amazing sequence which shows Thomas constructing his own filmic reality it is as though Antonioni is exploring the idea of visual communication as he uses his own camera to bring life to the sequence of still frames. Antonioni's cinematic language, then, relies not on words to communicate meaning to the viewer, but on images. *Blow Up* provides the perfect analogy for the way Antonioni wishes images to function in his films:

> 'The photographic images are, in effect, cinematic images; Antonioni wishes the audience to pay attention to the language of the image, and not the language of words. The images say much more than any words could. However, just like the humans in his films that can never say what they mean (or vice versa), images are not definitive and precise either.' (http://www.geocities.com/hollywood/3781/modernism.html)

However, although there is meaning created, it is not concrete and the more he blows up the images to find small details the more the reality dissipates. It becomes abstract, and as Patricia points out, it looks like one of Bill's paintings. In an age which began with such a definite idea of right and wrong, first there was a questioning of attitudes and power structures, now with *Blow Up* the process of analysis begins to question reality itself. The Sixties has moved into a phase of self-expression which has much to do with a complete re-evaluation of the world and the way in which it is experienced:

> '*Blow Up* is in fact a series of photographs about a series of photographs and so constitutes what might be called a metalinguistic metaphor, a highly self-conscious and self-reflexive meditation on its own process.' (Freccero in Huss, 1971: 118)

Thomas, whose name is barely mentioned throughout the film (another insignificance), is a figure who drifts through a dream-like reality where there seem few certainties. He inhabits a 'scene', the existence of which is questionable and is filled with people whose sense of reality is distorted, either by their living in this commercialised fantasy or by taking drugs to live in an alternate space. The way in which they experience the world seems central to the idea underlying *Blow Up* which makes it a highly ambiguous text. It has been subject to countless interpretations and it is this ambiguity, this sense of living in a lost void where meaning isn't clear that captures the moment so well:

> 'Antonioni managed to construct a brilliantly composed puzzle that permitted him to examine his own dilemma of artistic "truth." The photographer vainly trying to pry the hidden secret from the frozen moment of camera time was like the film director and his moving picture….' (Walker, 1974: 316)

Britain too has created its own reality but it is insubstantial and made by image-makers like Thomas – there is a lack of direction or certainty because everything has been questioned. The pleasures are now freely available but because there are no shared perceptions in this world of the individual, there has been something lost. What is life without meaning? There has to be some shared understanding, like the revellers show at the end. When Thomas finally joins them he shows a pleasure which is lacking through the rest of the film. This existentialist riddle expresses an age which for all its surface style has lost something vital.

The photographer phones his publisher, Ron, to tell him about what he thinks he has found. He is tremendously excited and tells him that something fantastic has occurred, thinking that he has saved someone's life by interrupting the attempted murder but he in turn is interrupted by the sound of the doorbell. It turns out to be the two aspiring models. He allows them in and the camera follows them as they run excitedly upstairs.

He tells them to make coffee but finding a rack full of fashionable outfits, they try some on and he returns to find one of them half-undressed. He pulls the outfit away and when her friend returns the girls begin to fight. He bars the door and eggs them on as they tear at each others clothes. Running excitedly from the room into his studio and still fighting, they pull down one of the backdrops, after which they strip *him*.

This scene of Sixties debauchery against a modish background of purple photographic paper is another of the defining images of the age but it is the power relationship between Thomas and the girls which points to its relevance to the times. Whereas Mark in *Peeping Tom* is dismissed and derided by his models, now Thomas' position as the powerful creator of 'fame' is not only appreciated but worshipped:

> 'As for the girls who come calling after hours, they epitomise …subservience at a comic level…the fantasy of male power associated with the camera. The mere promise of an eventual chance to model brings them stumbling out of their clothes in order to be sexually available to their benefactor.' (Scott in Huss, 1971: 93)

DISTANT

Having ordered the girls to leave, Thomas is blowing up another photograph, when he discovers that he didn't save the man's life as he had thought – he seems to have captured the image of his body. For the first time in the film, Thomas seems genuinely engaged with something other than his own fulfilment or personal gain and appears genuinely distressed. That evening he returns to the park and indeed discovers the man's dead body but hearing a noise in the undergrowth he runs away. Returning to his studio he walks around considering what he has seen before going to Bill's house where the door is open and he sees Bill and Patricia making love. He lingers momentarily and Patricia, seeing him, appears to be upset, perhaps even non-consensual, but Thomas, distant as ever, leaves.

Returning to his garret, he finds that the photographs he hung around the walls, like the girl, are now all gone. He discovers that in his absence the darkrooms have been ransacked and although he finds a copy of one of the photos, it isn't detailed enough to show the body with any clarity. The image is just an abstract form, without meaning.

He hears someone enter the building but it turns out to be Patricia and he asks her if she ever thinks about leaving Bill but she says that she doesn't. He tells her about the man that he saw killed this morning. She asks him who he was and he simply answers, 'Someone.' When she asks how it happened he says he doesn't know because he didn't see. 'You didn't see', she repeats quizzically.

'No', he answers.

'Shouldn't you call the police?' she asks and though he nods he shows no inclination to do so. He points to the photograph on the floor and she picks it up, commenting that it looks like one of Bill's paintings.

The conversation is stilted, another example of a lack of connection between two characters.

Their disconnection and their inability to express their own emotions emphasise their distance from the world around them. Patricia recognises the shape in the photo as being similar to one of Bill's paintings. They are both representations of reality but she is unmoved and Thomas's statement that it is just 'someone' dislocates them still further.

Adopting a look of steely determination, however, he runs to the phone and calls Ron, but he is out, and leaves to find him. Driving down the road he pulls up, seeing the mystery girl from the park outside a fashion store window. However, she disappears into the crowd and when he gets out following her she is gone again.

Running into a dark alleyway he finds himself in a club where a rock band is playing (actually The Yardbirds). They are dressed in mod fashion and the crowd are impassive, they are hypnotised by the performance. The guitarist begins to break up his guitar and throws it into the crowd, whereupon bedlam ensues. Thomas catches it and is pursued by crazed fans. Emerging onto the street he stands in front of a shop window full of mannequins in modish dresses. He tosses what is left of the guitar onto the pavement. It is picked up by a fashionable young man who inspects it before throwing it back down.

Thomas has entered a twighlight world of youth and they are portrayed like zombies, stood in an unthinking mass. There is no vitality here but rather the pop music so often identified with freedom and rebellion is here shown as having a controlling effect, reinforcing the negative side of the new mass entertainment:

'The young people among whom my film is situated are all aimless, without any other drive but to reach that aimless freedom. Freedom that for them means marijuana, sexual perversion, anything….' (Antonioni in Scott, 1971: 96)

When Thomas exits the club after being chased by those who know the guitar's connection to the band he then finds himself in a different place where the meaning of the item is removed, drawing attention to perception and cultural context in shaping our understanding of the world. Taken from its place, the artefact becomes meaningless.

The new culture, exemplified by youth, is not however completely confined to the young. The older generation too, or at least a privileged elite, has adopted their values and when Thomas then goes to a private house with wrought iron gates, the door is opened by a sophisticated looking man in a white suit. The room inside is full of fashionably dressed men and women of a wide age range. Thomas discovers Ron, stoned, in a room where people are laying on the floor, smoking marijuana. Verushka is there too and when the photographer comments that he thought she was in Paris, she answers, 'I am in Paris.'

The existential nature of Verushka's comment sees Thomas' 'investigation' become itself meaningless when reality itself has no meaning.

The photographer tries to explain his dilemma to Ron and persuade him that they must get a shot of the corpse but he is barely aware of what Thomas is telling him and instead persuades him to stay, Thomas effectively capitulating in his efforts to try and make sense of what he has seen and even, perhaps, make amends. The next morning he wakes, still clothed, on a mattress in one of the bedrooms and the partygoers have disappeared as though a dream.

He returns to the park with his camera only to find that the body is gone. He is at a loss and wanders around for a while but to no avail.

The peace and tranquillity of the park are now shattered by the sound of the costumed revellers who appeared at the beginning of the film. In their jeep, they drive around the park before stopping at the tennis court. Two of them mime a game while the others watch. They play a silent game in front of a silent crowd, their heads moving from side to side, before one hits the imaginary ball out of the court and the other gestures to the photographer to retrieve it. All eyes are on him. The camera follows the imaginary ball across the grass and Thomas goes to it. He mimes throwing a ball back and then his eyes seem to follow the ball in the recommenced game. We can now hear the diegetic sound of a ball hitting a racket as if a real game is now taking place (we don't see it).

Thomas' decision to become involved in the imaginary game, to take part in the shared reality is one which returns us to the idea 'what is actually real?':

'The final sequence of the film plays off this unstable nature of communicable "truth" within the photographic image... The audience may not see a ball, but the characters seem to, and the soundtrack seems to verify its presence. Does it really matter if the ball is there or not? The point, then, is that images are just as open to interpretation, just as fallible and unreliable as words are when it comes to their communicative powers.' (http://www.geocities.com/hollywood/3781/modernism.html)

An aerial shot of the Thomas sees him retrieving his camera from the grass. As the non-diegetic score fades up, Thomas himself slowly disappears from view, as if he were never there.

This puzzling ending has led many to conjecture as to its meaning but perhaps the most telling reaction was gained by Sarah Miles who played Patricia referring to the final sequence:

'I said, "Michaelangelo, what's this all about?" and he gave me the wickedest smile I've ever seen and said: "Sarah, it's for the critics." It was such a truthful, adorable comment that my heart opened up to him…..' (Sarah Miles, *The Observer Review*, 5 August 2007, p. 13)

SUMMARY

What seems to be an investigative adventure leads the viewer to expect resolution and revelation but this expectation slowly evaporates until the seeming central drama of the murder becomes irrelevant and instead is replaced by a philosophical exploration of how the world can be understood. Antonioni's paradox of an investigation into a pointless mystery is an existential conundrum which moves far beyond a portrait of Sixties London but nevertheless it is a movie which in capturing a moment captures *the* moment.

What could be more pertinent to a society that has created its own media world than an ending in which the media have to create explanations. It seems to be the ultimate joke on a nation which has believed its own publicity and as Alexander Walker points out, this is the very essence of *Blow Up*:

'It is about a society paralysed by its own distractions…The click of the camera is the only finite element in this world whose inhabitants' mode of life appears outwardly so glamorous, lucrative and successful but actually encapsulates a repetitive incompleteness and purposeless.' (Walker, 1974: 327)

Ironically one contemporary critic seemed to identify the very aspect of the film that enables it to pinpoint the age. John Russell Taylor, reviewing the film in *The Times*, commented that *Blow Up* was:

'ideally a film to talk about at smart parties, but when the party is over, disappointingly little remains.' (Taylor in Sandbrook, 2006: 405)

Blow Up evidences a shift away from the simplistic ideals of class struggle or youth rebellion. With the discovery of swinging London comes its death. Like Thomas' murder victim, it is questionable whether it ever really existed. Instead we are left with an idea and a realisation of a lack of substance. Antonioni, faced with negative reviews from critics who had missed the point, was left to:

'…laugh sadly at the irony of being berated by critics for getting "wrong" a reality which the whole film was designed to show as subjective.' (Walker, 1971: 331)

Antonioni claimed never to have tried to capture London but he did – by exploring the nature of reality. The undercurrent throughout the film is one of a fantasy world, a culture based in the new media, created and shaped by commercially-driven figures like Thomas. By making this existential movie in which nothing seems concrete or to matter, it indicated both the apex of the new culture and its end. Was Britain ever swinging, and does it really matter, if we *believe* it was?

CHAPTER NINE: DECADENCE AND REBELLION — *IF...* (COLOUR, ANDERSON, 1968)

Films to watch: *Performance* (1970), *Wonderwall* (1968), *Blow Up* (1966)

COUNTER CULTURE

There is very little in the way of counter culture in British cinema. The psychedelic haze of *Performance* (1970) is the closest British film came to the mind bending expression of Sixties rebellion but perhaps an indication of British cinema's inability to move on from the positive Sixties ideal was shown in the way this prescient film — made in 1968 — was shelved and not released until 1970. While America's *Easy Rider* (1969) became a huge hit in the States and paved the way for arguably the most exciting and inventive time of American cinema, *Performance* by Donald Cammell and Nicolas Roeg sat gathering dust.

By the time *Performance* was released it seemed to announce the death of the Sixties. It's a rather tainted and dark portrayal of the ideals of free love, lost in a haze of drugs hidden in a basement in Notting Hill Gate, its central character was a washed up pop star, the epitome of the soured Sixties dream. Like *Peeping Tom* (1960) before it, the film was met with a barrage of criticism that could neither understand nor was willing to comprehend its meaning. Like the character of Chas, a gangster looking for a hideout, *Performance* had seemingly been left behind by the times and was not well received in a country reluctant to admit that the film's portrayal had struck a rather inharmonious chord.

The counter culture, of course, was a product of those who wished to eschew society and reject its values. The idea of the swinging Sixties with all the associated optimism of Britain as a new and changed place had melted away and many were left questioning what had really changed. The old power structures remained intact and this was something that inevitably caused anger and disillusionment.

As John Lennon was to point out:

> 'Nothing happened, except we all dressed up,' he says. 'The same bastards are in control, the same people are runnin' everything. It's exactly the same.' (Lennon in Haslam, 2005)

This realisation that nothing much had changed, contrary to the media generated idea of a new liberal and classless society, indicated that the ideological constructs of upper-classes were very much intact. Despite the media revolution the reality was very different and this led young people to vent their disgruntlement at figures of authority.

The first generation to have grown up with television, to have experienced worldwide events from a shared perspective was seemingly beginning to develop a shared consciousness. The growth of globalisation was impacting on a generation who were disenfranchised and alienated from the aims of those in authority, discontent at a lack of social and political progress in this new modern world. For all the rhetoric of change people felt let down and the shared disillusionment suddenly seemed to manifest itself in insurgency.

Socialism was a growing force amongst those who felt this way and political activism was rising. Student protests in America and France which occurred in 1968 showed the strength of feeling, striking a chord internationally, and the rise of a new left-wing anti-establishment culture was beginning to pose a real threat to existing power structures the world over. Although the protests and uprisings which took place were not coordinated and shared no single cause it seemed as though they were all connected, part of a worldwide wave of discontent.

Britain, though it had a strong anti-war movement was by no means at the hub of this global movement and its time as a political force already ended, its time as a cultural leader was almost at an end too. The focus was inevitably moving elsewhere. As this awareness grew it served as an awakening to the reality of Britain's new situation and a gloom began to descend which would continue into the next decade:

> 'There was always a slightly diluted taste to the British version of 1968. Neither the number of people involved nor the aggressive purity of the confrontations with the (unarmed) British police matched the benchmarks set at the Sorbonne and Nanterre in France or Berkley and Columbia in the United States.' (Donnelly, 2005: 144)

However, one British film was produced and whose release coincided with these dramatic world events in such a way that it resonated globally while simultaneously reflecting British society. If... (1968) imagines a scenario in which that most British of institutions, the public school, is attacked from within, overthrown by its own pupils. This seditious conceit, like a latter day gunpowder plot, was seen as an attack on the ruling classes and the principles which underlie its dominance:

> 'It lays bare the process by which the system produces an authoritarian elite to govern the country, deals with dissidents and induces unthinking conformism.' (Aldgate and Richards, 1999: 204)

If... was concerned with the taken for granted, hegemonic rule of a privileged elite which had somehow stayed intact and remained almost untouched throughout the supposed Sixties revolution. By making the setting a public school, a world removed from outside society, it showed that the Establishment was still alive and much unchanged. The values, which had been dominant for centuries, would continue and those who would perpetuate them would continue to take up positions of power in society. In this way it articulated the discontent that Britain, for all its Sixties excitement had failed to bring about the end of the class system.

Ironically, it was the work of a film-maker who had been a part of the public school system and who had set out not to reflect the current civil disorder sweeping the world but to reflect on his own very personal experiences as a student. Perhaps not so surprising, however, is his place as one of the innovative directors of the 'Free Cinema' movement which played such a critical part in highlighting working-class life in the early part of the decade, part of the movement which had pointed out that British cinema '...was dedicated to an out of date national ideal' (Anderson in Hedling, 1998: 139).

Lindsay Anderson, whose film *This Sporting Life*, often the most highly praised of the British New Wave films is a director whose individual style was concerned with the British character and although part of the British new wave, Anderson's approach to film-making is difficult to limit to any particular movement.

This Sporting Life can be dealt with as a work apart from the other new wave films, filmed as it is with a series of flashbacks and mostly in the studio. Anderson, a theatre director had a vision of film which differed greatly with the new wave determination to relate everyday life through realism:

> '"I don't believe in naturalistic cinema. People being boring in front of the camera." Art thought Lindsay, was "an experience not the formulation of a problem."' (Anderson in Caterall and Wells, 2001: 53)

He considered film a poetic medium, allowing expression beyond the limiting space of the stage. For Anderson film could be used to express emotions through visual metaphor and construct narrative that was not dependent upon logic. In this way he forms a link between the theatrical film-making of the Sixties, the experimentations in form that can create new meaning and the highly individual film-making of the Seventies. *If…* is a film which captures a turning point both in attitude, in film style and the nation.

If…, like *The Knack* (1965), features experimental, Brechtian techniques, but it is quite different in that such techniques, with their combination of fantasy and reality, do not proliferate throughout the film and the techniques are not employed in the modish manner one might associate with the Sixties. His style is far more subdued and is often contrasted with the Sixties experimentation that preceded *If…*, Alexander Walker describes the movie as a 'relief from the frenetic trendiness' (Walker, 1974: 402) of British production at the time.

Anderson is not interested in creating any feeling of the swinging Sixties through film style, in fact quite the opposite, the place he creates is quite timeless and much of the film is shot in a very simple style while still crossing the boundary between reality and fantasy. Despite some crossover in technique indicating a departure from reality, the sensibility and dominant style he insisted was quite different:

> 'Stylistically I don't think *If…* fits very closely into a contemporary picture of film-making, except in so far as developments in the last…ten years have made it possible to work with much greater freedom in the cinema than before, and to be personal and not bound in to the traditional and conventional ideas of narrative construction and narrative style…The more what we might call "trendy", or eccentric, or showy technique has tended to become in the last few years, the more I have felt I wanted to make films with as much simplicity and as much directness as possible.' (Anderson in Aldgate and Richards, 1999: 212)

However, despite Anderson's reluctance for *If…* to be grouped with the 'trendy' films it is a piece of work which reflects the times. The use of adventurous film language to convey meaning links him to Sixties innovation because as he states, his film style develops as a result of Sixties changes. Though Anderson is loathed to be included with the swinging London cinema associated with Richard Lester, there is a striking similarity if not of technique then of influence that make both film-makers part of the same confluence.

Lester was, as we have already seen, heavily influenced by the Nouvelle Vague and he wished to emulate directors such as Godard in deliberately undermining the traditional and accepted codes and conventions of cinema. Anderson too acknowledged the influence of European art cinema in his work and the freedoms that these experimenters were bringing:

> 'The most important stylistic development is the escape from the straightforward narrative film, previously the basis of cinema (certainly of the American cinema). We have reached a point where the material of the film can be presented in more subjective ways…For me the cinema is a poetic medium.' (Anderson in Hedling, 1998: 59)

Anderson refers to his work in cinema as poetic while the cinema of Lester was associated with commercialism as his background was in television. Lester's American roots contrasted with Anderson's very British background but both directors try to break conventional boundaries of cinema, they both try to communicate Britain as a microcosm and both are influenced by the theatrical techniques, the use of space which is pointed out by Erik Hedling in his book about Anderson:

'The limited space theatrical space…incites co-operation from the audience according to a set of rules which expand the significance of the actions. Sign functions are created by means of the internal logic of the theatre, that a hole in the floor represents Yorick's grave in Hamlet…Theatre then is a spatial game based on the a conventional relationship between signifier and signified.' (Hedling, 1998: 58)

Neither of the directors works to create a literal narrative and instead the viewer is left to their own devices in creating meaning. Anderson's more subdued and simple approach indicates a movement toward the *auteur* dominated cinema of the Seventies where fantasy has ceased to be a novelty used for comic effect but is blended with reality to form a different and extremely individual perception of the world.

If… then is a sign of things to come and functions in the world of signs. It is a film which makes allusions to literature and employs theatrical devices to distance the viewer from the reality of what they are watching on the screen:

'Anderson shared Althusser's interest in Brecht, especially the use of "distancing" devices in his plays to encourage the spectator to think about the ideological implications of the action, accordingly "*If…*" uses a number of such devices to present the film as an allegory rather than a realistic depiction of school life.' (Leach, 2004: 191)

Of course the ideological content of *If…* too is also a reflection of the times, the prevalent mood in Britain was changing and the real world was beginning to break through the Sixties illusions. The sense of awakening is at the forefront of *If…*, of an angry awakening that spurs action and it is this that makes it such a powerful movie.

INSTITUTION

The title '*If…*' is one of the many literary references that exist in the text and Anderson uses this to frame the story of Mick and his friends who will have to face the challenge of a very British institution:

'It borrows its title from a poem by Rudyard Kipling, the author most associated with Britain's imperial past that describes the challenges a boy must confront if he wants to become a man.' (Leach, 2004: 191)

The film begins with the Paramount film company sign over which is played organ music. This is followed by a quote from the Book of Proverbs, Chapter 4, Verse 7:

Wisdom is the principal thing,

Therefore get wisdom

And with all thy getting

Get understanding.

That there is a lesson to be learned is clear and this both ironic and epic introduction precedes a film with intent to subvert. There is a palpable sense of unease. The rather pious quotation connects ideas of teaching, morality and religion with school though whether the wisdom will be gained through the teachings of the school is questionable:

'The wisdom that the college preaches leads only to conformity and dullness, the boys are encouraged to "understand" nothing, just obey.' (Graham, 1981: 103)

As the credits continue over a black print of school buildings, the title of the film appears in blood red, indicating the rebellion to come. Similarly the sound of a choir singing continues until this is replaced by the sounds of slamming, footsteps and boys laughing. This in turn is replaced by a rather sinister and threatening music. This enigmatic opening with its use of colours of anarchy (red and black), combined with the satirical use of the Kipling's 'If...' poem sums up much of what the film tries to communicate:

'Anderson was keen to point out that If... was not just about public schools, describing it as "a metaphor, if you like, of life in Britain today – the image of the school as a reflection of a certain British tradition".' (Murphy, 1999: 157–8)

Hence, the public school becomes representative of the nation. Here, where wealth and privilege thrive and where the next generation of society's leaders are educated, the school becomes a metaphor for the establishment and also shows a very definite power structure which had become for many unacceptable:

'Many felt...that the old elites remained in charge, adapting to, and accommodating, social and cultural change. The public schools were their bastion, and as the public sector of education went steadily comprehensive, the voices raised against the private sector became more strident. Gone was the desire for cautious evolutionary reform. Now the call was for the total abolition of those centres of privilege, power and class consciousness.' (Aldgate and Richards, 1999: 203)

Throughout the text there is a juxtaposition of the veneer of British tradition and the reality that underlies it principles. Elegant shots of grand buildings, ideals of religion and education conceal a structure that at its core is cruel and dehumanising. The choice to share Kipling's title clearly raises questions of patriotism and Empiric values, provoking reflections on how national identity is constructed. The boys who rebel against the conformity imposed by the school are often portrayed as embodying the spirit of freedom, that rather than rebelling against the school they are trying to reclaim its original values. Based on a story called 'The Crusaders' we can see that the original title connects the boys' rebellion to a just cause and patriotic heroism:

> 'I think these boys are traditional heroes. They become men. They stand up for their convictions and for themselves against odds that may be overwhelming….Now because the end is not literal, the end is plainly a metaphor.' (Anderson in Hedling, 1998: 104)

This of course, when read as a metaphor for England at the time it was unsurprisingly interpreted as a thinly veiled attack on authority and provoked angry responses in some quarters, Eric Rhode of *The Listener* describing it as the most 'hating film I know' (Hedling, 1998: 92). But the connection between structures of power and the construction of a dominant view of the world is something that is relevant to a Britain enslaved to ideals of tradition and heritage manufactured by a small elite.

One of the Brechtian devices Anderson chooses to employ is to divide the film up into titles, using placecards like the chapters of a book. This while in keeping with the literary references which proliferate the text also has the effect of distancing the viewer from the reality of the situation and is one of many devices Anderson uses in homage to other works notably, Jean Vigo's *Zero de conduite* (1933), another school film.

I. TRADITION – COLLEGE HOUSE

We see a busy corridor full of students dressed in traditional school uniform. This could be a scene from Tom Brown's *Schooldays* and immediately immerses us in a life removed from modern, common experience but also one bound in British culture and heritage. This environment is a world of its own and even has its own arcane language. However Anderson's intention to permeate the text with allusions and move beyond the story is made clear with a reference to a student called 'Machin', the name of the lead character from his previous film, *This Sporting Life*.

A frenetic introduction shows an overcrowded environment where there is a sense of chaos and the individual is lost. This establishment unlike so many of our Sixties films does not focus on individuality; in fact quite the opposite. *If…* considers the sublimation of the individual to organised authority.

On the staircase an older pupil, Rowntree, who is dressed in a flamboyant waistcoat and carrying a cane commands the pupils to 'Run in the corridor'. Emblematic of the system, he carries a box with the motto, 'Ancient age'. Some others are crowded around a noticeboard and one of the younger students, Jute, asks an older one, Stephans, for help:

'Excuse me, I can't see my name, I'm new', but the whimpering appeal for sympathy elicits none. 'You don't speak to us. You're a scum aren't you?'

'I don't know,' he answers.

'Of course he's a scum. You're blocking my view scum,' says Biles.

Thus the idea of status and hierarchy is introduced immediately. Jute, the new pupil, is at the bottom of the structure and needs to learn the way in which the organisation functions. He reappears throughout the film and we follow his process of integration until he disappears, overwhelmed and consumed by the system:

'Almost without realizing it, Jute becomes absorbed into the mass of undifferentiated boys and fades away as a center of interest in the film; by the end he is simply another standard-bearer. He is really the first casualty of the film, a prop for the clichés and outmoded rituals of the Establishment.' (Graham, 1981: 106)

He is labelled 'scum' as he has no status, whereas Rowntree whose outward appearance reflects his rank, has both privilege and power. How he uses this, however, is immediately questionable as can be seen in his instruction for pupils to run in the corridor. This, of course is at the very root of the film, as it highlights the abuse of power in a world of chaos. Rowntree commanding another student to 'Warm a lavatory seat for me, I'll be ready in three minutes,' sums up both his power and the rather ridiculous nature of this ordered environment where every action is controlled. Nonetheless it produces absolute obedience and even Biles, a character who is abused within the system, does not question its unfairness and actively reinforces it by bullying Jute and pushing him aside, passing down the actions and ensuring their continuance.

If… examines not only a system which imposes rules but the suitability of those who make them. The narrative which follows Jute's integration as well as providing insights into a range of characters who make up the system makes it clear that the Establishment is greater than the sum of its parts and that the hierarchy and rules by which it functions leave little room for consideration of the individual. But it is the way in which the systemic life the Establishment constructs which dehumanises those inside it contradicts the principles on which it is founded which makes the film such a potent attack. It is the way in which the higher principles expounded by those who control the system are shown to be completely hollow.

The system does not encourage free thought but values unthinking duty above all else. This sense of duty, so close to patriotic duty is examined in If… which demonstrates the questioning attitude toward education that would also be central to Ken Loach's Kes (1969), a film which also examined the social role of school in preparing the students to integrate effectively into society and the working world, a world controlled in western society by capitalist principles. This type of thinking brought to the wider public ideas popularised in new subjects such as sociology which questioned taken for granted structures upon which society is built and questioned who benefited through them. In *If...* school is structure, just like society:

'School takes control over all aspects of life according to a firmly set system of hierarchically organised rules and rituals. Even the ostensibly private is regulated.' (Hedling, 1998: 83)

Rowntree's position of dominance is enhanced for the viewer by Jute's mistaking him for a master and the representation of the prefects or whips as they're called is connected to the way in which power is enforced. Throughout the film they punish, cajole and bully under the protective umbrella of the institution's rules and are rewarded by their privileges.

Manning escorts Jute to the sweat room which is full of wooden desks and shelves where boys are involved in a variety of activities. Brunning calls to a bewildered Jute and allocates him spaces for his books, magazines, food and posters, reinforcing the control over the private with small concessions to the boys as individuals and the acknowledgement of an outside world:

'As an example of repressive tolerance, a few emblems of resistance are allowed in the "Sweat Room", the junior common room, like posters of Che Guevara and the Apache chief Geronimo.' (Hedling, 1998: 83–4)

Hierarchy

The way in which the hierarchy works is indicated as one of the younger boys, Machin, calls for silence and announces rules regarding tinned food. When they groan he tells them all to 'Shut up,' exhibiting exactly the same authority as Rowntree but within a slightly different sphere, thus as Biles conforms to the pattern so do the younger boys who imitate their elders and recreate the system at a lower level. The idea of personal freedom and the repression of such freedom can be seen as, left to their own devices, the boys exuberantly play.

On the staircase, a student, Bobby Phillips, passes downstairs before being obstructed by another, Keating. After allowing him to pass, he and his friend stop on the stairs and look at him. 'Come on up Bobby', he says. 'We want to stroke you,' says the other.

Another older pupil, the whip Denson reprimands them but then addresses himself to the other boy. 'And you Phillips, stop tarting.' He waves his cane at the back of his head and tells him to get a haircut.

The system of the school and the continual sublimation of one's own needs to the whole necessarily produce a reaction, and rebellion comes in all forms. Signs of repression are highlighted as Bobby Phillips is targeted for his appearance. His feminine looks and longer hair are shown to be unwelcome and threatening in this environment, which discourages any sexual activity. Those that show any sign of individuality are condemned and must be controlled, hence Phillips link with immorality in the form of a 'tart' or prostitute, nevertheless he is desired:

> '[t]he impulse for freedom naturally finds expression in emotional relationships as well as action. Perhaps the film suggests the link between sex and freedom…' (Sussex in Headling, 1998: 87)

Denson looks bemusedly at another student, who passes by, carrying a large suitcase on his shoulder. His face is concealed from his view but we can see that he is wearing a scarf wrapped around his face and a trilby hat. When he enters the room he pauses, and the student issuing orders comments, 'God, it's Guy Fawkes back again,' but as he passes through the dorm, other students seem pleased to see him.

The implications in this introduction of Mick Travis are clear, his dramatic entrance reminiscent of Hitchcock's 'Lodger' present him in an ambiguous manner that holds both threat and puzzlement. His masked face and hat immediately make his appearance subversive and Stephans even associates him with a figure of rebellion and attack on power, Guy Fawkes. Travis is also introduced as someone popular who has the respect of his peers, unlike Stephans, who aspires to power but is persistently disrespected.

Travis, the main instigator of rebellion is played by Malcolm McDowell, most famous for playing Alexander De Large in Kubrick's *A Clockwork Orange* (1971) and who would continue to work with Anderson on what became the Mick Travis trilogy of films over three decades. *If…* was followed by the less successful films *O Lucky Man!* (1973), followed by *Britannia Hospital* (1982).

In another reminder of the way in which the students lives are rigidly controlled, Stephans reminds them that they have 29 minutes left to unpack but his power is noticeably not that of Rowntree's as some of the older and now more aware students clearly do not wish to conform. 'Can it bog-face,' says Wallace while Johnny Knightly tells him, 'Come off it Stephans, it's getting monotonous already.' As Stephans badgers other students a shot of Travis' eyes emphasises his growing resentment.

Retreating to his study Mick looks at himself in the mirror before unwrapping the scarf and revealing a rebellious moustache, which he proceeds to stroke. The music softens and he sighs before beginning to remove it with a pair of scissors. Knightly appears over the top of a partition, commenting, 'God you're ugly. You look evil.'

'Yeah, my face is a never failing source of wonder to me,' Travis replies, indicating the power of image:

> 'Mick is searching for physical means of expression, metaphorically depicted in his study by the images in his study of predators and violence.' (Hedling, 1998: 84)

The decoration of the room, like that of the sweat room denotes this as their personal space and as the music changes it introduces this area as the home of sedition. The posters reinforce the themes of the film: the silent scream of frustration and mental torture, the dictator Mao, and the motorcycle as a symbol of rebellion, and famously ridden by Che. These posters form a commentary on the action and constantly link events within the school to the outside world. Travis will later be seen riding a motorcycle in a rare moment of freedom and his facial hair is an indication of his rebellious streak. Like so many other characters in the Sixties films, he is fascinated by his own image and identity and is aware of how it can be used for rebellion:

'...Mick Travers (sic) – enigmatic but passionate, scruffy but glamorous – was a perfect symbol for aspiring revolutionaries of 1968.' (Murphy, 1992: 158)

 Knightly clambers over the partition and asks him why he grew it. Travis answers, casually, 'To hide my sins'. The call of 'Scum' can be heard in the background, with the subsequent trample of feet, reminding them that they cannot wholly escape the rules that dominate their lives and now, with the beginning of a new school term, Travis' opportunities to 'sin' will be curtailed.

Knightly picks up some shells, like reminders of the outside world and then the magazine indicating a picture of an African freedom fighter. 'What do you think of him?' he asks. Mick turns and with admiration says, 'Fantastic. Put him right in the middle.' Knightly begins to tear out the page and tapes it to the wall as the dramatic and sinister music begins again. The picture is positioned between Munch's painting and a photo of some soldiers again indicating the rebellion to follow. Mick moves closer and repeats, 'Fantastic', staring at the image shown in close-up of the wounded man with a machine gun against a background of chaos.

The still images which form their own narratives are related to the events of the school and vice versa as Anderson uses techniques popularised in the Seventies where film narrative is expanded by additional imagery. This meta-language exists both as part of the text and has its own relevance. This post-modern film style can be seen to develop in the British film of the Seventies where the viewer is encouraged to move beyond the surface narrative of the film through intertextual references and allusion, something as we can see Anderson encourages and gives *If...* greater resonance:

'Mick and Co. are associated with third world resistance to the imperial powers.' (Aldgate and Richards, 1999: 215)

This is a key point and again the picture mirrors the story which, by the end, will see Travis in the role of the freedom fighter, machine gunning against the forces of authority. The ideals of the swinging Sixties of fun and freedom have dissipated and in their wake is only resentment and entrapment. Travis appreciates that he, like much of the country has not been able to avail himself of the new liberation but moreover recognises there needs to be full scale rebellion to affect real change.

The ringing of bells interrupts the boys' reminiscences of the holiday and reminds them of how removed they are from the outside world. Travis' final comment, 'When do we live…?' sums up his frustration.

The next scene re-establishes the idea of communal life as all students stand around tables in the dining room. Behind the head table there are paintings of former headmasters, emphasising the continuation of the system.

The diminutive Mr Kemp, the housemaster, played by Arthur Lowe begins to speak:

> 'This term I've just one thing to say to you. One rule, follow it and you won't go wrong. And it is this. Work, play – but don't mix the two.'

He talks to the younger students about the bewilderment they may be feeling:

> 'We are your new family and you must expect the rough and tumble which goes with any family life. We're all here to help each other.'

The cutaway shots show the detached faces of two older female staff and the threatening faces of some older students:

> 'You will find here, in college house the discipline not only to help others but to help yourselves. Help the house and you will be helped by the house.'

This scene perfectly conveys the underlying threat of the institution that the communal principle is one of conformity.

Next, Rowntree's own speech emphasises his already established dominance and the need for the 'whips' in the maintaining of order in the structure, the police of the school. Whereas the master tries to appeal to the students with words, Rowntree threatens violence ('I will come crashing down on offenders'). The whips' dominance even elevates them above the masters as is shown by the behaviour of the ineffectual Mr Thomas who has to defer to the head whip. Rowntree's speech partners ideas such as indiscipline with lack of spirit which demonstrates that discipline and conformity are valued above else and associated with strength of character.

He then tells all the assembled pupils to line up for their medical inspection. The other whips shout out a series of commands before two of them take their places behind a desk and ask a series of questions relating to the health of the students, whose genitalia are then closely inspected by Matron, played by Mona Washbourne.

If... combines cold brutality and cruelty with moments of comedy which parody the all too real. Surreal moments such as the health inspection and the pompous procession of the staff before the pupils only serve to emphasise the ridiculous and perfunctory traditions of the school which seemingly serve no other purpose than to bend the students to the school's will. It is through this that the film presents a picture of dangerous conformism and repression.

Following a scene in which an over-weight boy is belittled by other students, there is the first of the film's periodic black and white sequences. Mrs Kemp escorts the new under-master, Thomas to his bare room, which has no central heating. Mrs Kemp tells him the wonderful thing about the room is that it's completely quiet and has a view of the chapel spire; but there is a sense that he is being imprisoned. She asks him for a shilling, which she puts in the electricity meter before leaving him sitting isolated on the bed.

The sub-standard treatment of the new master shows that he, like Jute, is at the base of the structure. It also demonstrates that there is little emphasis on academic learning in the school. The education that takes place is that of socialisation and conformity where the students and teachers learn their place.

The use of black and white stock for the scene seems at first to emphasise the cold nature of the location but this use of monochrome for some scenes persists throughout the film and is another Brechtian, distancing effect on the audience:

> 'We felt that variation in the visual surface of the film would help create the necessary atmosphere of poetic licence, while preserving a "straight" quite classic shooting style, without tricks or finger pointing.' (Anderson in Sutton, 2005: 53)

Jute's dorm is inspected by a whip, who congratulates Machin on the standard of presentation. Meanwhile Travis is showing his contempt for the whips by delaying his going to bed. He is gargling and combs his hair and disrobes flamboyantly before hopping dramatically into bed just before the whips arrive. The chief whip greets Stephans. They walk around the room and Mason tells Travis to get his hair cut as it's still long. Stephans is congratulated by the chief whip, showing how the structure of power is reinforced by the whips.

The film focuses on and explores the divide in philosophy between the boys who are free thinking and do not conform to the expectations of the system and those who represent the system. Travis, Wallace and Knightly refuse to accept the standards imposed upon them and their frustration at rules which they see as senseless is manifest. Stephans, however, shows that there is another generation of whips in waiting and that the system will continue, irrespective of individual disobedience. To Travis and his friends Stephans is just part of the system while to Stephans the rebellious behaviour is pointless.

2. HERITAGE — COLLEGE: 'ONCE AGAIN ASSEMBLED...'

The establishing shot shows the playing field with the school and chapel in the background. Another shot of the inside of the building and the singing of a hymn is shown in black and white, characters we have already met are amongst the throng. 'Let us pray', comes the instruction.

The scenic shot of the school emphasises ideas of heritage and tradition so often featured in British film and carry much of the same beauty but here they seem rather distant to the people who inhabit the buildings and the deliberate juxtaposition of the everyday events makes them seem almost aloof:

'...one could also read these images in "If..." as contrapunctal commentary, as beautiful images, contrasting the exterior with the brutality of and stupidity of the interior.' (Hedling, 1998: 91)

The students make their way to class. Travis' class walk into a lesson and one of the students bemoans the fact that there are no girls in the orchestra this year from 'Springfield', showing more signs of the sexual repression.

The teacher is heard singing 'To be a pilgrim' before we see this eccentric, cycling down the corridor and into the class, ordering the windows opened to allow in 'freedom'. He begins handing out essays by throwing them around the room. He tells Travis that he thinks he lost his essay in the Mont Blanc tunnel but is sure it was good. He begins to talk about the growth of nationalism, newspapers, railway, communication and how it led to World War I. He then puts forward the view that they may prefer to believe 'that history is a simple matter of evil dictators rather than whole populations of evil people, such as ourselves'. He is deliberately provocative, keen for the students to voice their opinion and asks whether this view of history is facile. Giving up, he sets them an essay title on George III.

The entrance of this cavalier history teacher tells us much about the school. His manner is individual and idiosyncratic and yet he cannot engage the boys in individual thought and he does not wholly fit into the school. He favours Travis, in whom he recognises a freer spirit, but this is one of the few times we see the students being taught and they are unenthused by the prospect of actually exploring ideas:

'Significantly, given the traditional public school commitment to character-forming rather than academic attainment, lessons only occupy a small part of the film, and the boys are seen as unresponsive and apathetic during them.' (Aldgate and Richards, 1999: 204)

The younger class is being taught Maths by the Reverend and as he instructs them he hits Brunning and he puts his arm around Jute's neck and chokes him. This depiction of the Reverend again shows how power can be abused. His sadistic manner demonstrates that religion and religious beliefs are used to benefit the dominant view and must be subservient to the organisation. While the Reverend continues to serve the school outlook, he will get away with this abuse of the children:

'The targets for their satire (Anderson and writer, Sherman) were the same: the state, the Church and the military.' (Hedling, 1998: 97)

Meanwhile the Head is giving a talk to some of the older students, walking them around the school and talking animatedly of the role of education in society. He lectures them on class and the responsibility entrusted to the middle classes. He talks about the modern world and how education must respond to this and how college is an exciting place:

'Britain today is a power-house of ideas, experiments, imagination, on everything from pop music to pig breeding; from atom power stations to mini-skirts, and that's the challenge we have got to meet.'

The Headmaster's speech about progress seems to link him with Harold Wilson, he is a rather liberal character but also a self-indulgent one, who views the world from the comfort and security of the school. His desire to teach a fashionable subject and to talk of a changing world, reflect his trendy views and methods. He wishes to be seen by the students as witty, approachable and modern but he is an anachronism. His view of a changing world is spoken from inside a school that clearly *doesn't* move with the times. What is apparent from his talk is that although he recognises that the customs are 'silly' he believes that the future of the country lies with these middle classes and their associated values.

Jute is being tested by Brunning and another pupil from his cohort. They ask him a series of questions about the school and its traditions, which Rowntree will test him on but they are angered when he makes small mistakes because as they explain, the whole house will be punished and he'll have to retake the test:

'The school is a rigidly ordered society with an unshakeable hierarchy from "scum" to "whips". Its exclusivity is reinforced by its arcane and self-perpetuating slang, in which we see a new boy instructed. He is made aware that it is not just content, but style which is important here.' (Aldgate and Richards, 1999: 204)

In contrast, a montage of images of war and religion is shown against a bookcase in Travis' room. He listens to some tribal music while lying on his bed and cutting out another image, of a lion, from a magazine:

'He listens constantly to the Sanctus from the Congolese Missa Luba, with its throbbing, exciting, primitive rhythm, speaking of rebellion, vitality and youth of an emerging continent.' (Aldgate and Richards, 1999: 215)

Travis is interested in primitive culture because it is the exact opposite to the stifling atmosphere of the school. He yearns to be wild and free, to express himself and cast off the oppressive shackles of the school. At a time when many of the Empire's countries are rejecting Britain's rule, Travis recognises the same culture of superiority being engendered in the school and similarly rejects it.

 Biles is chased through the gym by a group of other students before being carried to the lavatory where his head is flushed down the toilet. They tie him upside down. Wallace, who has been playing his guitar, gets him down after the boys leave. Biles stands with soaking hair and he says rather thanklessly, 'Excuse me, please, you're standing on my clothes.' Biles' acceptance of the situation shows that his integration into the system is successful. While bullied, Biles does not rebel against it, but rather maintains an unemotional politeness that is so ridiculous as to be almost surreal.

3. REPRESSION — TERM TIME

A game of rugby is being played. This is followed by a shot of the exterior of the school at night where Matron is laying out bedding. In the whip's office, Phillips is toasting what should be muffins. Denson, who harbours feelings for Phillips, is staring at him. Rowntree criticises Phillips for giving them crumpets before sending him away.

The transparency of the whip's loyalty to any cause but their own is highlighted as they talk about the obviously coveted Phillips and how another house has asked to swap him for a boy called Taylor. They laugh at Denson who doesn't like their lecherous conversation, calling him 'purity Denson'. He argues that it is their duty to uphold standards, as that is why they receive their privileges. However when he criticises their 'homosexual flirtatiousness', Rowntree exposes his protestations by calling Phillips back and making a gift of his services to Denson. When Phillips leaves, he turns to Denson and tells him to 'Say thank you.'

Denson's repressed homosexual desires are uncovered by Rowntree, who toys with his feelings but their laughter at Denson's expense forces him to point out that their privileges come in exchange for their service. This, however, is abused by the whips and it is clear that whatever advantage they can gain is the true object. This selfishness is encouraged by a system that rewards self-interest and once someone reaches the top of the hierarchy they are free to take advantage of others without hindrance.

Another montage featuring Marilyn Monroe and other images of the popular culture indicates a return to Travis' quarters. Knightly is reading *Women's Own* against a background of a topless model. He reads the horoscope to Travis: 'No matter how strong the urge, resist any temptation to go into battle this month. Otherwise you run the risk of not only being on the wrong side but possibly in the wrong war.'

The attitude of the rebels is in contrast to the whips, whose repressions have led to them substituting boys for women. Travis and his friends who refuse to accept their place in this society look to the outside world for comfort with images of Marilyn Monroe and a woman's magazine reminding them of the women outside. The dramatic irony of Knightly's horoscope demonstrates that Travis as an individual is destined to lose his battle against society and that the dominant rules will triumph in the end, but he seems to already know this: 'The whole world will end very soon, black, brittle bodies, peeling into ash.'

Wallace looks in the mirror, and in a portrait of adolescent angst fears he is going bald, suspecting they put something in the soup and complains that he will be senile before he leaves the school. Knightly reads out a problem page while Wallace begins to worry this time about having bad breath. Travis, however, continues:

> 'There's no such thing as a wrong war. Violence and revolution are the only pure acts…War is the last possible creative act.'

The feeling of losing life is tangible to the rebels and their talk often centres round their own hopeless situation but it also has a wider application. They are appalled and fascinated by decay. Their conversation is full of the moribund melodramatics that are a feature of teenage conversation but there is a hopelessness in their conversation that reflects depression brought on by the school and their situation. Travis' answer to these problems lies in aggression and death.

When Denson enters the room they deny drinking and when he asks Wallace to breathe he demonstrates contempt by showing that he has a mint on his tongue. Denson makes them stand up and tells them they'll have a cold shower the next morning for having hair that's too long. He then spots the chain of teeth around Travis neck and is disgusted. He tears them from around Travis' neck and calls him a degenerate.

Denson's fear of the rebels manifests itself in aggression. Travis' necklace of teeth is an outward message that he accepts he has a primitive side and dismisses this constructed civilisation which dehumanises. The rebels' long hair is another reflection of this as well as associating them with the Sixties rebellion in which people tried to free themselves of the strictures of society.

An exterior shot shows the outside of the building again and a bell is ringing. Bobby Phillips is carrying a bowl into Denson's room. He opens the curtains and Denson watches. He then applies shaving foam to his face. Denson's lecherous behaviour shows the desires he harbours beneath his façade of respectability which may well be the cause for his aggression to the rebels who unlike him can accept their feelings.

Travis, Knightly and Wallace take their cold showers under Denson's supervision. Denson sits in a bath and issues orders as Phillips brings him a cup of tea. When it is Travis' turn in the shower, Denson ignores him. He gets out of the bath and gets dressed while Travis says, 'My time's up you bastard.' But Denson tells him to 'Stay there till I get back.'

The relationship between the hateful Denson and the rebels demonstrates much about the structure of power. Denson recognises Travis' behaviour as a threat to his position, which is emphasised by his taking a bath while the others shower. The attitude reflected by his bathing while being waited on as a servant reinforces the rebels' association with the third world and the whips with the Empire.

4. HEROISM – RITUAL AND ROMANCE

In the gym a teacher is instructing the students to vault over the horse and then the boys run away to get changed. Bobby Phillips, to the sound of sinister music, goes to the balcony to watch Wallace on the parallel bars. Once again the music turns to that of wonderment as he sees Wallace below. He readies himself for his gymnastics but then turns and smiles at Bobby before beginning his routine. The slow motion and emphasis on the graceful movement of Wallace's routine show the connection between the two characters. The bond between Phillips and Wallace is one of mutual attraction and fondness, rather than one of repression or resentment and is in contrast to Denson's rather furtive glances.

The rebels position as heroic heroes can be seen as Wallace engages Knightly in fencing before Travis enters the fray by means of a gym rope and they fight each other shouting dramatic dialogue. Here the extent to which the text uses intertextuality and allusions can be seen as the literary references proliferate:

'The fencing scene provides an anthology of English poetry which renders explicit the strong sense of tradition in the search for freedom.' (Hedling, 1998: 93)

Wallace quotes Richard III, Johnny from Blake and Mick quotes Byron, Tennyson and Kipling as the boys are seen (or see themselves) in the heroic manner of those whose quest is to battle for England. Their romanticism conflicts with the Headteacher's attitude:

'…the boy's attitude can be contrasted with the petty bourgeois philosophy of the school.' (Raine, 1968: 268)

They run into another room and colour returns. Finally Travis is beaten to the floor and checking his hand he points to a wound, fascinated, 'Blood, real blood'. The result of their fighting has brought signs of life and is another indication that Travis will bring life through battle.

The crowd as instructed by Rowntree cheer the rugby and matron is seen shouting aggressively for 'fight'. Travis and Knightly use the match as a chance to escape unnoticed and meanwhile run through the town. They are seen crossing a roundabout which is being tended by two workers. They are handcuffed together, playing the role of escaped criminals in a scene reminiscent of The Beatles' escapes in *A Hard Day's Night*. The shop windows show Sixties fashion, lingerie and silverware as the outside world finally makes an appearance in the film. Travis watches a girl as she passes and then he and Knightly stage a play fight with Knightly falling to the ground and an old lady coming to check on him.

Travis and Knightly's youthful exuberance can be seen as reflecting their feelings of escape. Their joy at freedom gives rise to playful games and the sequence is filmed in a vérité style that also serves to contrast with the rigidity of their school. They steal a motorcycle from a showroom and are shown careering through the countryside, the music reflecting their sense of adventure. Point-of-view shots through the trees to the sky reinforce the feeling of freedom and resemble the free spirited camera work of the French New Wave.

Pulling up outside a roadside café (The Packhorse Café), the film returns to black and white and the seditious sounding music plays. The café is empty except for the young woman who works there. Travis and Knightly order two coffees. As she pours them, they look over the counter at her body.

She serves them as if in a western, sliding them along the counter with disdain. Travis asks for sugar and then grabs her arm and kisses her but she slaps him. The antagonism between Travis and the girl is like a mating ritual. The girl comes up behind him and puts a hand on his shoulder. He turns to face her and then she confronts him:

'Go on, look at me. I'll kill you. Look at my eyes.' With the framing accentuating the girl's eyes, she continues, 'Sometimes I stand in front of the mirror and my eyes get bigger and bigger and I'm like a tiger. I like tigers.'

She roars and he tentatively sniffs her before swiping at her with her hand and snarling. They begin to circle each other and bite in a mock fight to the sound of intense drumming before falling to the floor. Suddenly they appear naked continuing to snarl as the music reaches a discordant crescendo.

This sequence is strongly reminiscent of one featured in *The Knack* where the characters mimic animals and one can again see similarity between Lester's and Anderson's work.

The bizarre sequence is both strange and fantastic, seemingly taking place in a void – neither in the hermetically sealed school nor the outside world. This seems to be a key point in the film. The love-making is not gentle but rather it is frenzied and aggressive, with Travis and the girl behaving like animals. This primitive action is instinctive and primal, an awakening and has significance beyond a simple sexual encounter. Within the school there is no sex because there is no life ('when do we live?'). At the café Mick makes his dreams a reality in what Hedling describes as 'mental process narration':

> 'Mick and the girl imitate the predators (a lion and a tigress) from Mick's study walls; the beast of prey is the ultimate metaphor for the physical satisfaction Mick is denied by the rigidities of life at the school.' (Hedling, 1998: 87)

The tribal music sounds as the three are seen again in colour, racing across a field on the stolen motorbike. The girl stands between Travis and Knightly with her arms outstretched the crucifixion pose that will reappear later in the film when Mick is punished. The unspoken agreement is apparent.

This memorable sequence of sex and rebellion seems a metaphor of change. The western inspired café, the juke box, the introduction of a female character, the aggressive mating ritual seem to be symbols of freedom and they are indicated in a changing style that comes to dominate the latter stages of the film, departing from reality and entering into a realm where events are no longer restricted by the real world.

5. DISCIPLINE

The church bells give way to a shot of a rifle rack, more signs of war. Wallace and Phillips are talking in the arsenal and smoking. Phillips explains his ambition to be a criminal lawyer in California:

'I believe in having a goal,' says Phillips. 'That way you'll succeed.' He tells Wallace that his trouble is that he is has no ambition. 'No, I know,' he replies.

Wallace and Phillips' intimate conversation again suggests changing times. For Phillips, the future lies in America. This awakening of Britain to the new world opportunities is featured in other movies of the time, like Performance, which begin to recognise that it is America which will become the global influence and that Britain is a rather anachronistic country. Wallace, the older and more complacent character seems like the older generation, already left behind.

The pair are interrupted by the sound of footsteps and Wallace ushers Phillips to hide before Denson enters with his flashlight. He asks Wallace to explain himself. In close-up he asks who Wallace was with and he defiantly tells him, 'No-one'. The antipathy between the two characters who court Phillips' attentions is emphasised.

A close-up of the war collage in Travis' room (to violent music) is followed by a shot of Travis with a cellophane bag over his head. The music intensifies before fading and Knightly, holding a stopwatch, pulls off the bag and asks him what it felt like. 'Like drowning,' he replies, which initiates a discussion on violent death. Their youthful fascination with the subject will shortly be put to the test as the antipathy between their way of living and the establishment's begins to be recognised as they prepare themselves for death.

The elder prefects are having dinner with Mr Kemp, served by his wife. Rowntree talks about the existence of a 'lunatic fringe' at the school and how it may be necessary to make a few examples of what he terms a hard core, as he cracks a nut. Mr Kemp warns him that the Headmaster doesn't like too much thrashing but Rowntree counters by warning him of the dangers of the house getting a reputation for decadence.

The use of the word 'decadence' in particular makes the conversation relevant to the outside world. The Establishment is here questioning the behaviour of the rebels whose ruthless attitudes they find unsettling. The Establishment's response to the perceived threat is violence and one can see how it could be seen as a symbol of protest and connected to the riots which were happening across the world as youth stood against what they saw as an unjust establishment – be it against an unjust war (America in Vietnam) or repressive regimes in Eastern Europe.

Mr Kemp asks about the juniors and, again, Rowntree warns of unruly elements that threaten the stability of the house, advising that it is 'best to nip them in the bud'. The noticeably uncertain Kemp then tells them that 'they must do what they think best', thus abdicating himself of responsibility for their actions. This ineffectual authority figure gives *carte blanche* to his police force of whips and in doing so will inflame matters, again reflecting the actions of the leaders of the outside world.

The younger pupils are shown in their sweat room and Peanuts is seen with his microscope surrounded by photographs of the universe while a call goes up in the background for Travis, Wallace and Knightly. They make their way along the corridor to Rowntree's quarters where there is a group of whips brandishing canes. They are viewed over the shoulders of the whips and the intended intimidation is clear. 'Good evening', Rowntree greets them and explains to them that the reason they have been called is because they are a 'nuisance' around the house.

This confrontation between the rebels and the whips is the meeting of two forces. Again reminiscent of real-world riots, the whips are armed while the rebels stand up to authority.

Travis questions this: 'What do you mean being a nuisance? What have we done?'

'Done? It's your general attitude. You know exactly what I mean?'

Again Travis queries this: 'Attitude?'

Rowntree continues and tells them that they've decided to beat them for it.

Denson then begins a tirade against Travis, telling him:

'There's something indecent about you, Travis. The way you slouch about. You think we don't notice you with your hands in your pockets. The way you just sit there looking at everyone.'

This vague accusation shows the fear that the whips have of Travis' 'threat'. Their arbitrary punishment is unilaterally decided but the crime is not specified because it is merely the trio's possession of a different set of values. Travis' mere demeanour shows his disapproval of their methods and is a constant reminder of the way in which they abuse their power.

Rowntree tells them that they have become a danger to the morale of the house but when Travis smiles at this, Denson again attacks him for his attitude:

'You can take that cheap little grin off you mouth. I serve the nation. You haven't the slightest idea what this means have you. To you it's just one bloody joke,' he says pulling at the badge on the breast of his jacket.

Travis is dismissive: 'You mean that bit of wool on your tit.'

The whips' justification that Travis and his friends pose a threat to morale only goes to highlight that what they really threaten is respect for the values and beliefs that the school structure tries to instil. The outward signs of respect for authority such as Denson's badge reinforce these but Travis scoffs at it, bringing it down to its base material. Travis recognises that the nation isn't what he is attacking; it is the dominant order that use 'the nation' to justify their position. Travis has no time for such justifications and recognises that the hierarchy is not based on any merit.

The three schoolmates wait in the vestibule while the whips enter the gym. Wallace is called in first and as Knightly and Travis wait outside, the sound of footsteps and the striking of a cane can be heard as Wallace is thrashed four times. Wallace laughs on his return and Knightly is called.

The scene is particularly memorable and effective as its use of space, time and sound all combine with the visuals to communicate the viciousness of the punishment. While Knightly and Wallace are caned the camera waits outside and the sound of footsteps and the cane are heard while, like Travis, the audience is kept from the gym.

Travis, however, does not wait to be summoned. He enters just as his name his called and he throws the door open in dramatic style. He stands at the door and for the first time we see inside the gym. He smiles and walks in front of the whips. Rowntree instructs him to take his coat off and walk to the bars. Travis leans against a long horizontal beam facing them before he is told to bend over. He stands over it before positioning himself face down and arms outstretched, the very image of martyrdom.

Rowntree runs at him and canes him while the younger students in the sweat room are shown listening to the sounds. Travis gets up to go after the fourth stroke but Rowntree, losing control shouts at him to 'Wait 'til you're told. Get down.' Knightly and Wallace peer through the door as Travis receives more beatings. We see his face in close-up as he takes Rowntree's assault and we also see Stephans chewing contentedly on a sweet as he listens. As the sounds continue, Peanuts looks up from his studies at the microscope and then we see through the microscope as cells divide.

The beating's impact is shown as the sound reverberates around the school. As we see inside Peanut's microscope we are reminded of the consequences of the actions – as the organisms breed, so will violence beget violence. The arbitrary number of strokes Rowntree inflicts is a reminder to all that the whips can do as they please.

The beating is the act of an order whose power is based on fear and though Travis subjugates himself to Rowntree as tradition dictates, the use of force here will have major repercussions.

6. 'RESISTANCE'

Once again the exterior of the school is shown and the sound of singing is heard. In a class a teacher smoking a pipe asks Fortinbras to translate from Plato's 'Republic', a metaphorical story which shows the impact of violence and educating students in war, part of the role of the school in a larger system of duty and patriotism:

'…the boys are educated to become a philosophical elite, to govern warriors and manufacturers.' (Hedling, 1998: 95)

As the sinister music sounds again, we see Travis shooting a gun at the pictures on his wall, a cigarette hanging from the side of his mouth. He reloads and fires again, the darts from his gun hitting pictures on the wall. There is a variety of pop culture imagery that includes Lenin, a large breasted naked woman against a backdrop of police in riot gear, a dog, a cigarette packet, a celebrity couple, a family in bed and another scene of violence, a topless model and a large red jelly, a man running with arms aloft against a background of a conference, Harold Wilson, Big Ben, Martini glasses against pictures of starvation and hardship. He pauses and takes aim carefully before hitting a picture of the Queen's carriage and bowler-hatted gentlemen with umbrellas who can be seen through the carriage.

Travis thus wages war on everything, on life itself, but significantly targets not the Queen but the bowler-hatted man who represents the Establishment; for it is the structure, the class system which upholds the power (the monarch) that Travis wants to attack.

Travis is draining the bottle of vodka with Knightly and Wallace, sharing it out: 'We're on our own now,' he says.

'What are we going to do?' asks Wallace.

'Trust me?' he asks.

'Of course,' answers Knightly.

'When are we going to do it?'

'When I say', he reaches inside a drawer and pulls out a razor. He slices their hands as they swear, becoming blood brothers.

'Death to the oppressors.'

'The Resistance.'

'Liberty', Wallace says and Travis tells them, 'One man can change the world with a bullet in the right place.'

The underground sedition of Travis and his friends contrasts with the ordered celebration of the house thump. The loud chanting of approval, which shows those who are integrated is in contrast to the quiet planning of those who are removed. Their alienation from the school has been made complete by their punishment and they swear allegiance to each other.

Travis reaches outside the window and hands the others real bullets.

In a fantastically surreal moment, Mr Kemp is seen sitting on his bed singing, while his wife plays a recorder. Meanwhile the Matron lies asleep in her chair with a smile on her face stroking the chair:

> 'The sexual adventures of the boys are contrasted with the characterization of the Kemps…whose sexuality is reduced to symbolic gestures. Kemp an archetypal product of repression at the school, is clearly impotent.' (Hedling, 1998: 87)

In black and white we see sleeping students and Wallace and Bobby sharing a bed, looking a picture of contented innocence. We then see the stars in the night sky and Peanuts looking through his telescope. Travis joins him at the window and Peanuts tells him that space is expanding at the speed of light and that it's a mathematical certainty that somewhere there is a planet where English is spoken. Travis hands him a bullet but Peanuts hands it back. He invites him to have a look but Travis doesn't look at the stars, he tilts it down toward another building and sees the girl from the café, leaning out a window, brushing her hair. She stops, looks directly at the camera, smiles and waves.

Peanuts' role of looking at micro and macro elements of the world – either through his telescope or through his microscope – serves to marginalise the conflict in the school. It will, however, continue and the girl's rather surreal and theatricalised appearance in the telescope signals the strengthening of the fantasy world in which the conflict will take place.

7. 'FORTH TO WAR'

The exterior of the chapel is shown in colour and the chaplain, in black and white, is giving an aggressive talk to the students, who are dressed in uniform, about the expectations of being a soldier. He says there is one failure, one crime, one betrayal that can never be forgiven, that of desertion. The deserter should expect to be shot. 'Jesus Christ is our commanding officer,' he says and if we desert him we can expect no mercy and 'we are all deserters', he concludes. Watching him timidly is Jute.

The Reverend's manic speech exemplifies how the religious aspect of the school reinforces the dominant values and shows how both guilt and bullying are used to foster respect. The authority of Jesus is linked with the authority of the army in a preposterous way that gives the scene its comedy; but the pathos of Jute's presence leads one to think of the innocent children being given their taste of war in Fortinbras' reading from 'The Republic'.

Outside, in colour, the students march in uniform behind a leader on horseback. Drums are being played. Meanwhile back in the peace of the school (in black and white) we see the Head of House's wife walking naked along a corridor. While the school's passion for war continues unabated, and the students play war games, Mrs Kemp's repressed sexual desires are expressed.

The chaplain leads the march on his horse and again we see Mrs Kemp as she goes through the boys' dorm. Emphasising the pointlessness and ridiculous nature of the exercises, Denson commands 'B Section' to attack a bushy topped tree. Travis, Wallace and Knightly make their way from the fighting up a hillside while the others continue with the manoeuvres. Reaching the top of the hill, they seem to be attacked by some younger pupils but they are recalled by their leader, Peanuts, who tells them to do it again because they forgot the 'yell of hate'.

Travis, Knightly and Wallace watch a group attack a house. They are then attacked by the new undermaster who throws a grenade. They don't move as it explodes while he triumphantly announces, 'You're all dead. I've won.' The chaplain rides by and Travis looks hatefully at him.

The war games are ridiculous especially when viewed in the context of the images of violence from Travis' room. There are new battles being fought in society and yet this public school seems to be reliving former triumphs. The regimented games have more to do with ritual than training and the rebels pass through their midst without incurring suspicion, a new type of enemy.

Travis, Knightly and Wallace, now concealed in the bushes, shoot at the tea urn and while the students fall to the floor the chaplain strides through, commanding them to show themselves and to give him the rifle. They stand at the top of the hill but as he approaches, Travis walks forward and seems to shoot him, before screaming and pointing the bayoneted gun at him while he squirms helplessly on the ground.

This prelude to the real rebellion acts as a warning to the school of the rebels' behaviour, but the ineptness of the 'soldiers' response points to their lack of preparation for real conflict and the Reverend's 'command' of the situation is that of a school teacher, not a soldier.

In his office, the Head lectures the boys and tells them to apologise to Reverend Woods. He pulls a drawer open in his office and the Reverend is inside. He sits up and shakes their hands in turn. The Head closes the drawer and then begins to talk to the students in an understanding way:

'It's a natural characteristic of adolescence to want to proclaim individuality. There's nothing wrong with that it's a quite blameless form of existentialism. This, for instance, is what lies at the heart of the great hair problem. I think you boys know that I keep an open mind on most things and on one thing I am certain, short hair is no indication of merit. So often I've noticed, it's the hair rebels who step into the breach when there's a crisis, whether it be a fire in the house or to sacrifice a week's holiday in order to give a party of slum children seven days in the country. But of course there are limits scruffiness of any kind is deplorable, I think you'd go that far with me.'

The Head's presumptuous talk ironically emphasises his *lack* of understanding. He tries to intellectualise, while the students seem puzzled. He does not recognise or understand their alienation or its potential danger but instead associates their rebellion with kindness, about which again he himself shows little understanding. Instead of 'punishing' them he gives them work to do – cut to a shot of Phillips reading as Knightly emerges form beneath a trap door in the stage wearing a gas mask. He is struggling with a stuffed alligator.

Wallace comes to help and with Travis they carry it out to a fire in the playground. The sinister music begins again as the boys are shown in black and white clearing the space under the stage. Knightly finds a locked cupboard and Travis uses an axe to open it. Inside they find jars of specimens from science. Travis removes a foetus and looks at it, this metaphor for the boy's lack of life:

> '…they do not live a life, but are human embryos, as the one seen in the glass jar, or nearly choked to suffocation, as illustrated in the scene where Mick puts a plastic bag over his head.' (Hedling, 1998: 93)

Wallace comes down the ladder and Travis lights the way with a match before the girl turns on a light. In this space there is an arsenal of weapons. They inspect the bombs and guns excitedly before the screen fades to black.

8. CRUSADERS

'Guard of honour', 'shun' comes the call against a Union Jack fluttering in the breeze. The camera zooms out to reveal the tops of the school building, and the familiar sound of the chapel bell is heard. Students dressed in military clothing welcome a guest from the army, General Denson (illustrating the family traditions and continuation of the elite) who arrives at the school in a green car flanked by motorcycles.

He inspects the boys before being greeted by Rowntree and the bishop, who already knows him. The choirboys lead a procession into the packed hall as the congregation sing a hymn. On the stage there is the Head and assorted staff. Some members of the procession are dressed as knights or the Crusaders of the original story but their dress is reduced to a ridiculous symbol. The Head speaks to the crowd in Latin, greets a member of the royal family, the bishop and General Denson before ironically making a speech about the school's rapid change.

The Head introduces General Denson as a 'national hero and an old boy', his intimated relationship to Denson, the whip, illustrating the continuity of values maintained by the elite. The General speaks to the boys and demonstrates that he is a product of the system that he considers essential:

'It's a very sad thing that today it is fashionable to belittle tradition. The old orders that make our nation a living force are for the most part scorned by modern psychiatrists, priests, pundits of all sorts but what have they got to put in their place? ... Never mind the sneers of the cynics. Let us just be true to honour, duty, national pride. We still need loyalty; we still need tradition, if we look around us at the world today, what do we see? We see bloodshed, confusion, decay. I know the world has changed a great deal in the past 50 years but England, our England doesn't change so easily and back here in college today I feel, and it makes me jolly proud, that there is still a tradition here which has not changed and by God it isn't going to change...'

The General keeps speaking before belatedly noticing that the room is filling with smoke.

His speech, unlike the Headmaster's earlier claims to modernisation, underlines the real purpose of the school – not to move with the times but rather to stay still in the face of change. The stubborn refusal to move on shows the true outlook and the perpetuation of a privileged elite. His oblivious determination is emphasised by the continuation of his speech in the face of the flames rising from beneath the stage.

The crowd evacuates the hall, coughing and shouting into the open. Suddenly an explosion detonates, followed by a hail of gunfire. The camera zooms in on Travis, sitting on top of the roof opposite, firing a machine gun. He is flanked by the girl from the café. The crowd flee into the open and run around in panic as Knightly fires and runs across the roof.

As members of the school and crowd fight back – notably an older woman who screams 'Bastards, Bastards' while firing a machine gun – the Head pleads for the rebels to stop. He calls out, 'Boys, boys, I understand you listen to reason and trust me, trust me.' The girl draws out her pistol and shoots him through the head.

The organ music plays as the whole school gathers on the grass to return fire. The final shot is of Travis relentlessly shooting at them.

The close of the film is poignant while as Travis tries, seemingly in vain, to stem the counter-attack, the organ music seems to denote a return to 'normality'. Travis' revolution is doomed to failure as he cannot possibly defeat the Establishment:

'As Anderson observed on 1969: "it doesn't look to me as though Mick can win. The world rallies, as it always will, and brings its overwhelming fire power to bear on the man who says 'No'." In reality too the Establishment was fighting back. In 1970 the years of Labour Government came to an end with the reflection of the Conservatives. The years of prosperity drew to a close and recession set in.' (Aldgate and Richards, 1999: 216)

SUMMARY

If... is a film that has a very Sixties identity: for some a revolutionary classic which captures the moment of Sixties rebellion; but for others an overblown combination of allusions and references that errs too much toward pastiche or homage, veering dangerously into parody and surrealism, never really succeeding in its own right.

The messages are confusing and there is a real sense that the film which is obviously steeped in British tradition and heritage is exploring the structure of a Britain in which the conflict of previous ages was clashing with the modern world.

It also captures the spirit the alienation of some who realised that, in the wake of the liberal revolution, little had actually changed and, in focusing on the hierarchical structure of a public school, it, like Peanuts' microscope and telescope, was looking both at the micro and macro elements of society.

Like Philips, it also points towards America as the future. Britain was no longer the centre of excitement and fashion, as had been depicted in Darling and Blow Up. Its temporary position as the cultural centre of style was a short-lived phenomena and now with counter-cultural, political revolution taking place around the world, the set-in-its-ways Britain could no longer represent the modern world.

What was left would be a slightly altered Britain, one which had new traditions and which would now be packaged and sold, with its Queen alongside its queens, its Rolls Royce alongside its Mini, its Big Ben alongside its Beatles – and reality need no longer apply.

CHAPTER TEN: BRIT-FLICK — *THE ITALIAN JOB* (COLOUR, COLLINSON, 1969)

Films to watch: *The Long Good Friday* (1980), *Lock, Stock and Two Smoking Barrels* (1998), *Austin Powers: International Man of Mystery* (1997), *Snatch* (2000), *Layer Cake* (2004)

STYLE

This final film of the book serves as a precursor for the way in which Britain would adapt, following the upheaval of the decade and to an extent, present itself to the rest of the world thereafter. It is a combination of assumptions and anachronisms which serves to pigeonhole this new Britain and assimilates most of the ideas of the age until the Sixties rebellion, such as it was, is reduced to a stylish essence, that has become a self-parodying media package.

The film is a glossy American financed, action and crime caper that draws on a variety of stylistic influences. It obviously features many of the archetypes of the British crime movie but also incorporates the eccentricity of Ealing comedy, the humour of a 'Carry On...', the imagery of the swinging Sixties and the action of a Bond movie. Not only this but it is self-aware and plays on ideas of nationalism and star image with irony that makes it clear that it is not to be taken too seriously.

Of the wave of Sixties British films discussed herein, *The Italian Job* is perhaps the closest in tone and content to much of today's British cinema. Tellingly it has been remade, along with *Alfie*, as the cycle of British nostalgia for the Sixties shows little sign of abating. At a time when the nation again seems to lack a fixed identity, where increasingly British society looks to America for not only political but cultural leadership, we once again turn to the Sixties for reassurance. As a result, we are possibly even more deluded than before about an era, the remakes presenting little new or edifying.

The Italian Job is an archetypal presentation of a Britain of cockney gangsters, mini-skirts and Mini motors. A fantasy of British ingenuity gaining the upper hand over foreign cousins, a cartoon of comic capers that has been reproduced in recent films such as *Lock, Stock and Two Smoking Barrels*, a figurehead for a new generation of very British film criminals, in a country desperate to relive former times.

At the close of the decade the idea of swinging Britain is just a style, there is no longer any rebellion or subversion but the Sixties attitudes and fashion are now completely acceptable and absorbed by an industry looking to package and promote a culture. The Sixties end finds the country exhausted as a source of innovation and inspiration, the American money beginning to leave the British film industry. According to Steve Chibnall in his essay on *The Italian Job* the film squeezes:

'…the remaining drops of madcap frivolity from the husk of "swinging London", but *The Italian Job*, in particular contains intimations of the sombre diet to come…there is a hint of desperation in its joie de vivre, a sense that the good times might not last, the party might be closed down.' (Chibnall, in MacFarlane, 2005: 146)

In *Performance*, a gangster does battle and merges with the counter cultural figure of a pop star, two characters by now central to Britain's film industry and both of which continue into the next decade and beyond. In the Sixties of anti-authoritarianism, the British gangster movie developed from *The Criminal* in the early part of the decade to *Performance* and *The Italian Job* in the latter part and the public perception of gangsters changed with it, particularly in the wake of the Great Train Robbery of 1963, when the audacious nature of the robbery made violent criminals seem more like latter day Robin Hoods (although there seemed little intention to redistribute the ill-gotten gains).

By the decade's end, British cinema's gangster was less a criminal outsider than a conservative figure who embraced capitalist values and whom also had an abiding respect for traditional values and status. This well-suited and elegant figure became an embodiment of a new Britain, a working-class character with aspirational qualities, recognising that money and power equate to success and, in a culture which respects the accumulation of wealth, *how* it is accumulated became less important. In this sense, Charlie Croker (Michael Caine) is a not-too-distant relative of *Room at the Top*'s Joe Lampton, sharing the same wish to get on and reinforcing the continued importance of status in a society where class was still important. Nevertheless there had been changes forged by the Sixties' attack on the establishment.

> 'This questioning of authority led to a less clear cut distinction between hero and villain. The sophisticated gangland set produced a new kind of leading man.' (*Hollywood UK* BBC4)

Gangsters, then, became the lovable rogues of cinema. With their working-class roots and anti-establishment attitudes, they showed that success can be achieved with style, charisma and enterprise rather than the old values of deference and hard work. In *The Italian Job*, this is achieved by instigating a military style campaign against another nation thus appealing to another strand of British pride:

> 'The Italian Job (1969) is really a war film...the planning, preparation and execution of the raid conforms precisely to generic conventions of the "special operation" behind enemy lines depicted in countless films about the Second World War.' (Chibnall, in MacFarlane, 2005: 146)

In *The Italian Job* a collection of gangsters have become brave heroes, representative of a new Britain, as they come from a variety of social backgrounds, to team up to fight against DeGaulle's resistant Europe. The period of domestic internal strife and fighting authority has ended and *The Italian Job* shows a country coming together, as in war time, to fight a common enemy, reviving ideas of patriotism while integrating the new ideals of the Sixties liberation.

So it was that British film returned to fighting a war while in real life as the country somewhat reluctantly but necessarily and inevitably drew closer to its foreign counterparts. This movement was beginning to breed resentment and fear. The UK had twice been refused entry to the Common Market by 1967 and it was beginning to look increasingly isolated. With a dwindling Empire, exclusion from a European Union and an economic and political dependence on America, dark times appeared to be ahead:

> 'In the film the criminal underworld represents the Eurosceptic flip side of Britain, the vein of patriotic isolationism that runs deep beneath the surface of an island race...This truly is a self preservation society, determined to be distrustful of "Johnny Foreigner" and ready to exploit his weaknesses.' (Chibnall, in MacFarlane, 2005: 149)

The film reflects a traditionalism – albeit one tempered by modern commercial realities – in which there is a belligerent reluctance to accept that the world beyond the UK's borders has anything to offer and despite all the changes that have taken place, presents a framework through which the British viewer can once again take pride in the nation's traditions and heritage. With recession on the horizon and an uncertain future, the return to traditional values was one embraced and saw the return of a Conservative government.

Instead of rebelling against the British establishment, as in *If...* and questioning the hierarchical structure of society, *The Italian Job* encouraged viewers to uphold the idea that the British in all their variety should gather together and demonstrate to Europe their superiority by embracing the standards of an earlier generation. Charlie, the working-class hero, still has to respect Mr Bridger's old school authority and know his place if he is to succeed, and the film shows a microcosm of British society through the depiction of the criminal fraternity where there is a clear hierarchy which will enable and ensure the future success of the nation.

As expressed by Hebdige in his book *Subculture*, the rebel style must be incorporated back into the culture to fit with the existing framework and dominant ideology. This can be seen in the way Bridger, a figure of the underworld, far from seeing himself in opposition to the state has adopted the ways of regal superiority:

> 'In the film's distorted lens, Bridger represents the traditional ruling elite of Britain.' (Chibnall, in MacFarlane, 2005: 150)

He worships the Queen, behaves in a superior way and is waited on in the same manner as Royalty, his first concern for the nation.

The presentation of the gang, however, is representative of a new Britain that has emerged from the cultural revolution. But any true movement towards an integrated culture is belied by the gang's use of the stereotypes that would be such a feature of British comedy in the next decade:

> '…in *The Italian Job* and its ilk exciting action sequences enliven the dull interplay between poorly developed characters…, [the film] has a vulgar package holiday vitality….' (Murphy, 1992: 218)

The film has of course prospered as a cult text and Michael Caine became something of a postmodern figure of traditional masculinity in the 1990s, lauded by magazines such as *Loaded* as an icon. This idea of British 'ladism' has firmly established the film with a particular audience who see it as a reflection of Britain at its greatest. Modern reinvention of the British identity has seen a rise in a more aggressive patriotism which with the rise of multi-cultural Britain has often been a source of contention. There is no doubt that *The Italian Job*, like James Bond films plays up to and has been appropriated by those whose beliefs include Britain's innate superiority which often verges on the racist:

> 'Italy is a…complacent culture, less adaptable than the new post-Imperial Britain. The new Brits are quick-witted, light on their feet and still blessed with a devil may care attitude to danger that helped to build the Empire in the first place….Cheeky and irrepressible the patriotic Minis are the mechanical projections of Britain's 1960's spirit.' (Chibnall, in MacFarlane, 2005: 151)

Thus, for all of the film's kinetic energy, its attitude is actually one of stasis. Britain is losing its status as a centre of culture and instead opts to fall back on safe notions of itself, in terms of war and insularity, trying to bend the recently developed excitement of change back into a safe and ultimately conventional vision of Britain.

COMIC

The film begins with a panoramic view of the Alps, through which a red sports car is driving. The car enters a tunnel but there is heard the sound of skidding tyres and we see an explosion at the end of the tunnel. A suited man carrying a wreath can be seen next to a black car waiting outside as a bulldozer backs out of the tunnel having blocked the sports car's path. Another man in a grey suit, Altobelli, gives the order for the crumpled car to be disposed of over the edge of the mountainside.

This swift and merciless murder comes as quite a shock after the beautiful mountain views but it sets up the film as the merciless, black-clad Mafia show themselves as a uniformed, largely faceless mass, well organised but without charm. This portrayal of the 'enemy', as efficient but characterless, is consistent with war films as the English will have to beat them with innovation and character.

Charlie Croker in contrast is introduced in close-up with the now familiar grin of Michael Caine as he leaves his prison cell. His cheeky, down to earth, persona is enhanced as he calls out his goodbyes to his fellow inmates. His manner is different, however, when saying goodbye to Noel Coward's character, the formally addressed, Mr Bridger to whom he is considerably more deferential, subdued and polite. Bridger, with an air of superiority however, ignores him. Bridger clearly perceives himself as from a different class than Charlie and, despite his supposedly equal position as a convict, does not allow this to reduce his standing.

The introduction of two of Britain's most well-known figures of stage and screen sets the tone for the film as we are encouraged to engage with them not only as their characters but also star figures. The film's possible interpretation in patriotic terms is balanced by its ironic tone and self-deprecating humour. Here is the very best of Britain, past and present, showing the world that its post-empiric identity has actually made it stronger, combining old traditions with modern attitudes to produce a new contemporary Britain in which young and old, working-class or upper-class, rich or poor can live together.

Caine, rapidly becoming a British icon is associated not only with the carefree identity of Alfie, Harry Palmer and sexual freedom but is also associated with national pride and bravery from his performance in *Zulu* (1964) and simultaneously embodies colonial strength and tradition. Similarly Coward's image too is multi-faceted, a playwright and composer, famous for his songs of national identity, including 'Mad Dogs and Englishmen', 'London's Pride' and 'Don't Let's Be Beastly to the Germans' reinforces English theatricality and tradition.

Thus beneath this comic portrayal there are strong ideological ideas being presented that demonstrate how the new Britain will function. There has been social movement but the idea of class is reasserting itself in a bid to re-establish the social order upon which Britain was once powerful. Where the Sixties has bred uncertainty, a combination of archetypes and stereotypes is attempting to restore order and some sense of national self to the nation.

Outside the prison gates, the organ music conjures up the swinging lifestyle that awaits Charlie on the outside. He is met by his glamorous, fun loving girlfriend Lorna. When Charlie asks her why she hasn't visited him in the prison, she responds that visiting with all the 'weeping wives' with their 'howling kids' is not her 'scene'. Her American accent picks her out as a cosmopolitan character suggesting that the idea of a swinging lifestyle that is no longer confined to Britain and her seeming rejection of family ties reinforce her connection to Sixties values. However, it is her partnership of trans-Atlantic convenience with Charlie that embodies the future for Britain.

Charlie, then, has missed the Sixties party, locked away while his American girlfriend has had fun and this very much reflects the experience of many Sixties Brits, who felt that the whole 'scene' had passed them by and that it was only an idea invented by Americans to drag Britain into the age of commercialism. The feminine figure of Lorna can thus be associated with consumerism and as such is a bad influence and not to be taken too seriously, with male values being reasserted after a time of flamboyant irresponsibility.

This impression is reinforced as Lorna immediately encourages Charlie to spend on his appearance. She explains that she has booked him an appointment with a tailor. He, meanwhile waves a flag he has found in the car at her and questions where she obtained it. The car it seems, belongs to the Pakistani ambassador. 'I just wanted you to come out in style, baby,' she replies. Riding roughshod over ex-empiric nations, Lorna personifies America's new globalised dominance as well as convention breaking rebellion.

At the tailor's shop Charlie explains how he has been in America but the tailor is clearly complicit in the lie. Charlie is informed that times have changed while he has been inside and they give him a flowery shirt associated with the more decadent, psychedelic style of the later Sixties. However despite buying these, it is a rather more subdued suit that he emerges in, re-establishing his image and affirming Britain's reluctance to follow the wilder excesses of the counter culture and the feminine ideas associated with American consumerism.

Charlie then collects his car, a very British Jaguar, which has been in storage at a garage. The assistant knows him as 'Captain Croker' and Charlie adopts a rather well-spoken accent as he collects cash which has been hidden inside the car engine. His story this time is that he has been in colonial India, shooting tigers, and when he hands the surprised attendant two hundred pounds in cash, Charlie telling him he was paid a bounty for his work.

Charlie's irreverent cheek shows his rebellious spirit and his masquerading as a military officer shows he understands that Britain's society is still very much class-led and perhaps reflects his own aspirations (as well as being a sly nod to Caine's breakthrough role in *Zulu*, perhaps). Charlie may show respect for his superiors and is keen to attain their status – but in doing so, the wartime British sense of fair play must necessarily fall by the wayside.

At the hotel, Charlie moves upwards through the ranks and introduces himself as Lord Croker at a reception where a message is waiting for him to meet someone named Beckerman in another suite. Inside his own suite, however, he has a surprise waiting. Greeted by Lorna who is surrounded by girls in underwear, she asks, 'What would you like?' 'Everything,' he answers. Like James Bond, Charlie is a character who is only too willing to embrace Sixties values of freedom when they promise him pleasure. The girls are treated as commodities, and it is his American girlfriend who presents them as such with Charlie as the consumer.

Thus the amalgamation of the traditional and modern stereotypes of Britain continues, as the film tries to construct the male audience. The idea of Charlie as a reckless and insouciant everyman is established while ideas of class values are reinforced. He is both traditional in his taste in cars and his tailoring, eschewing the fashionable excesses of Sixties and yet, like Bond he knows how to enjoy the sexual permissiveness that the age's liberation has allowed. Like Bond he is a character that portrays a masculine fantasy.

Later, the dishevelled hero emerges from the hotel suite and, reading the message left at reception, makes his way to the suite for the arranged meeting. Inside he is met by another young woman who holds him at gunpoint. Having expected her late husband Charlie asks 'Where's your old man?' and she clarifies the narrative, recalling the opening scene and telling him that he was killed in a car crash in the Alps, explaining how it wasn't an accident, before presenting Charlie with the plans to an audacious robbery and a room for the night.

This is not the experimental narrative of the more adventurous Sixties films and shows how the Sixties ideals are being adapted to the classic Hollywood narrative. Charlie's cheeky everyman character is not one who embodies a new British classlessness, but is instead and attempt to create a new British stereotype, a cheeky chancer, a development of both Alfie and Harry Palmer, a gangster to rival Bond's national protector, the emphasis on self-interest.

PATRIOTISM

Charlie rides home on the back of a milk float looking at a reel of film in which Beckerman tells Charlie about his plan for a heist that will bring in four million dollars.

The money is transported in a convoy through busy Turin traffic and the plan is to hijack it as it will be stuck in a manufactured traffic jam created by their breaking into the traffic control centre in Turin and controlling the city's roads.

Charlie interrupts a board meeting for Bridger's concerns led by a young man named Camp Freddy and tries to persuade him of the merits of his planned robbery. Camp Freddy, however, is unconvinced by Croker who he clearly considers a chancer.

Bridger's role as an Establishment figure and patriot is here reinforced as his concern for his country outweighs any idea of personal gain while Charlie's upstart persona is demonstrated in his having to make a business-style proposal. In this new Britain of dubious moral values, there is one unifying factor and that is the need to accumulate wealth but this is not outweighed by the loyalty one owes ones country and that capitalism must exist hand in hand with patriotism is clear. The outward respectability of Bridger's criminal gang is contrasted against Charlie's breezier and rather more selfish attitude but it is clear that Charlie must learn through his experiences and become a responsible leader.

Thus the bank job provides Charlie with an education about himself and his relationship with his country. Bridger is like the officer that has the right to send his troops to war through his standing and thus he is portrayed as someone of experience and status. Like most gangster figures, Charlie is keen to make money and to be on an equal standing with those above him but though his aspirations and initiative make him a very enterprising character, he has to learn the value of the Britain that he represents and thus in the same way as the war tested the resolve of patriotism, Charlie has to learn his devotion to his country through his mission on foreign soil.

The strength of his determination is shown as Charlie breaks back *into* the prison to converse with Bridger. In this reverse of the war time escape attempt, Charlie enters the prison as Bridger is going to the lavatory in his smoking jacket, escorted by two guards one of whom is carrying his newspapers and toilet roll, his status is comically reinforced, underlined by the tune which accompanies his walk, 'The British Grenadiers', rearranged as chamber music. Thus from early on in the film, Charlie is associated with the ingenuity and anti-authoritarian strength of the prisoners of war, with Britain itself becoming ruled by those who are incapable of effectively doing so. If Britain is to move on it has to embrace the young entrepreneur.

Bridger is upset to find Charlie inside his cubicle, finding his unexpected visit an affront to his privacy. Charlie tries to tell him about the plan, speaking of Europe and the Common Market and making clear the metaphorical connection between his plan and Britain's entry into the European Union. The guards call to see if Bridger is alright and he flushes the toilet before emerging, again to the patriotic tune. A disconsolate Charlie is left in the cubicle talking of showing the plan to the Americans because they recognise young talent and are prepared to give it a chance, reinforcing their position as leaders of global capitalism.

Bridger then visits the prison governor, played by popular comic actor, John Le Mesurier. The gangland boss sits down at a large table, forcing the governor to join him. As he does so Bridger waves his hand to grant him permission to sit, reversing the power relationship between the two. He sits at the large table, forcing the governor to come out from behind his desk and join him. Bridger reports that his toilet was broken into the previous evening. The governor apologises. 'There are some things', he explains, sitting beneath a picture of the Queen, 'that to an Englishman are sacred'. His connection with the patriotic symbol of the Queen emphasises Bridger as a character of old British power and associated values.

He tells the governor that he isn't doing his job properly. 'You are symptomatic of the lazy unimaginative management that is driving this country on the rocks.' The governor asks Bridger if he recognised the intruder that so upset him and he lies, indignantly and convincingly, 'I have never seen the man before in my life.'

Bridger's assumed superiority over his jailor further emphasises his status: although he is a criminal, it is clearly irrelevant to his position in society. Bridger may be a representation of the Establishment but it is an Establishment which retains its traditional values whilst recognising the need for competition. He is a successful businessman, able to adapt to the times and his criticism of the governor is framed in business terms. He is certainly not to be associated with the fuddy-duddies who are symptomatic of Britain's decline. And it is very much this message that comes out of this American backed film, that to survive Britain must wake up to the need of the modern capitalist world.

Whereas the beginning of the decade began with the reservations of how American cultural attitudes would impact on British culture, The Italian Job spells out how the two must sit side by side if the country is to succeed. While like Charlie, Britain stood still, the ideological battle of the Sixties took place and it was won by American style capitalism and now Britain, as it had to do in the Second World War, has to battle for its very survival. It will of course receive the backing of the States but tellingly the battle will judge Britain's capacity to indulge in theft.

This combination of new and old values is emphasised in his conversation with the romantically named Keats where the combination of hard-nosed businessman and criminal is apparent. Bridger tells him to give Croker a good going over. The obsequious assistant tells him he will and eager to please, again reinforcing the importance of Britain's future relationship with America, tells him that he has also got him two volumes of the Anglo American Trade and a copy of the balance of payments 1966 and 1967. Bridger is keen to help the country's financial situation and will see Charlie's plan as an opportunity. Keats has also obtained *The Illustrated London News*. When Bridger asks why, he answers that it has a picture of the Queen, which pleases Bridger whose love for the monarch emphasises his patriotism.

Perhaps the reference to the *Anglo American Trade* is as much an allusion to the future of British cinema as it is to British business but there is no mistaking that the film is describing a changing world. Bridger's keen business acumen makes it clear that though he retains the important aspects of the country's heritage he is keen that Britain moves forward by its business dealings. In short it has to fully embrace the capitalist values that are so much a part of the gangster identity. He may not admit this to Charlie who ruefully reflects on his lack of American style opportunity but it is clear that he has a dual outlook. He mercilessly punishes Charlie for getting beyond his station but begins to research the younger man's plan.

Charlie's girlfriend Lorna, meanwhile, provides a contrast to the male world of business deals as she drives through a busy Portobello market place. She turns the corner before parking the car and the camera focuses on her lower half, clad in the fashionable leather mini-skirt and boots as she jumps out of Charlie's sports car. She walks in through a door which is guarded by a life-size model of a Grenadier guard creating the impression that swinging London is still alive and well. She is followed by a van carrying Camp Freddy and some of his accomplices. They are keen to get inside but Freddy tells them to wait and suddenly screaming girls in underwear run out of Charlie's flat, while Lorna angrily throws their clothes over the balcony and shouts at them not to come back. Camp Freddy is amused as Charlie has been 'caught on the job'.

Inside his bohemian pad which is decorated in the most colourful and fashionable way of the younger generation, Lorna shouts at Charlie for his indiscretion and berates him for leaving her after being caught with the ambassador's car and for not paying the hotel bill. 'You know how the game's played Lorna,' he tells her. And it is a game in the same way business is a game. And Lorna and Charlie's Anglo-American relationship is more like a business agreement. There are rules by which they have to abide and Charlie's infidelity is not excused on this occasion as it has not been mutually agreed.

A knock on the door, however, has her portrayed in a more conventional manner and the so far fearless and independent female quickly leaps to Charlie for protection, fearing it's 'the law' but it turns out to be Camp Freddy and the other gangsters. They tell him they've been sent by Bridger and considerately apologise for having to give him a beating. There is it seems honour amongst these very British of thieves and like Charlie's seemingly 'open' relationship with Lorna there are rules to be obeyed. Traditional British life is orderly and structured, this must be reinforced by the hierarchy. As Charlie reinforces the rules to Lorna, Bridger does the same to Charlie and he must unquestioningly accept it.

Another sign proclaiming 'Harley Street' relocates us back to a more traditional area of London wealth and privilege. Two security guards stand on the pavement, indicating Bridger's presence and his ability to move beyond the prison gates when it suits him. A taxi pulls up outside one of the buildings and Camp Freddy goes inside, where the sound of a dentist drill can be heard. In the lobby are another two security guards but inside, despite the sound of the drill, the 'dentists' are sitting around, smoking and playing cards with Bridger.

He tells Freddy to go back and see Charlie about his plan. Bridger despite issuing the instruction to have Charlie beaten confirms his interest in the plan and the source of the gold bullion (Chinese are giving Fiat $4 million in gold as a down payment on a car plant that they are constructing near Peking) is confirmed. And thus it is that we see how old enemies will be scuppered. The Italians who were often perceived in Britain as being weak during the Second World War and the familiar enemy of Bond films embodied by communist China are placed like so much else in the context of a business/war alliance. Charlie's mission will be part robbery and part reflection of a wider ideological battle.

INVASION

Bridger assures Freddy that despite his reservations, Charlie is a worthy investment and his mission will coincide with a very British invasion of football fans as there is even a match the day before the delivery between England and Italy ensuring there will still be plenty of supporters in Turin afterwards. Thus the film again plays up the audience by combining as many national archetypes as possible and reframes the football fans as foot soldiers to Charlie's special force. They will provide the cover for the robbery and also the nationalistic triumphalism which forms such a key ingredient of the film and has seen its continued popularity into modern times.

Bridger tells Freddy that he needs a computer specialist for the heist and one of the dentists tells him about the country's leading specialist, Professor Peach (played by comedian Benny Hill). Bridger tells Freddy to get him but Freddy protests that he may not be 'bent' seemingly a prerequisite to succeed in this new climate . Bridger, however, tells him that 'everybody in the world is bent', reinforcing the more pragmatic view of the capitalist culture.

The operation that will take place is a fantasy robbery, which contrasts with the reality of a Britain unable to compete on equal footing with its European counterparts and provides the success of material gain with a combination of initiative, determination and enterprise. It will in the world of cinema reassert new Britain as a thrusting force which will incorporate all social groups which is embodied in the gang itself:

'It is a melting pot in which issues of class, race and sexuality are largely subordinated to questions of professional expertise.' (Chibnall, in MacFarlane, 2005: 149)

Charlie holds a meeting at Bridger's office and he introduces members of the team which includes stereotypes of a variety of backgrounds. The subsequent montage shows preparations and the difficulty of removing the gold from Turin and featuring the famous, "You're only supposed to blow the bloody doors off" while emphasising the threat and presence of the Mafia.

At a pre-arranged 'funeral' Bridger also warns Charlie of the dangers of the job which he says will, if it succeeds, be an insult to the Mafia, before giving a Henry V-like speech to the gang who are about to do battle with the enemy. He pays tribute to his 'Aunt Nellie', who he says brought them up properly and taught them loyalty but also warning them that if they don't come back with the goods Nellie will jump out of her grave and 'kick their teeth in'.

Thus battle commences and Charlie is seen on a typical wet British day, like a general, jacket draped over his shoulders, waving the buses on to the ferry whose name emphasises the metaphor of business — The Free Enterprise, which we see cutting through the water to the strains of the anthemic 'Rule Britannia'. This cuts to a red, white and blue bus driving through the sunny Alps against a background of Italian-style music as we are returned to the location in which the film began. Charlie gets off to direct the vehicles involved in the job to Turin, making sure that the take different routes. The Minis, the final ingredient of this patriotic showcase of British tradition and identity are unsurprisingly painted a patriotic, red, white and blue. The invasion is underway.

The sports cars which head the invasion however are the first casualties. They have to stop as they encounter the Mafia on the bend of a road. The now familiar sight of the black-suited gang on the mountainside spells trouble for the visitors. Charlie and Lorna get out of the first car to speak to their leader, Altabani. He demonstrates to them how Beckerman was killed by crushing one of the cars and pushing it over the edge. He then quizzes Charlie about how he intends to take the bullion, sceptically asking whether Bridger thinks he can take over Europe from a prison cell.

Despite the further destruction of more cars indicating the seriousness of their intent, Charlie warns Beckerman that if they are killed, Italians working in England will be made to suffer. He tells him that there are a quarter of a million Italians working in Britain. In a show of Churchillian bravado he warns him that 'Every restaurant, café, ice cream parlour, gambling den and nightclub in London, Liverpool and Glasgow will be smashed. Mr Bridger will drive them into the sea.' The Italian leader in turn tells him that it's a long walk back to England and bids them a good morning.

Altabani's warning to Charlie brings out those belligerent British qualities associated with war time Britain. He refuses to be intimidated by Altabani, who questions Bridger's plans for Europe, thinking him helpless because he is incarcerated. This restriction on Bridger can be seen as comparable with Britain's exclusion from the Common Market and robbed of cars, they seem to have little hope of success but, with the war-like determination Charlie exemplifies, success for the underdog is still possible. The idea, however, of a more integrated and multi-cultural modern Britain seems less likely, as Charlie's threat to all Italian run businesses in the country shows a Britain still struggling with its new multi-cultural present.

In contrast to the depiction of British borderline xenophobia, the Italians are hosting some American guests. They toast Altabani and his wife and Altabani is complimented on how he handled the 'English mob' that morning. Altabelli, however, is cagey and warns him that they are not as stupid as they look.

Charlie, meanwhile, in a scene very similar to that of a war time operation, cycles through the night to a power station and causes an explosion which allows his gang into the traffic control centre. A shot of a dinner party shows a close-up of Altabani who realises the significance of the blackout while Charlie's gang are shown making their way through the inside of the centre.

Professor Peach substitutes one of the reels of tape and while Charlie makes his way on foot through the night he is passed by two police cars. The next day we see an airport filled with the Italian military as the security van goes to pick up the bullion from the waiting plane. Charlie is in the terminal giving instructions to Lorna, telling her how to get on the plane without drawing attention to herself. She is complaining as she wants to stay but in a demonstration of his traditional male dominance, he is sending her home out of harm's way.

The Italian Job, of course, is a male fantasy incorporating cars, football, patriotism and a strong sense of masculinity. In Lorna's dismissal, Charlie is making a masculine statement but it may also be read as a need for Britain's need for independence from a clearly not to be trusted America and a return to war time mentality. He may need her but he must also maintain his individuality. He tells her that he'll meet her in Geneva – historically a place of war time neutrality – and reinforces traditional values by asking her to have a cup of tea ready. She indiscreetly shouts her loving goodbyes while Charlie tries comically to remain anonymous, but Altabani appears beyond the fencing, watching the plane.

Charlie enters an Italian palazzo and tells his gang to get rid of any fingerprints in the house. Charlie gives some last minute instructions to the drivers, one of whom asks if they should synchronise their watches: 'Nuts to your watches,' he replies. 'You just be there by quarter to, and don't get stuck in the traffic jam neither.' Charlie sends them away before stopping them for a last-minute reminder – 'in this country they drive on the wrong side of the road' – to a collective groan. The superficially haphazard nature of the planning is reflective of an adamant refusal to submit to the qualities of efficiency and precision associated with mainland Europe. Success will be achieved through British determination and spirit, not through synchronised time-pieces.

Dressed in blue jump suits the team leave for the heist. Altabani is watching the security convoy and Charlie leaves their hideout. Shots of the control centre and the military convoy are seen. A member of the gang dressed as a football fan asks for directions but is annoyed by the man he asks: 'Bloody foreigners,' he remarks; comically, perhaps, but a not inaccurate depiction of the time of an Englishman abroad. He lumbers around the city grumbling as he puts devices in bins which interfere with the traffic control centre security cameras.

The computer programme planted by the Professor begins to work and malfunctioning traffic lights cause chaos in the city. Altabani himself is stuck in traffic and complains that they have lost the convoy. Jams begin to develop all over the city and a cacophony of car horns is heard, while Charlie's jeep makes its way steadily through deserted backstreets. They sit in wait for the security truck and then pull out behind it as it struggles through the traffic, putting on their baseball helmets.

Camp Freddie watches over an archway ironically proclaiming Italia Vittoriaas, while below, two members of the gang wait in vehicle carriers. Dropping smoke bombs they pull out to stop the convoy and Charlie's van pulls in front of the van and they hijack it. The Minis are seen waiting in an empty building and the gang drive the van to the waiting cars to unload the bars. They blow the doors open and begin to unload the gold.

The police arrive and try to break down the doors with one of the vehicle carriers. The Italian police are shown as incompetent, in contrast to the ruthless efficiency of the Mafia. They are no match for the British gangsters who have swung into action. They run to a Dormobile decorated in football paraphernalia and escape dressed as football fans in scarves and hats, while the Minis escape. The police break open the doors only to find the gang has disappeared along with the gold.

The Minis meanwhile make their way by unconventional means through the city – through buildings, shopping malls and town squares before disappearing down a subway. The van makes its way back through the route by which it arrived and the Minis are seen in ever more dramatic stunts and unusual places as the Italian police try in vain to catch them. They bounce down church steps, drive on top of a building and hide in a car lot.

In the traffic jam we see familiar Italian stereotypes – choir boys, a man drinking wine and an amorous man being slapped by a woman. The control centre is in a panic and the staff are told to stop the gang leaving the city. Altobelli is also trying to stop them and gets his gang to reconnoitre ways out of the city.

The Minis are visible, metaphorical signs of the English 'victory' as they brazenly drive triumphant to the capitalist anthem, the 'The Self Preservation Society', splashing through water and through tunnels in carefree fashion. Truly this is a moment for jingoistic celebrations and, like a sporting victory on foreign soil, the news spreads with similar effect. Bridger is informed that the team have pulled off the heist and the prison inmates celebrate. Charlie waves to the celebratory crowd while the Minis drive onto the back of the coach.

As it drives into the mountains, winding its way around the roads they dump the Minis by pushing them out of the coach, in an echo of the Mafia's earlier vehicular destruction. The team meet up with the van and everyone gets on the coach where they celebrate; but as they drive around corners at speed the gold is thrown around and the coach skids off the road, its rear end hanging over the edge of a cliff.

Charlie orders the gang to the front of the coach but the weight of the gold pulls it over the edge. As Charlie crawls toward it, he orders the gang as far back as they can go but as he edges closer, the gold slides to the end of the bus, making it even more unstable.

'Hang on a minute lads, I've got a great idea,' he says as we see the coach teetering on the edge, the camera pulls back and in a long-shot we end the film with the panorama of the mountains.

SUMMARY

The Italian Job cynically exploits the tastes of a male British audience, playing up to a range of stereotypes of British life, combining the war with the Sixties and the Queen, trying just about everything to amalgamate the past and the present to create a new capitalist vision of the country. In so doing it has become a much loved comic romp that has not just spawned a remake but has also been imitated, parodied and adapted. Its cockney infused songs have been adopted by football fans and adverts alike. In short it has become part of the fabric of the nation, a celebration not of Britain perhaps but the media fantasy of Britain. As Steve Chibnall so eloquently explains it is:

'...Englishness in a bottle. Granted it may be bottled myth, and for some it might smell like sweet perfume, while for others it might stink like stale urine, but it is there for all to sample.' (Chibnall, in MacFarlane, 2005: 148)

This representation has been embraced by a nation seeking a return to better times and it is a comforting portrayal of national cohesion that for many seems to capture the optimism of the Sixties. It is a text which mythologises the spirit of the war and the spirit of the decade, combining the old and new in a comic story which provides both security and comfort. The film presents like the Sixties a unifying explanation to a decade of disparate forces and reconciling them.

'It somehow has come to represent the sixties, even though it is a kind of a fantasy version of it.' (Troy Kennedy, DVD documentary, 'The Making of *The Italian Job*' in Michael Caine 3 disc box set)

It is a success, and like the British film industry in that it probably has America both to thank and to blame. And so the decade ends in glorious failure, the coach balanced precariously, just as British film teeters similarly on the edge of a new decade.

CONCLUSION

The much derided Sixties British film, with its London landmarks, Hammond organ music and 'cut-up' editing style is not surprisingly, like the idea of the swinging decade itself, a constructed and illusory image which is the result of an age of great change and conflict. Even *The Knack…* which includes all of the features that supposedly constitute the dire excesses of the Sixties film does more than merely reflect the hedonistic excitement associated with the age and instead articulates its conflicts. Like much of the cinema of the decade, it deserves reappraisal.

In many ways the films are rather more conservative than one might expect and instead of revelling in the excitement of hackneyed ideas – a liberal attitude to drugs, free love and the dream of a society of classless inclusion – they recognise the construction of the media myth and focus upon that. Far from being shallow, multi-coloured montages of the London 'scene' popularised in *Life* magazine they actively examine the creation of the media Sixties, the processes by which Britain is being represented to the world.

Significantly the American magazine is part of the process by which the previously powerful empiric Britain became colonised by pop culture and the films of the time show this. From its early stages in Free Cinema, it traces the rise of mass culture and examines how this new, American inspired culture is changing the nation. In this sense the films provide an interesting and self-reflexive perspective on media dominance over our understanding of the nation and its place in the world.

The simplification of the Sixties into the fantasy of *The Italian Job* is now the established 'reality' and films which question it or provide us with the conflict that is at the heart of the mythic revolution are now hidden, marginalised or dismissed precisely because they fail to reinforce the dominant view of the Sixties as a decade-long party. Of course the media's distaste for complexity and the ideological struggle of the Sixties are not readily acknowledged.

But the representation presented by the cinema of the period is one of confusion rather than pleasure, a time in which possibilities far outweigh fulfilment, and there is a great sense of disillusionment and emptiness when the realisation that the optimism is perhaps misplaced. Those characters who fall foul of the Sixties dream are shown to do so for a variety of reasons but their experiences are not always coherent; rather they often provide a rather fragmented and partial picture of a complex puzzle.

One theme apparent is of the country's movement from community to commodity as it became in thrall to American consumer culture and it is this shift that is also apparent in the films. Supermarkets, shop windows, billboard posters, jingles and advertisers are all part of a new Britain in which the characters are often framed within a consumerist world and some characters are themselves defined by their own commodity and the media is instrumental in creating this. Recurrent images of shop window dummies point to the alienation of young people in this new society.

From Arthur Seaton, who is only too aware of his value to his employers, through the bored and feckless Diana Scott, to the thrusting enterprise of Charlie Croker we see characters whose worth is measured commercially. Far from an age of freedom, it is in fact an age of imprisonment, showing trapped characters who yearn for freedom, whose hopes and dreams cannot be fulfilled by the trappings of this consumer society.

And ideas of nationality and patriotism are naturally questioned in a society where obedience to others and a sense of community is diminishing. The importance of national heritage and tradition is faltering in the face of the modern world. Images of Queen Elizabeth's portrait, national dress and famous landmarks all appear reframed in a number of circumstances often indicating the waning of Britain's influence or the anachronistic nature of a modern United Kingdom and it is this conflict that many of the films confront as the battle between new and old values raised in earlier in the decade has to be resolved.

The dominance of London to the idea of Sixties film has tended to marginalise the important contribution of the British new wave and is edifying in showing how media representations dominate our understanding. The new wave films are hard-edged social criticism and radically different from the movies which preceded them; but their stories are set outside the capital and therefore cannot apparently be considered representative. Their adventurous style, natural locations and their determination to present life beyond the south belie their easy categorisation of 'kitchen-sink' and reveal a power structure at work in the way the country *is* represented. Their vital contribution to advancing the idea of the working-classes as real people and starting a long tradition of social realism cannot be underestimated, even reemerging at the end of the decade in Ken Loach's *Poor Cow* (1969), and provides a greater revolution than the 'swinging London' films.

The reaction to this realism, and perhaps its threat, was a London-centric fantasy which reclaimed the youth market and presented a new and vibrant capital; but the influence of the new wave films continues as even the so-called swinging London films are often not the superficial montage of images that many believe. Far from being films that were complicit in an illusion of a party, they question the media's role in construction of that fantasy. Schlesinger's *Billy Liar* and *Darling*, especially, remain pertinent in examining the illusion of this media fantasy and even The Beatles' *A Hard Day's Night*, which is a film of unquestionable exuberance, focuses the viewer's attention on the band's constructed image – so where exactly is the party?

The answer is that it is gone before it has even begun, disappearing into the ether, like Thomas in *Blow Up* and along with the *The Knack…* and *If…* – all Palme d'Or winning films which use fantasy to communicate meaning, they all translate similar feelings of disenchantment with a country suffering from its own delusion. The country has been caught examining itself through the media, trying to make sense of the impact of pop culture and while greater ideological changes took place Britain was hypnotised by its own image, frozen in time.

But it was apparent from the outset: *Peeping Tom* warned of the dangers of the camera. When this movie pointed the lens at the audience, pointing out their complicity in the construction of reality, it caused great consternation. By the time liberal values were embraced it was too late for a film that correctly identified the dangers of the audience pleasures to come.

BIBLIOGRAPHY

Aldgate, Anthony and Richards, Jeffrey, *Best of British Cinema and Society from 1930 to the Present*, IB Tauris, London, 1999

Ashby, Justine and Higson, Andrew, *British Cinema Past and Present*, Routledge, London, 2000

Barrow, Sarah and White, John, *Fifty Key British Films*, Routledge, Abingdon / New York, 2008

Black, Jeremy, *The Politics of James Bond*, University of Nebraska Press, Lincoln, 2000

Caterall, Ali and Wells, Simon, *Your Face Here*, Fourth Estate, London, 2001

Donnelly, Mark, *Sixties Britain*, Longman, Harlow, 2005

Glynn, Stephen, *A Hard Day's Night*, Turner Classic Movies British Film Guide, IB Tauris, London, 2005

Green, Jonathon, *All Dressed Up: The Sixties and the Counter Culture*, Pimlico, London, 1999

Hedling, Erik, *Lindsay Anderson – Maverick Film-maker,* Cassell, London, 1998

Huss, Roy, *Focus on Blow Up*, Prentice Hall, New Jersey, 1971

Lay, Samantha, *British Social Realism: From Documentary to Brit Grit*, Wallflower, London, 2002

Leach, Jim, British Film, Cambridge University Press, Cambridge, 2004

Lidner, Christopher, *The James Bond Phenomenon, A Critical Reader*, Manchester University Press, Manchester, 2003

McFarlane, Brian (ed.), *The Cinema of Britain and Ireland*, Wallflower, London, 2005

Murphy, Robert, *Sixties British Cinema*, BFI, London, 1992

Murphy, Robert, *The British Cinema Book*, BFI, London, 1997 (third edition, 20009)

Sandbrook, Dominic, *Never Had It So Good A History of Britain from Suez to The Beatles*, Little Brown, London, 2005

Sandbrook, Dominic, *White Heat, A History of Britain in the Swinging Sixties*, Little Brown, London, 2006

Sargeant, Amy, *British Cinema, a Critical History*, BFI, London, 2005

Sinker, Mark *If…* BFI Film Classics, BFI, London, 2004

Street, Sarah, *British National Cinema*, Routledge, London, 1997

Sutton, Paul, *If...*, Turner Classic Movies British Film Guide, I B Tauris, London, 2005

Walker, Alexander, *Hollywood England: The British Film Industry in the Sixties*, Michael Joseph, London, 1974

INDEX

STILLS INFORMATION

The publisher has attempted to correctly identify the copyright holders of the images reproduced herein and believes the following copyright information to be correct at the time of going to print. We apologise for any omissions or errors and will be delighted to correct any errors brought to our attention in future editions.

Peeping Tom © Studio Canal/Joel Finler Archive; *Saturday Night and Sunday Morning* © BFI Stills; *Billy Liar* © Studio Canal/Joel Finler Archive; *A Hard Day's Night* © Miramax/Joel Finler Archive; *Goldfinger* © MGM/UA; *The Ipcress File* © Lowndes Productions Ltd.; *Darling* © Studio Canal/Joel Finler Archive; *The Knack... and How to Get It* © MGM/UA/Joel Finler Archive; *Blow Up* © Warner Bros./Joel Finler Archive; *If...* © Paramount/Joel Finler Archive; *The Italian Job* © Paramount/Aquarius Collection. Framegrabs interspersed within each chapter are taken from the respective Region 2 DVDs of the films.